THE BOOK OF
WESTON-SUPER-MARE
with Worle & Uphill

THE BOOK OF
WESTON-SUPER-MARE

with Worle & Uphill

Somerset's Holiday Gem

SHARON POOLE

HALSGROVE

First published in Great Britain in 2004

British Library Cataloguing-in-Publication Data.
A CIP record for this title is available from the British Library.

ISBN 1 84114 343 X

HALSGROVE

Halsgrove House
Lower Moor Way
Tiverton, Devon EX16 6SS
Tel: 01884 243242
Fax: 01884 243325
email: sales@halsgrove.com
website: www.halsgrove.com

Title page: *May Day celebration on the Grand Pier, 1949.*
The pier owner, Mr Brenner, can be seen behind the float.

Printed and bound in Great Britain by CPI Bath.

CONTENTS

ACKNOWLEDGEMENTS

I wish to thank everyone who responded to my requests for memories, pictures and ephemera, as well as all my friends whom I have bored over the last year talking about Weston's past. I hope everyone will enjoy the result. Particular thanks go to:

Mrs Adams, Mrs Addicott, Brian Austin, Mrs Bennett, Alfred Bishop, Roy Brunker, Mr Buchanon, Marina Coles, Ruth Coles, Mrs Compton, Eileen and Laurie Crews, Michael Dauncey, Nancy Davis, Ann Fewings, Madge Frankpitt, Michael Freedman, Annette Gibson, Hilda Goold, Alison Harvey, Mrs Harvey, John Hess, Rosemary Hodges, Carolyn and Keith Hollands, Ena Howe, Pat Johnson, Pat Jones, Joy Kenward, Ken Long, Peter Nisbet, North Somerset Museum Service, in particular Liz Neathey and Nick Goff, Eileen Oxley, Maurice Pitman, Ollie Pratlett, Dave Portch, Chris Richards, Sue Robinson, Jennie Rossiter, Sue Ryall, Jane Saker, June Stephen, Catherine Stevenson, Ruth Sutton, Stan Terrell, Joe Thomas, Robert Tinker, Mike Tozer, Joan and Dave Tyler, June Venn, Elizabeth Warwick, Robin Wild, the community of La Retraite.

Sharon Poole, 2004

INTRODUCTION

'Weston has no history!' Those who know me know that I have spent most of my working life battling to refute this claim, yet it was still being made as recently as 20 years ago or less. What people think of as history can vary, of course, but fundamentally it is times past, whether 100 years ago, or yesterday. The problem, however, is that history changes, or rather that new things are discovered that impact on what we thought we knew, which force us to reappraise past events in the light of new ideas. It can be easy to think that there is nothing more to discover about Weston's past yet we constantly uncover new revelations. Just by compiling this book I have learned about things of which I had never previously heard, such as the Children's Church in Swiss Road, which only closed as recently as the 1980s. Not only had I had never

come across it before, but neither had another local historian to whom I mentioned it.

History is not some abstract idea either, but the doings of men and women just like you and me, and in this respect this book is truly the story of a community. You will not find within these pages a neat chronological account of Weston's rise to popularity. Nor will it tell you a great deal about anything before 1900. This is because it is very much a people's history – a written record of memories, anecdotes, ephemera and all those little snippets of information that so often get left out or lost in more serious volumes. Alright, so memory may not always be totally accurate, but that does not negate its value in building up a picture of a place and providing a record of a time – a period when life could be hard but pleasures were simpler and life was still fun;

Wedding of Mr Charles Oxley and Miss Eileen Beach, c.1929. Charles Oxley was born in the Royal Arcade. He later played water polo for Weston. Eileen Beach was born in 1911 in Amberey Road, and owned a greengrocer's shop in Clifton Road.

a time when children roamed free and safe in the school holidays; when work was physically demanding but jobs were often for life; when home cooking was the norm; families sat down together and when take-away meant fish and chips and fast food was a salad!

I have not lived in Weston all my life. I moved here at a period of great change in the town. The 1970s saw a new phase of development. Vast new housing estates were beginning to cover the ancient farm land at Worle. The large Victorian houses were being sold for conversion into flats, or worse – demolition – and old established family shops were closing in favour of national multiples. I believe I was fortunate in having a great curiosity in old property and attending many closing-down sales and house auctions, when the contents of a house were sold in situ. This is something that has sadly died out today, probably due to the difficulty of policing such sales and the limited space for the buyers. However, it gave a wonderful glimpse into another time and another life, where the plain green or cream walls and cracked lino floors of the pantries, kitchens and servants' bedrooms contrasted with the carpeted and wallpapered parlours and best bedrooms of the family. The clutter and intimacy of a long life laid bare for all to judge, reduced to the banality of the auctioneer's lot number. I was recently lent the catalogues for some of these house sales and it is sobering to realise just how much furniture and equipment it took to run these households in the way they were originally managed. In 1949, the contents of Caerleon, at 4 Queen's Road, took two days to sell. It was a five-bedroomed house with two reception rooms, a study, kitchen, scullery and basement. Included were huge amounts of linen, books, glass and china (among the latter being tea and coffee sets, dessert sets, breakfast sets and no less than five dinner services). Everything was for sale, from the wardrobes in the bedroom to the three hip baths in the scullery. In 1951 the contents of Uphill Grange were auctioned by Lalonde Brothers & Parham of Weston. In this instance it was a seven-bedroomed mansion with maids' rooms, a china pantry and billiard room. Among items in the coach-house, was a 1946 Standard 8 drop-head coupe motor car. I wonder how much it sold for?

As I have mentioned, to write this book I have enlisted help from the whole community. Many people have come forward with anecdotes, photographs and other souvenirs of their lives and connections with Weston-super-Mare, Uphill and Worle and I am greatly indebted to them. It is mostly their memories that I hope you will read and enjoy, and maybe they will, in turn, spark memories of your own. The chapters are certainly heavily weighted with memories of wartime and schooldays, but I do not apologise for that. What is here is what was important in people's lives and what they remembered most vividly.

CATALOGUE

OF THE

Antique and Modern

Appointments

and EFFECTS

AT

The AUCTION ROOMS,

Station Road,

Weston-super-Mare.

TO BE SOLD BY AUCTION ON

TUESDAY, 3rd APRIL, 1951

commencing at ELEVEN o'clock sharp

On View : Day prior to Sale from 10 a.m. to 4 p.m.

Auctioneers :

LALONDE BROS. & PARHAM	**J. H. PALMER & SONS**
18 Boulevard and Station Road	Bank Chambers,
Weston-super-Mare	Burnham-on-Sea
and at	and at
64 Queen's Road, Bristol 8.	Highbridge, Cheddar and Bridgwater.

Price 6d.

Catalogue for a sale of antiques and household furnishings at Lalonde's salerooms, Weston, 1951.

Chapter 1

A Short History

From the eighteenth century onwards Weston began to grow from a village of about 100 farmers, fishermen and their families, to a large bustling mid-Victorian resort of nearly 20,000 people. In 2004 the population is over 70,000. Luck and situation had a lot to do with this growth, but so too did the vision and drive of the townspeople and their willingness to grasp every opportunity, not just for personal gain, but for the good of the town.

People have lived in the area for many thousands of years. We still have the evidence around us, not only in the form of occasional finds of pottery, coins and bones, but also the massive stone walls of the Iron Age settlement on the hill behind the town. Worlebury hill-fort was built over 2,000 years ago. When it was excavated in the 1850s, human remains were found, many showing evidence of a violent death. We may never know why this settlement was attacked, but over the years people drifted back and when the Romans left Britain in the fourth century AD, there were isolated farmsteads again covering the hillside.

By the time of the Saxons, Christianity had arrived and the Church was the centre of village life. Thatched cottages were built along what is now the High Street, while streams and reed beds criss-crossed the village.

In 1568, the mineral calamine was discovered on Worle Hill, the first place in Britain it was found. This type of zinc ore was vital for the production of brass and mining began very shortly after its discovery, continuing well into the nineteenth century. Galena, a lead ore, was also mined along the hillside and remnants of this industrial activity can still be seen in the pits and spoil heaps along the hill.

In 1696 Weston Manor was bought by Colonel John Pigott of Brockley. He built himself a summer holiday cottage in The Grove, Weston, next to the Old Rectory and Parish Church. In 1791, the Revd Leeves of Wrington followed Pigott's example and built his own seaside cottage on the dunes. Part of this cottage can still be seen today as The Old Thatched Cottage Restaurant. The Pigott family held the manor until the estate was sold in 1914 to pay debts and nothing remains beyond the title, lord of the manor of Weston-super-Mare, which was also sold.

By the middle of the eighteenth century, doctors began to explore the health-giving properties of sea water. King George III tried bathing at Weymouth in 1789 and so set the fashion. Weston was conveniently within a day's ride from Bristol and Bath and also offered the then popular attraction of romantic and windswept scenery. The first visitors rented rooms or a house from the locals. Not until 1810 was a hotel opened, which is now part of The Royal Hotel.

As well as bathing in the open sea, indoor spa baths were popular and Mr Howe, a Bristol umbrella maker, opened the first complex on Knightstone in July 1820. From the *Bristol Mirror*, 18 May 1820:

The Public are most respectfully informed, that early next Month the HOT and COLD SALT WATER BATHS will be completed at KNIGHTSTONE, WESTON-SUPER-MARE, 22 miles from Bristol. The advantages which Visitors to the healthy and delightful Village will derive from such an Establishment require no comment. The Reservoirs, to receive the Water during the flow of the Tides from the Sea, are excavated in a solid rock and will contain upwards of 1,000 Hogsheads of Water, which will purify itself, and thence be admitted into PRIVATE BATHS, each Bath to contain 12 Hogsheads of clear Sea Water, and fresh supplied for every Bather, at any time of the day. The Hot and Shower Baths are on the same plan as those of the Bristol Infirmary. There is a House built on the Rock; part thereof will be appropriated to Lodgings for Invalids, and the other part for a public Tea and Coffee-Room, where the London, Bristol, Bath and other Papers will be taken in; thus adding great attraction to this already much frequented Summer Resort.

N.B. Those families who intend visiting Weston-super-Mare this Season, may be accommodated with Houses in Sea View Place, comfortably furnished, by early application to J. Howe, No. 1, Belle-Vue, Weston, or at his Parasol Manufactory, Dolphin Street, Bristol; where a large assortment of PARASOLS are now selling at very reduced prices.

Knightstone was an island and bathers were ferried over by local boatmen. Later a stone causeway was built, which is still in use today. Ten years later Dr Fox of Bristol purchased Knightstone Baths and

Some of the men who built Marine Lake. The named men were all Weston quarrymen. The others were fishermen as well as volunteer lifeboat men. Left to right: ?, ?, ?, ?, ?, ?, ?, ?, William Day, N. Haydon, Henry Baker, William Henry Day, ?, Lou Smart; on the roof: ?; seated on the ground: ?.

'Sketch plan of the picturesque houses which are being rapidly erected in the Station Approach.' This area became known as the Ellenborough estate and was one of the many housing and other developments that took place in Weston in the 1930s. The rural feel of this 1934 drawing is in sharp contrast to the same setting today, which is a mass of road junctions and the railway station car park.

developed it further, building an elegant new bath-house, recently restored and awaiting a new use.

When Isambard Kingdom Brunel extended his Great Western Railway from Bristol down to Exeter in 1841, Weston nearly missed its main chance of success. Not wanting 'noisy smelly steam engines' in the then fashionable resort, the Town Commissioners declined a mainline station, opting instead for a branch line from Weston Junction, and initially using horses to pull the carriages the one-and-a-half miles to the small station where the Floral Clock now stands. Eventually they realised their mistake and purchased a small steam locomotive to replace the horses, but it was 40 years before a loop line was laid into the town so that mainline trains could deliver visitors to within a short walk of the beach itself.

Birnbeck Pier was opened in 1867 during the great era of pier building around the coast. Meanwhile the town was growing as new villas and crescents covered the hillside, and terraces and shops began to fill up the centre.

As a new century dawned, so a change began to take place. Society was much more relaxed and new entertainments, such as moving pictures, were being invented. On the beach the bathing machines disappeared as mixed bathing became acceptable. Another pier was thought necessary, closer to those visitors arriving by train, rather than steamer, and in June 1904 the Grand Pier opened. Instead of fairground amusements as on Birnbeck Pier, the Grand Pier had a large theatre offering all the top musical stars of the day.

Weston played an active role in the First World War. As men left for the battlefield, so unexpected opportunities opened up to women. Indeed, Weston was home to the first female tram drivers in the country. The beach was put to use for recruits to practice digging trenches before they were shipped to Flanders.

After the First World War the confident 'Roaring '20s' led to more leisure development taking place. The Marine Lake, Central Picture House and Winter Gardens and Pavilion were all built during this period, followed in the 1930s by the Open Air Pool, Odeon Cinema and an airport. Many South Wales miners took

Advertisement for new houses in the Devonshire Road estate, 1933.

to flying over to Weston on Sundays. It was quick and cheap, but the town's pubs were the main attraction as the Welsh ones were closed on the Sabbath.

In 1937 the town was granted borough status. It is interesting to read the comments in the special souvenir supplement to the Weston Mercury newspaper that was produced to mark this momentous event, particularly the question, 'Has Weston a future or, as a local pessimist recently suggested, will the town become a distressed area within 20 years?' The worry was that 'gigantic schemes involving the expenditure of vast sums of money have been carried out, with the result that the financial position of the town gives cause for concern.' This is a reminder that at this period, most of the new developments, such as the Winter Gardens and the swimming pool, were instigated by the local authority and funded from the rates. With the wonderful benefit of hindsight we know that Weston enjoyed a very prosperous period before and after the Second World War and that these worries were unfounded but balancing the books

Building the Grand Pier. This pier took just seven months to construct, from driving in the first piles in November 1903 to the opening in June 1904.

Staff at Henlys Factory, Oldmixon. This was a Ministry of Supply works, run by Henlys, where combat vehicles were overhauled or rebuilt. The factory serviced everything from RAF refuellers to DUKW amphibious vehicles. It opened in 1948 and closed in 1965.

remains an annual problem for councillors today.

War was looming again and by late 1939, huge numbers of evacuees arrived in Weston from London and other large cities. As well as pregnant women and children, whole schools were also evacuated, for example, the Weston County School for Girls took staff and pupils from two London schools, Barking Abbey, and in late 1940, Mitcham Secondary School. There were many bombing raids but the worst blitzes took place in January 1941 and June 1942, when large parts of the town were destroyed.

When hostilities ceased, the council was faced with a decision about what to do with the various bomb sites and had to plan for the future success of the resort. War had brought new industries to Weston, leaving vacant factories available, and the Borough Council promoted the area heavily as an ideal base for light industry. Until this point, tourism

had been the major employer in Weston and it was felt that new industries could offer a valuable source of employment in a declining holiday market.

By the late 1960s foreign holiday destinations had become easier and less expensive to reach and British seaside resorts began to lose their appeal. This has meant a struggle for economic survival. It is no longer enough to offer basic hotels and a few attractions. People are more sophisticated and expect the same level of service and accommodation that they get abroad, often for less money. Hard decisions will have to be taken, but there is no reason why Weston cannot regain a measure of its past glory. In 2002 over 4.5 million visitors came to North Somerset, generating over £181 million for the area and giving employment to 5,000 people. These figures were an increase on the previous two years, suggesting the start of a reversal of decline and giving strength to the notion that people still want to come to the seaside. However, they now come for short breaks rather than the traditional two weeks by the sea. This means that the town has to adapt what it offers to attract the new kind of tourist. For example, in a recent survey by the English Tourist Board, shopping and eating out came above attractions and beaches in why people choose a short-break holiday destination. Food for thought indeed.

Uphill and Worle

Uphill was very much a maritime village. Its harbour was once an important port and the River Axe was a commercial artery inland as far as Axbridge. It was not until the floodgates were constructed at Bleadon in 1808 that the river ceased to be navigable. It is thought that the Romans exported the lead ore mined

View of Uphill village from the hillside, c.1910.

Mr Howe and his son Charles outside The Old Hall, Beach Road, Uphill. Charles lived to be 92. During the Second World War he was head of the local ambulance service.

from Charterhouse on Mendip, through Uphill.

In the Domesday Book Uphill is spelled Opopille, possibly originating from the name of the Danish Chieftain, Hubba and therefore meaning Hubba's pill or creek. In the late-seventh century Vikings were sailing up the Bristol Channel and launching raids inland along rivers such as the Axe. The Anglo-Saxon Chronicle records that several Danes took refuge from the Saxons on the islands of Flat Holm and Steep Holm, from where raids were launched on the Somerset coast.

In 1592 the French ship *Greyhound* out of Bayonne, was attacked and damaged by one of Sir Walter Raleigh's men-o'-war and had to put in to Uphill for repairs. In 1645, during the English Civil War, an unsuccessful attempt was made to land Royalist reinforcements at Uphill to strengthen the garrison at Bridgwater, then under siege.

The Old Church of St Nicholas and Uphill Quarry. In this rare view it is possible to see the roof of the cottage, long-since demolished, on the slope below the church.

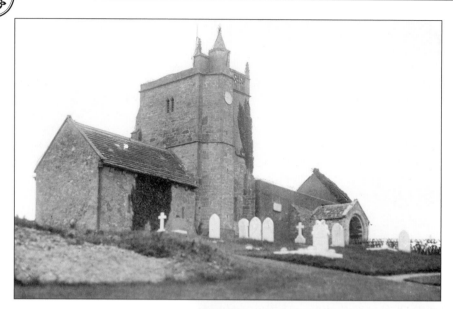

The Old Church of St Nicholas, Uphill.

The interior of the New Church of St Nicholas, decorated for the Harvest Festival, 1922.

The Every family in their garden at Sandcroft Cottages, Uphill. **Left to right, back row:** *George Every, his wife Ellen (the village midwife), Alice Blunt (née Every), Jack Blunt, Joyce Every;* front: *Grace Every.*

In later times, cattle, coal and slate became the most common legal cargoes (smuggling was rife along this coast in the late-eighteenth and early-nineteenth centuries) traded between Uphill and Wales. In 1860 over 16,000 tons of coal were imported through Uphill. The quarry was also important to the local economy. Quarrying began on the hill in the village as early as 1826. The limestone rock was quarried using gunpowder. When an Inspector of Mines and Quarries called at the quarry in the 1920s, he asked where the explosives were stored. The manager replied that they were kept in the box on which the Inspector was sitting! The construction of a proper magazine was ordered, the ruins of which can still be seen on the left of the track running south just beyond the quarry. Quarrying finished at Uphill in about 1939.

For a time there was also a tile- and brickworks in the village, on the level land at the foot of the hill. In fact Uphill Brickyard was probably one of the oldest in the area. When the Revd Skinner visited Uphill in September 1829 he wrote in his diary:

We spoke to the Brickmakers who have sunk fifteen feet below the deposit of the Severn and they think it is upwards of five feet more before they come to the bed of the estuary.

By 1843 the yard was being run by Charles Whitting. In the 1851 census he is listed as landowner, coal merchant and brick maker employing a total of 16 men. In 1861 Thomas Whitting & Company were working the yard but three years later the works had passed to the Gould family. Most of what is now Thornbury Road, Berkeley Crescent and Beach End Road were once clay workings. The brickworks closed early in the twentieth century but their roof tiles may still be seen on a number of buildings in the Weston area.

The Old Church of St Nicholas stands on the hilltop, as it has done since the Norman period. For hundreds of years its tower, the western side then whitewashed, served as a landmark for sailors. The new church, also dedicated to St Nicholas, opened in 1844 and the old church fell into disuse. Its roof was partially removed in 1864, although the tower still retains its bells, four of them cast by the great bell-founding family of Bilbie at Chew Stoke in the eighteenth century. Today the building is looked after by the Churches Conservation Trust.

Nowadays the oldest building, besides the church, is Uphill Manor. Recently acquired by the charity Weston Hospicecare as an in-patient and day unit, it dates back to the sixteenth century. The two inns in the village, now The Dolphin and The Ship Inn, were once known as The West and East Inns. During the eighteenth century The Ship Inn was also called The Crown and later, The Lamb. In 1826, when The Strand Hotel was built on the site of what is now

The Royal Sands development, The Dolphin lost its licence as the new pub was also in Uphill parish. It was 1860 before it gained a full licence again.

Brunel's Bristol & Exeter Railway skirts the village and what was officially Uphill Station was actually closer to Bleadon. There were once, however, traces of a station at the junction where the loop line into Weston joins the mainline at Uphill. It was said that the Uphill landowner drove a hard bargain, selling his land to the railway company on condition they built him his own private station. This was agreed, but nothing was said about trains calling at the station, and despite a court action, the landowner lost his case and not once did a train stop at his station.

By virtue of its geography, Uphill has managed to retain its village feel. There is a distinct break between it and Weston-super-Mare and, as the main road bypasses the village and there is little available land for house building, there is no reason it will not continue to do so.

At Worle it is a different story. The one-time village of Worle has kept its name unaltered since the times of Domesday (1086) when Walter of Douai held the manor. A wooden fortified manor-house was built at Castle Batch in the late-eleventh or early-twelfth century. William I had these fortified homesteads built all over the county (another was at Locking Castle) as part of the defences against a possible invasion by King Harold's son. The main village of Worle grew up along the southern slope of the end of Worle Hill. Foxglove Cottage at the top of the Scaurs, with its medieval cruck-frame structure, is probably the oldest domestic building in Worle. St Martin's Church dates to the twelfth century and has some lovely surviving architectural features including a squint (a 'window' in a column so that the whole congregation can see the altar) and some medieval carved wooden misericords or fold-down seats in the chancel.

The wedding of W.L. (Jack) Blunt and Alice Every, Uphill, 19 May 1923. Left to right: George Every, Ruth Tucker, William Blunt, Alice Every, Alice Stevens, General ?. Miss Stevens was the daughter of the village policeman.

B 18753   CERTIFIED COPY of an   ENTRY OF MARRIAGE.   [Printed by authority of the Registrar General.]   M. Cert.
Pursuant to the Marriage   Acts, 1836 to 1898.   A.P.

Marriage certificate between William Leonard Blunt of Sandcroft Cottages and Alice Grace Every, 1923. They were married in the Wesleyan chapel in Uphill. William's father was listed as 'riding master', whilst Alice's father was a quarryman.

Gradually the village spread to the lower-lying land at the base of the hill. Worle was on the main route to Weston and all visitors to the resort had to pass through the village until the railway was built in 1841. The New Inn (now The Woodspring), built in 1815 at the bottom of the Scaurs, was a staging post where horses could be changed. Opposite the pub was the village pump, still in situ until lost to road widening in the 1960s. Other public houses in the village included The Lamb and The Golden Lion, both in the High Street, The Old King's Head in the Scaurs and The Valiant Soldier in Church Road. In 1859 there was also a reference, discovered by researcher Brian Austin, to The Pig and Whistle in Leather Lane, Worle. This referred to a 'nuisance abated by committee' with the result that the pub was taken over by Dan Gill in 1869 and the church bells rung to celebrate!

The area's oldest shop was at the top of the Scaurs. Variously known over the years as Henville's, The Worle General Supply Stores, Manchester House and Gunnings, this store sold pretty much everything, from candles to calico, mutton to muslin. The complex included a store, granary, bakery, slaughterhouse and butcher's shop. Customers came from far afield as it was the only shop for many miles until Weston began to develop in the 1830s. It sadly closed in 1985 and was converted into housing.

Worle remained very much a distinct and 'olde-world' village until the 1960s when much of the High Street was demolished for new shops and other facilities such as a branch library and health centre. Since then it has become more like a suburb of Weston, with little to distinguish the boundary of the old parish.

Station Road, Worle, 1964.

The eastern end of Worle High Street during the laying of new sewers, 1960s.

Chapter 2

'Air Like Wine'

Despite the fact that Weston developed as a salt-water spa for invalids, as did all English seaside resorts, the health aspect of holidays is often lost today in a haze of ice-cream, candyfloss, donkeys and piers. Early visitors came to the town to restore their flagging spirits and cure their ailments, real and imaginary. Only those able to afford the time and money to travel and stay away from home could take a holiday at that time. It was not until the Bank Holiday Act of 1871, together with special cheap excursions run by railway companies, that ordinary working folk could also enjoy the delights of the seaside, unless of course they lived there, and so holiday resorts gradually adapted their facilities to meet the needs of everyone, rather than just the privileged few. It was at this time that the spas, bath houses and reading-rooms began to give way to piers, theatres and pierrots!

As comparatively late as 1938, however, Weston was still being promoted for its health-giving aspects. That year the Borough Council published an advertising leaflet aimed solely at medical professionals. It listed Weston's facilities and natural advantages that would aid the sick and convalescent. With the strict environmental controls we have today, it is easy to forget that many of our towns and cities were then polluted with smoke and smog and in contrast, Weston's clean fresh salty air must indeed have been a tonic to the sick.

The booklet described the climate of Weston-super-Mare and its therapeutic effects and specified the types of patients who would benefit from a stay here. It also included, unusually, those unlikely to do so. Weston was, the leaflet claimed, ideal for the patient who needs:

... a temperate, tonic winter climate, but cannot afford to go abroad. Weston air works wonders. Weston-super-Mare's outstanding asset is its remarkably invigorating, recuperative and health-giving climate, which is temperate and equable, yet very bracing. Taking the year through, Weston has one of the finest tonic climates in this country. It approaches the 'optimum' for human health and efficiency.

... the town is sheltered from northerly winds and enjoys singularly warm and sunny winter days. Some

districts face directly south, but all are fully open to the Atlantic Ocean with its sunshine and fresh breezes. It is these breezes which constitute Weston's 'Air like Wine', and provide what is seldom found at south-western or southern resorts, a non-relaxing climate. They disperse the heat of what otherwise would be sultry summer days and temper winter's cold, thus making the climate cool in summer and warm in winter. Therapeutically they are very important, for the researches of Sir Leonard Hill... and others have shown that the cool air and continual breezes of the seashore deepen the respiration and, in children, favourably alter the shape of the chest... and generally improve metabolism.

In the 1930s, sunbathing was thought to be a very healthy occupation with no consideration given to hazards such as sunburn and skin cancer.

Sunshine is abundant, sufficient to satisfy the most ardent sunbathers. Last year it totalled 1,541 hours and during the five summer months Weston, with 778.6 hours, led all the resorts on the western seaboard for recorded sunshine. From November to March (the Invalids' winter), when sunshine is so deficient in industrial centres, there is an average of 2.4 hours of bright sunshine per day in Weston...

The mildness, dryness and brightness of the town's winters are becoming increasingly appreciated, and many people do as well at Weston as on the Riviera where, despite sunnier and slightly warmer days, the evenings are chillier, the nights much colder and the winds often troublesome. Snow is almost unknown and there was absolutely none last winter, even in December when most of the south country was snowbound.

Beach Road on the sea front and the roads immediately behind it are specially beneficial to asthmatics, probably because the prevailing sea breezes are free from pollens and dusts. Weston is also notably effective as an 'after-cure' to tone up patients who have been lowered by eliminative spa and bath treatment.

Neither Weston nor any other resort suits everyone, and its climate is too stimulating for acute or haemorrhagic pulmonary tuberculosis, or for acute mental and other diseases needing a relaxing or sedative climate.

The town provides all facilities for obtaining general

and specific medical and physical treatment. The General Hospital has a modern and well-equipped Electrical and Sunlight Department which caters for private patients; massage, sunlight and other treatments may be obtained at private clinics and nursing homes. Many hotels and boarding houses provide for those needing special diets.

The Council's Medicinal Baths at Knightstone supply foam, vapour, hot sea water, seaweed and other medicinal baths. Open all the year round, they have a great reputation in the treatment of all rheumatic conditions, and are popular with those training for sports and athletic competitions.

Reading some of the claims in this leaflet today one wonders why anyone would want to holiday anywhere else, let alone why any of us ever get ill!

For this reason the town was chosen as the site for many convalescent homes. As well as the Sanatorium, which, incidentally, never took infectious cases such as tuberculosis, a special convalescent home opened in Walliscote Road in 1895 just for children, taking boys and girls from the ages of three to eleven. In the 1930s the Kewstoke Convalescent Home was built by the Birmingham Hospital Saturday Fund and in the 1950s the British Legion opened a home in Claremont Crescent as a County War Memorial. In 2003 the British Legion announced plans to replace this home with a new Somerset Legion House in Beach Road on the site now occu-

pied by the derelict Sandcroft Convalescent Home. At the time of writing it is planned that the new building will have 52 twin-bedded ensuite rooms together with public lounges, a library and a cinema. Knightstone was offering medicinal baths, such as hot sea water, seaweed and vapour treatments well into the 1960s. It has always been my hope that the baths complex, currently derelict, would be converted into a modern hydrotherapy spa, but it seems an unlikely prospect.

Local health care has always incorporated a high degree of community involvement. Until the mid-nineteenth century all health needs were provided by private doctors, surgeons or pharmacists and people were cared for in their own homes. If you were unable to afford their services you either got better naturally, or you died. A free dispensary was opened in Alfred Street in 1847. This helped those suffering from disease but could offer little help for the injured. In the 1850s, a local labourer fell from scaffolding and broke his leg very badly. His obvious suffering at having to be taken by horse and cart the 20 miles to the free Bristol Infirmary led to Weston's first cottage hospital being built. It opened in 1865 on what were then the outskirts of the town, in Alfred Street. It offered seven in-patient beds and an out-patient unit. In 1887, the women of Weston raised sufficient funds to add a separate children's ward and by 1900 there were 35 beds, caring for 300 patients annually. The hospital was funded entirely locally. It had a small income from invested property but the remainder of its running costs came from donations and fees. In the 1881 census, the staff on duty consisted of Welsh house surgeon Hugh Rowlands, matron Victoria Byrn, 15-year-old cook and general servant Sarah Phillips, and one nurse per ward (there was a male ward, a female ward and an infectious ward) as well as one night nurse. There were 24 patients, of which seven were female domestic servants and six were children. Of the remainder, one was a dressmaker and the rest working men, such as a wheelwright, a soldier, and a mason's labourer.

By the 1920s, the population of Weston had grown fourfold and the cottage hospital could no longer cope with demand. An extensive fund-raising drive, led by local entrepreneur Henry Butt, raised £50,000, a huge amount of money for the time, which earned Butt the nickname the 'King of Beggars'. Not only did it pay for the building in full, but there were sufficient funds to furnish it with all the latest equipment. It was built in the Boulevard, and connected with the old hospital by a passageway at the back. The opening day of 6 July 1928 was a general holiday in Weston. This new Queen Alexandra Memorial Hospital was opened by the Duke and Duchess of York, later King George VI and Queen Elizabeth – the town's first official royal visit. The couple arrived by train at 3.40p.m. and were greeted by 3,000 local children. They were then

Advertisement for the medicinal baths at Knightstone, during the 1950s.

driven on an extended route via Walliscote Road, Moorland Road, Uphill Road, Beach Road, Regent Street, High Street and Waterloo Street, so that as many people as possible would be able to see them. Reports say that 100,000 people lined the route. Since Weston then had a population of around 32,000, they must have come from far and wide. When the royal couple arrived at the hospital they were taken on a tour of the building and performed the opening ceremony with a solid gold key. They then left by car, leaving the town via Alfred Street, Locking Road, Jubilee Road, Baker Street, George Street and Swiss Road, before finally driving along Milton Road, to take them past the new council-houses at Milton.

With various additions and alterations over the years, this hospital served the people of Weston and district well. However, services had become scattered all over the town as other buildings were acquired to cope with the growth in population. For example, the maternity unit was in Ashcombe House, while the Royal Hospital, originally the Royal West of England Sanatorium, housed acute medical and geriatric beds. Eastern House in Landemann Circus provided 36 convalescent and recovery beds. The situation was not ideal. In 1986, all units were

Henry Butt, businessman, councillor and first mayor of Weston, 1937. It was his drive and vision that saw the successful building of the Queen Alexandra Memorial Hospital in 1928.

finally brought under one roof, when the present hospital was built at Uphill. All the original buildings have since been converted into private housing with the exception of Ashcombe House which was demolished.

There were times when Westonians lost hope that a new hospital would ever be built, and it was a triumph for local campaigners when the Duchess of Gloucester arrived in Uphill on 28 April 1987 to perform the opening ceremony. In the intervening years medical care had been transformed. The new hospital, Weston General, boasted nine wards as well as an intensive care unit with a total of 252 beds. The Hospital League of Friends had contributed almost £250,000 for beds and equipment. The *Weston Mercury* ran a huge fund-raising drive with its 'Buy a Bed' appeal. Today, of course, with the increase in population following the construction of the new housing estates at Wick St Lawrence and Locking Castle, even the new hospital is proving too small, and there have been almost constant additions over the years. The latest has been new oncology and day-surgery units, made possible by a legacy left to the Trust by the late Sybil Jackson Barstow. These were officially opened by Prince Edward, the Earl of Wessex, in September 2003.

Souvenir of the opening of the Queen Alexandra Memorial Hospital, Weston-super-Mare, 1928.

The first phonograph in Weston, c.1892. The tall man in the bowler hat in the centre of the picture is Walter Gage. He is said to have brought the first Edison phonograph to the West Country from America. In the picture he is demonstrating the machine in the Royal Arcade in Weston. The audience is listening on headphones, for which they were charged a penny.

Meadow Street, decorated for the coronation of King George V, 1911. Hopkins Street is on the right.

Chapter 3

Down Memory Lane

The accounts in this chapter relate the personal memories of people born or who lived or visited Weston and who knew it as a very different town from that of today. Charles Bidwell was born in Worle in 1905 and Madge Frankpitt was born in Meadow Street, Weston, in 1909. Both have very contrasting memories of life during the early years of the twentieth century. Also in this chapter is an account by Mr Portch of Bristol, who first visited Weston in 1919 aged 11 and Nancy Davis, in her nineties at the time of writing, who came here for annual holidays from Wales with her parents from before the First World War.

Madge Frankpitt

Margaret Payne, as she was named then, was born over her father's grocery shop in Meadow Street in 1909. Madge recorded her memories on tape in 2002 and it is a much-edited version that is reproduced here. The original contained nearly 30,000 words! The following account records Madge's own words and takes the reader back to a gentler age when children wandered the town, beach and woods alone in perfect safety, when couples 'courted' and when luxury was an indoor toilet!

A Place to Call Home

It has been suggested by family and friends that I talk onto a tape and tell the memories I have of the past 93 years. It seemed a daunting task at the outset but I've decided I will try. I was born over my father's grocery shop, Harry Payne's Stores, in Meadow Street in 1909. My brother Jack was born there six years later. I looked at those two shops the other day, and they're just the same as they were 100 years ago. I think two new doors have been put in but at least the structure is still the same and I often look up to the windows over the shops and remember our home as it was. It was a warm comforting home.

I was born into a loving family, Mother and Father and two half-brothers. Father had been a widower when he married Mother. He had been married to Georgina Shorney who came from a family of builders in Weston who lived in Victoria Square in a big house called Brynmor. When he married her he bought a house in Baker

Street called Grosvenor Villa which faced what was to become Swiss Road. But Georgina wasn't happy there, it was too far out in the country so they moved back and lived over the shop. She died quite young when there was an epidemic of typhoid in Weston. Father also lost his elder brother, Walter, who had a tailoring shop on the other side of the road to him in Meadow Street. It was later taken on by Stockers, the newsagent; a few years ago when they were doing some alterations there they found some old leaflets that Uncle Walter had had printed, advertising flannel trousers. However, Father had two young boys when his wife died and with the help of Granny Payne, his mother, who lived around the corner in Alfred Street, he brought them up.

When I look back on our home behind and over the shop, I can't believe how primitive it was, but to us in those days we expected nothing different. There was a sitting-room behind the shop and that was cosy. There was a table and chairs and two comfortable armchairs for Mother and Father and a fire. There we used to have our meals and after dinner – we didn't have luncheon in those days – Mother would always bring out a board game of some sort which we would play. There was also a cupboard under the stairs off that room. In that cupboard Mother used to develop her films – she was very keen on photography, and she used it as a darkroom amongst other things. There was always a great big crock of eggs in isinglass [a preserving agent] and jams were put on shelves. Then along the passage you came to the kitchen. It was quite a small room, but oh, how primitive. Just a little Belfast sink with a cold-water tap and a gas cooker, a table and some shelves. There were usually some Christmas puddings on the top shelf, as I remember, and the door led out into the back yard which was whitewashed. In those days, there were no such things as refrigerators, freezers or washing machines; there was just a mangle there in the yard and a safe [a small wooden cupboard with a metal mesh door] in which we used to keep the meat, butter and milk. There was also the outside lavatory, and as I'm thinking about it, I don't believe we ever had toilet rolls. We must have had newspaper cut up in squares.

That was the downstairs. When you went upstairs there was a door on your right leading into our best sitting-room. On the left were two bedrooms. You walked along the landing and came to another door which led to Mother and Father's bedroom. I had a cot, I remember it quite clearly, in the corner, a white enamelled cot, and off that bedroom there was a little room which they used as a dressing-room. Of course we had no bathroom. Friday nights the tin bath was brought in and we were bathed in front of the fire, which was very comfortable, but it was all as I say, very primitive. The best sitting-room was used on Sundays, and party days and Christmas, of course. Mother was a great one for parties so it was used quite a bit. There was a three-piece suite upholstered in red moquette, very uncomfortable and tickly on your legs. There was a china cabinet that used to fascinate me. I wasn't allowed to open it but I could look in through the glass and there were my parents' wedding presents. There was a lovely silver sugar basin with a red liner, which used to fascinate me, a butter dish with a rollover top, which I still have, and a coffee and tea service in silver plate, which I also still possess. There's no plate left on it now but it's a reminder of those old days over the shop.

Then there was the piano. I remember as a little girl learning [to play] the piano. I was sent upstairs each evening to do my scales and practice and it was jolly cold up there but somehow there was a warmth about the place. The street was lit with gas lamps and there was always something going on. People did their shopping quite late at night and with the horses and cries of the newspaper boys, it was a warm comforting feeling. On Saturday nights the band used to play. There was a German band and it used to play on the corner of Alfred Street, Baker Street and Meadow Street.

Harry Payne's Stores

Father was apprenticed to a Mr Dashwood who had a big shop at the top of Meadow Street, and Father must have been quite young because he used to tell me that very often, of a Saturday night, Mr Dashwood, who was a very upright Christian man, had a little boy who would not be more than 12 or 14 who he would send with the sack trucks to deliver some sugar right up to Milton by The Windsor Castle. Father said that very often [this lad] was so frightened to be going out at night that he would go to Alfred Street to ask his father to go with him.

After Father finished his apprenticeship he went to Wedmore's in Bristol, wholesale grocers, and there he learnt tea-tasting and general grocery before coming back to Weston to open up his shop at the bottom of Meadow Street. In those days it was a busy little road because one of the buses used to come up from Milton Road through Baker Street and decant a lot of passengers as it turned up Alfred Street. These people would make their way up Meadow Street and pass Father's shop, and so he was very busy. The two shops were divided. One was the provisions, where they sold the bacon, etc., and the other was the grocery and there was a lovely smell about the shop. The grocery side had a wooden floor and every morning the assistants would

scatter sawdust over the floor and then turn the coffee-grinding machine to give it a sense of smell and comfort. And then there were the spice drawers. Behind the counter there were two rows of spice drawers and they gave out a lovely smell. There were chillies, cloves, pepper, coconut, bicarbonate and nutmeg and then under the counter itself were big drawers full of currants and sultanas and great big fat raisins and cap peel, which you don't see these days. Big caps of orange and citron peel and there were always lovely lumps of sugar in it. Then, of course, there were the brass scales and the little wooden till with a paper roll in it. It was very primitive. Outside the shop was a storeroom and every Monday morning I remember a sack truck would be wheeled in with a sack of sugar on it and the assistants would stand there weighing up sugar, one pounds and two pounds, in blue bags, which were stacked on the shelves in the shop. There was no such thing as Nescafé. I can remember the red and white blue tins of chicory and coffee, that would be the instant coffee of the day, and Camp Coffee, and big caddies of tea. People would buy their tea loose and Father would have his white paper with his name and address on and that would be put on the scale and then [the assistant would] pick down one of the big tea canisters and shake the tea into the paper on the scale and they used to say 'and a little bit of dust' and that was another finer tea

The cover of an account book given to customers by William Payne in 1899.

and then it was flat wrapped. And all the fruit was wrapped in blue demi paper and flat wrapped.

There was no heat there and in the days when I joined the shop during the Second World War we had one little round oil stove and that was the only heat we had in the shop and we were frozen but Father always wanted the doors open. He said it encouraged people to come in. And if we grumbled he'd say 'I've been in the shop and seen snow at the doorstep so you can stick it a little bit longer.' On the other side – the second shop – was bacon [the sides of which] would be hanging up at the back of the shop and big slabs of butter and lard and margarine and the bacon slicer. The cheese was always cut with a wire cutter. Everything was fresh and sliced immediately; you ordered your bacon according to the thickness that you liked. The sides of bacon were quite heavy to lift down and cut in half and then it all had to be boned but we had assistants there who could do it quite efficiently. I always remember at Christmas time, my brother Frank was in charge of the provisions side, and his window at Christmas was always lovely. He would have sides of smoked bacon at the back, decorated with laurel and holly and there would always be pork pies in the front and a big Stilton cheese which was broken in half and put in the middle in pride of place, because there wasn't much variety in the cheeses in those days. We just had Gorgonzola – I always remember the firm, it was Mattia Locatelli and it was beautiful – and just Stilton and Cheddar.

I remember Father used to buy his cheeses just twice a year. He had a very good reputation as a grocer. The ethics of the commercial travellers were that if there was a commercial traveller in a shop you wouldn't go in, you'd wait outside with the result that very often on a Wednesday, which was half-day in Bristol, we had a lot of commercial travellers in Weston; I remember seeing perhaps half a dozen of them outside of the shop. Father would go outside and say 'I want to see you and you but I won't see anybody else' and they would pack up their bags and off they would go. We had our favourite commercial travellers. There was a Mr Sage who used to come every Wednesday and he travelled for Ashton Vale Biscuit Co. There was Mr Bosanquet who I was always very frightened of. He wore a bowler hat and always had a rose in his buttonhole. Quite a lot of them became family friends.

There was lots of storage space at the rear of the shop. Behind the shop itself there was a place where we used to pack up the sugar and all sorts of orders were put up. People used to hand in their orders. Beyond that was another store and I can remember the vinegar barrel was there and it used to get very dirty. When I think of the hygiene, it just didn't exist at all. And then beyond that was the yard and then a big store and then up a flight of steps to a workshop and it was up there, at Christmas time, that Father would insist on cleaning all his own fruit and he used to go up there in the coldest of weather with cans of boiling water and wash all the fruit and then sprinkle it with a sort of sugar solution and then put it in a box in the window. It used to shine and look beautiful but his poor hands, they were pitted with the little stalks from the currants and sultanas and I often think what hard work it must have been in those days. What a far cry from the supermarkets of today. If I could have one wish I would have Father back just for a day and take him to Tesco, just to stand and watch. I remember when we used to go on holiday to Bournemouth, in the Arcade there was a beautiful grocers' shop called Williams & Treadgold, and whilst Mother and I were pottering around the shops, Father would just stand there looking in admiration at this beautiful shop. He always had a walking stick, and he'd lean on this stick and stand there quite happily watching the people going in and out, he was quite a character, was Father. He chain-smoked Gold Flake and he always wore a cap. I remember he never went shopping anywhere and when he needed a new cap he would send a messenger up to Cecil Walker for a box of caps to be sent down, which was done. Father would stand in front of the mirror and he'd pick up one and flop it on his head, 'no', and then another one, 'yes', and then another one and he'd go through the whole box and choose two or three and then send the rest back. That was the extent of his shopping.

So those were the two shops. We had a side alleyway, and in the early days we just had sack trucks and ordinary trucks to deliver all the groceries. Later, many years after, we had an Austin Seven and then we moved on to a Bedford van.

Back at the shop, Arthur, Frank [Madge's stepbrothers] and Clifford [an assistant], used to go out every morning collecting orders from various customers. They would bring the orders back and they would be put up by the staff and delivered. Father, until very late in life, kept Monday mornings for his two or three special old customers. Father had a bicycle and I remember he would mount it from the back. He would stand on the steps which stuck out from the back wheel and then lower himself onto the saddle and then off he would go, sometimes with me on the crossbar. I remember his first port of call was a Mrs Pople in Oxford Street. There was a little cottage there where the ambulance hall is now, and he would call there and take her order. From there we would go to part of the High Street, which was then Union Street, which was, I suppose, if you could call it so, our slums. It was a little narrow street. There was Tremlett's, the farrier and Noah Brown who was a local celebrity, who was always getting drunk. I think he appeared before the magistrates about 300 times for drunken behaviour, but he was a china riveter, and it was said that he never once broke a piece of china, although he was such a rumbustuous man. He used to sit in the window of his little cottage there in Union Street and do his riveting. And there was also another shop that Father used to call on – a little sweetshop run by Mrs Tripp. I remember the things she sold. I used to be fascinated – little strips of liquorice, bootlaces and sherbet dabs, some dreadful chewing gum that was like wax, but she always used to give me some, then there were dolly mixtures and wine gums. It was a really old-fashioned sweetshop. Father used to take an order from her. And then from there we went to his prime customer, which was the York Hotel where Mrs Thorn-Evans, the owner, used to have us in her sitting-room. She would give Father her order and then we would get on the bike again and come home.

The Payne Family

Father's mother lived in Alfred Street and she had come from Frome. Her name was Annie Burr and she married James Payne who came originally from Wolvershill, Banwell. He died quite young which left Granny with three sons. Uncle Walter was the eldest, then my father, Harry, and then the youngest, Sylvester. Walter married Lilla Hurman, who lived in one of the tall houses at the bottom of Alfred Street, and she too was a tailoress. They had this shop in Meadow Street, but when Uncle Walter died she moved to a house in Walliscote Grove Road with her two sons, Sylv and Cecil. Then there was Father who married Georgina Shorney and had Arthur and Frank. Father's younger brother Sylv married Lily Morris. She worked in Coulstings, the toy shop in the High Street. She was a sweet woman, so gentle. She looked after Granny Payne until Granny died.

Granny Payne was a tailoress who specialised in making waistcoats and Father told me that very often, when he was quite a young lad, he would bank the fire up for her at night and she would sit up all night and make a waistcoat. It was sent up a couple of doors away to another woman who would do the buttonholes, for which she was paid, I think, a farthing a buttonhole. And then in the morning father would take the waistcoat, which was by then finished, to Mr Salisbury who had a shop in West Street. He was paid 1s.6d. and that meant they would have some money to buy some food for the day.

But Granny Payne was a complete character. She made all her boys' clothes, of course. They went to Christchurch School, all three of them, and on Saturdays, she would put their best clothes on, because in her words, 'One day my son you might be Mayor of Weston and no one's going to say you ran about with the seat out of your pants.'

Granny Payne lived around the corner in Alfred Street, and Father set her up in a little grocery store, a little hucksters shop. She was very happy there looking after all her customers in Alfred Street and I always remember the shop. It used to have cards hanging up around the inside that held perhaps little round pill-boxes of Beecham's Pills or Daisy Powders for headaches and another card had dummies on it. On the occasions Mother went up to London, I would go up to Granny Payne's to be looked after with Jack [Madge's younger brother] and when Mother came back I was

there with a dummy in my mouth and I must have been about six or seven and she was horrified but this card of dummies always fascinated me.

As was the custom then, at Christmas, Granny Payne used to give her best customers a little parcel and she used to do up perhaps a pound of sugar and a quarter of tea and a bit of butter or something like that. There was one family in Alfred Street who always owed her money and it was said that Granny said to Florrie one year, 'Florrie come in here'. She had a little sitting-room behind the shop and on the table were all these parcels and Granny says, 'Now look Florrie, that's for Mrs Westlake and that's for Mrs Tanner and that's for Mrs Bennett and that's for Mrs Gould and that's for Mrs Hurman.' She pointed them all out, 'but there isn't one for you but I'm going to knock 2s.6d. off your bill', and that was Florrie's Christmas present.

During the First World War one morning there was an explosion. Granny thought the Germans had come, so she put her bonnet on and her coat and she marched off down Alfred Street to her son's shop. She thought the Germans were bombing the town and said she wanted to die with her sons, but it was an explosion at the gasworks!

We used to go and visit Granny every Sunday night and we would sit in her sitting-room behind the shop and she would be in her chair with her feet on a foot-stool, with elastic-sided boots and a black bodice and her hair in a bun. Uncle Sylv used to play the harmonium while we stood round singing hymns. One thing I do recall was that Granny Payne had a phonograph. It was a little machine with a cylinder and on the top was a sort of needle that came down and the records were cylinder-shaped too, made of the same shellac that the 78s were made of. I don't know how it worked, we must have wound it up by some means because there was no electricity and these records would slot onto the cylinder and then this raucous American voice would come on and it would always start off 'This is an Edison Bell Record', and then we would have songs like 'Nellie Dean' and 'Bicycle Made for Two'. It was quite a treat to go to Granny's and listen to those records. I used to stay there when Mother went on holiday and I always remember the bedroom. We had to take a candle up to bed because there was no gas upstairs and in the bedroom where I used to sleep there was a great big print of 'The Monarch of the Glen'.

This reminds me about some of the pictures which were in our own home. In the sitting-room behind the shop there was a great big black-and-white print of King George V welcoming Lord Roberts after the Relief of Ladysmith. It wasn't a very pretty picture but Frank took great delight in pointing out to anyone who looked at it that if you looked very carefully you could see 'OXO' all the way round the frame. Mother used to get so annoyed that he would always point this out. It was obviously a present from the OXO firm. Upstairs in the best sitting-room there were two pictures, one showed a little boy, a little girl and a pony. The little girl had an apple behind her back and it was called 'A Tempting Bait'. In the other one, the little boy had managed to catch the pony and mount it – the scene was called Bravo. I always remember those two and in fact about 50 years later, I found a picture postcard of 'A Tempting Bait', which I have still got somewhere. The other picture I remember was 'Little Speedwell's Darling Blue' and it was a pretty little girl sitting in a field of blue flowers but there was a wall all around her and it used to worry me how she was going to get out.

The Gibbs Family

Now I must talk about Mother's family. Mother was born in Taunton. Her father owned a drapery shop there. Her mother died aged about 32 leaving Grandfather Gibbs with five children which was a dreadful thing. [He ran a] busy business and staff who lived in and he had these five children, Margaret, Effie, Alan, Olive and my mother, Nell. Mother used to tell the story of how he was a Victorian father, very strict. If the shop wasn't very busy he'd go along behind the counter pulling out all the packets, because in those days lots of things like stockings and underwear came in white packets and he'd rip them open and make it look like they were busy and ruffle up the baskets of odds and ends that were on the counter.

When he decided to sell the business and come to Weston, he bought the Princess Alexandra Hotel [commonly called The Alex], which was the pub opposite Father's shop in Meadow Street. One afternoon Mother and her two sisters had gone for a walk in the woods and they were late getting back. They were frightened that their father would be cross with them so they took a cab at the Old Pier to come back to Meadow Street but as they passed the end of West Street they saw a crowd there and they stopped to look; it was their father who had died there. He had had a heart attack. So these three girls were left to run the public house. They had never had more than about a shilling a week pocket money but the magistrates granted Aunt Effie the licence which was a ridiculous thing to do, so you can imagine they ran riot and in no time the place was getting run down. Mother had to go out and do a job. She went to Colmers of Bath and then came back to work for William C. Thomas, which was where Burtons is now [the corner of High Street and Regent Street]. She lived-in there and that was when she met Father.

At that time Effie and Margaret were both courting and subsequently got married. Aunt Effie married Bob Vowles. The Vowles were a family in Weston who owned horse brakes which used to ply from Alexandra Parade. They lived in a cul-de-sac which is where Peacocks is now, and at the end of this road was a pub called the Waggon and Horses and it was here that Mrs Vowles and her two sons ran their coach business. These two sons were very handsome, tall and good-looking, and at that time they had just come back from the Boer War. Bob, who was the younger of the two, had been driving Lord Roberts in South Africa and he came back quite a local hero, and very handsome! Wally was the other one. When Bob Vowles and Effie got married Bob took over the licence of the Princess Alexandra Hotel. Margaret, Effie's younger sister, became engaged and married Bert Allen. The Allens were quite successful builders in Weston. They lived in a house on Beach Road called Cromwell House and Bert worked for his father. When he married Margaret they moved to a cottage which was just behind where the Sands Night Club is now. It was called Portland Cottage and it was here that Aunt Margaret had two children, Irene, who was born with a tubercular hip and always walked with a limp, and Douglas who went to Kingsholme School and then worked for the gas company.

My mother, as I said, was working in Bath and she came back at weekends and holiday times. She and her sisters were having a roaring time and my father was living opposite with his then wife. Subsequently Father's wife died. I don't know how the friendship with Mother blossomed but obviously they met and courted, as it was in those days, and got married. So Mother took on two boys, Arthur and Frank. It wasn't an enviable task to take on two stepsons but they were lovely boys and I adored them.

Arthur and Frank

The First World War had begun when Arthur became 17 so he joined the Royal Flying Corps, as it was called in those days, with his friend Reg Davis, and he was posted to France quite quickly. He used to drive the big transport lorries which were carrying the observation balloons. Fortunately he came through the war without a scratch so that was a mercy. Frank joined the Dorset Regiment when he was 17 and he was sent to France, from where his regiment moved to Italy. I remember him telling us he was in the big battle of the Crossing of the Piave River. It was quite an event and he said he could see some of his friends being swept away as they crossed the river. He came back across Europe in a cattle truck without taking his clothes off for the whole journey. It must have taken a long time and his legs were very badly injured with ulcers as a result. But they came back and both of them went into the shop to work.

I used to love it when they came home on leave. They had a friend called Bunny Young. He was a brilliant pianist and played at the local cinemas. He would visit us and I would join in with these boys as they stood round the piano singing all the songs of the day. It was such a thrill to have them home on leave, and when they were demobbed it seemed so lovely to have them permanently here. Arthur looked after the grocery side of the shop and Frank went into the provision side. Mother thought that it would be good for Arthur, who was very artistic, to have a bit of experience outside of Father's shop and he went to a very exclusive shop in Clifton in Bristol for a time and learnt another side of the trade.

Above: *Meadow Street looking towards Regent Street, 1950s. On the right is Mr Whitton's butcher's shop and W. Salisbury's outfitting business, where Madge Frankpitt's parents got their overcoats made.*

Left: *Advertisement for Lewis Wing, chemist, 1934. This picture shows the three shops that the firm operated, in the Boulevard, Regent Street and Walliscote Road. The wooden sign from the Boulevard shop is now in North Somerset Museum. Madge Frankpitt's mother used to buy her favourite perfume, Mendip Lilies, from Lewis Wing.*

But Father, like his mother, was a great one for his family and wanted his boys around him all the time, which really wasn't a good thing for them. They should have been pushed out of the nest, but there we are. So Arthur came back and finally he got married. He was a lovely man but he was a chain smoker like his father and he contracted lung cancer and died very young at 47. It broke all our hearts.

Mother and Father

Mother was a tall lady and always very smartly dressed. She used to wear costumes which were made by Mr James Salisbury, my father's tailor. She and Father always wore overcoats made from a local fabric called Mendip Cloth. It was very hard wearing. I used to go and watch them being fitted. I was fascinated to see the little pieces of tailor's chalk which were pink and shiny. They used this chalk to mark alterations on the cloth as they were fitting costumes on the customers.

I can also remember the way Mother did her hair. I used to sit on her bed and watch her sitting at her dressing-table. She used to brush her hair up from the nape, a parting one side and then a parting the other side and one across the back. And then the two side

pieces of hair were back-combed and brought up onto the top of her head, first one side and then the other. The back piece was back-combed and brought up to the top to cover the join between the two side pieces and finally the front piece was taken back over and fastened with hair pins – no Kirby grips in those days – and it used to look so smooth and pretty, I used to admire it tremendously, it was so neat the way she did it. Then she would put a little perfume on a handkerchief and that was her toilet done. She always used a perfume called Mendip Lilies. It was made by a local firm of chemists called Lewis Wing who had three shops in Weston – one in the Boulevard, one opposite the Floral Clock and another one in Walliscote Road on the corner of Albert Road. The choice of perfume in those days was very restricted. There was Yardley's Lavender and 4711 Eau de Cologne and apart from that the choice was very small. I remember my Auntie Lil used to use Californian Poppy which I hated. Then there was Evening in Paris and Ashes of Roses and Ashes of Violets but not the choice that we have today. Coty made some nice perfumes and when I was older I always used L'Origan.

I also loved Grossmith's perfumes – they were very eastern in their scent. One was called Phul-nana and

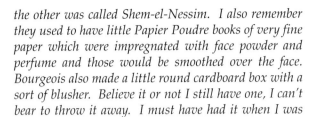

the other was called *Shem-el-Nessim*. I also remember they used to have little Papier Poudre books of very fine paper which were impregnated with face powder and perfume and those would be smoothed over the face. Bourgeois also made a little round cardboard box with a sort of blusher. Believe it or not I still have one, I can't bear to throw it away. I must have had it when I was about 16 or 17.

My father had a moustache and the ends of it were waxed with Hongroise. I can't think where the word Hongroise came from (was it the firm?) but he had this little tube and he would put it on the ends of his moustache and twirl them and the ends would stay stuck together.

Mother would take me to the hairdresser to have my hair cut. They would take pieces of hair and twiddle them into little tight pieces, rather like the dreadlocks of today, and then they would have a taper, which they would light, and run the taper up and down this piece of hair and singe the ends to encourage growth so they said. Whether it did or not was another thing. Of course permanent waves weren't known in those days. I had to be about 16 or 17 I suppose before I had my first permanent wave and that was a trial of strength. The firm was called Eugene and there was a stand with a circle on the top holding silver cylinders. Your hair would be washed and wound onto curlers and then these cylinders would be drawn down from this apparatus that was hanging over your head and clamped onto the curler. The electricity was switched on and those cylinders got hot. It was alright if they stayed upright on your head but sometimes they would get a bit slack and fall onto your scalp. You came away with lots of curls but also some burnt patches. We also had Marcel waving, which was done with hot tongs and some of the hairdressers were very adept at it. When I was 18 I would go every Wednesday evening after work and have my hair Marcel waved. I used to go to a dance at the Winter Gardens on Wednesday evenings.

Mother had a great zest for life. She loved parties and any occasion – picnics, birthdays, Christmas parties – nothing seemed to tire her and this went on right to the end of her life; she died in July 1952 when she was 67 and her joy of life lasted all that time. I remember my birthday parties; on one occasion she hired a cab and took us all out to Ashcombe Park for a picnic, which was lovely. Another time she hired a cab and took us to Brean. Then there would be parties in the best room over the shop. We always used to start off with 'Chase the Slipper' and 'Hunt the Thimble', musical chairs, then the dreaded 'Postman's Knock' where you always sat around the room, fearing that your name would be called, or that it wouldn't be called. Then when we were all hot and flushed and excited, Mother would come around with a plate of orange slices to cool us down. Then some more games, 'Pass the Parcel', etc., and then we would all troop downstairs to the sitting-room where the food would be laid out. It wasn't the sophisticated food they have today at parties, just jellies, blanc-

manges, cakes and things like that. The friends that we had lasted many years.

I remember my parents' 25th wedding anniversary. Mother had a party at the Winter Gardens and Freddie [Madge's fiancé] and I took advantage of the occasion and celebrated our engagement at the same time. When I was 21 she organised a lovely meal in the south foyer at the Winter Gardens. All my friends came along and then afterwards we went into the ballroom for dancing, and when the evening came to a close we went back to where we were living in Walliscote Road, where we had cake and champagne and the evening continued. It was all very exciting. Father went along with all this. He was always agreeable to anything that Mother did.

Mother used to love to go to London for the day. We would set off about seven o'clock in the morning and on arrival at Paddington we'd take the bus and go to Oxford Street for Selfridges and then walk down to Regent Street for Swan & Edgars and then across to Soho. In Wardour Street there was a restaurant that we used to frequent called Pinoli's and for 2s.6d. you could get a three-course lunch which we used to enjoy. I can always remember the great big trolleys of hors d'oeuves that they used to wheel round. The smell of it was delicious. Then, after lunch, we would walk across to Piccadilly and catch a bus and go over to Kensington where we liked to go to Barkers' & Pontins and spend the afternoon there, and then back on the tube to Piccadilly and back to Pinoli's for dinner. After dinner we would go and queue for one of the theatres. In those days people used to queue for the pit and the gallery and things like that and you could rent little stools to sit on because sometimes you had to queue for quite a long time. I remember one occasion we went to the Empire in Leicester Square where Fred Astaire and his sister Adele were performing in Lady Luck. There was a great big commissionaire on the door and he was standing with his arms akimbo. We went up to him and Mother said, 'Can you tell us where we queue for the pit?', and he, from his great height, looked down and said, 'Madam, there is no pit', and of course we fell about laughing and finally found our seats in the stalls. I remember all those lovely theatres that we used to go to. After our evening in the theatre we would catch the bus to Paddington to connect with the 11p.m. train home.

Father used to love a holiday and he would very often take me away. Several times we went to London. He wasn't very conversant with the tube and the buses so we always had taxis everywhere, which was lovely for me, I used to enjoy that. One lovely holiday in June the debutantes were presented at court and all their carriages would queue up along The Mall. Father and I were walking along rubbernecking into the carriages and in one carriage there was an old girl with her tiara on and she looked at Father and bowed very graciously and said, 'Good Evening' and Father raised his hat and bowed back to her, which I thought was very funny.

Along with friends, Hetty Wreford and Dolly and Flo Sleep, Hetty's two maiden sisters, Mother used to go off and follow the Banwell Hunt. With their walking sticks they'd go tramping over the fields and I've got some lovely snapshots of them, it really was funny, but as I say, there was this lovely zest for life.

Mother was a very proud person and very proud of the way I was dressed and how Arthur and Frank were dressed, and Father too. I mean, he had to be looking smart all the time, but one blow to her pride was when I was not more than a baby. Her friend Mrs Warrilow lived opposite and she had had a baby girl and they had bought a beautiful coach-built pram, I think they called it a Dunkley in those days. She and mother used to push us babies out together, but poor Mother, she had to make do with a basketwork pram for me, which Father had taken in lieu of a shop debt and Mother's pride was cut to the quick because she had to push this basketwork pram along the streets alongside Mrs Warrilow with her beautiful coach-built pram.

Burton House School

When I was five, the First World War had broken out and it was time for me to go to Burton House School. [My parents] really wanted me to go to Rossholme but Rossholme wouldn't accept me because we were living over the shop. When I think of the snobbery that existed in those days, it was terrible really. There was a boys' school at the top of Ellenborough Park South called Etonhurst, now a block of flats, and at the top was a big board which read 'Etonhurst School – For the sons of Gentlemen'. I've often wondered how Mr Wollen, who was the headmaster there, adjudicated between a

gentleman and a non-gentleman. Was it breeding or was it money? But of course Weston was full of schools in those days. For girls there was Beaurivage on Uphill Road North and I remember Joyce Bisley, a friend of mine, went there. They used to wear pillbox hats made of black astrakhan. Then there was Burton House [which taught boys in the kindergarten only] and Rossholme, Stanmore in Royal Crescent, Athelstan, Eastern House, La Retraite, St Faith's and, overlooking the Old Pier, Westcliff. For the boys there was Lewisham, where Jack went, Kingsholme, which is now flats, Brynmelyn in Landemann Circus, Brean House in Montpelier, Clarence House in Clarence Road South and Etonhurst. On Sunday afternoons you would see the crocodiles of schoolchildren walking up and down the promenade. We used to play hockey on the sands, where the pitches stretched from the Sanatorium right up to West Street.

All these schools made Weston a very busy place and I remember we used to have inter-school sports. We had a cup for hockey, one for swimming and another for tennis and that made for a great community spirit. I think Miss Chass, who used to referee some of the matches, was always accused of favouring Burton House. Whether it was our ability, or Miss Chass' propensity for making her own school the best one I don't know.

My school-days in Burton House were very happy. Burton House School was owned by a family called Weir who were Irish so, of course, our school colours were green. There was Mrs Weir, a dear little old lady with a lace cap who didn't take much active part in the school,

Beaurivage School, Uphill Road North, c.1909.

but she had three daughters, Miss May who was the headmistress and Miss Chass, a sweet soul who we used to play up. She was so gentle and kind. She had wispy grey hair and pince-nez glasses and used to take us for English and Geography. Then there was Miss Tilly, the youngest one, who took us for music. When you started music lessons, you were taken by a Miss Kirk, who used to teach us on one of the older pianos, but as you got better you graduated to Miss Tilly, who took her classes in the drawing-room. It was so cold in there, even though she used to have a fire burning in the grate. It seemed to be full of those egg-shaped pieces of coke and she would stand there and kick it to try and get some semblance of flame but it was very cold and cheerless.

Miss Lee was one of our teachers as was Mr Callow, a bearded gentleman who was the choirmaster and organist at Christ Church. He used to thump our morning hymn out on the old piano; Miss Chass used to wince with pain. In those days we could choose a hymn each day for our morning service and of course we used to choose all the heavy ones such as 'Stand Up, Stand Up for Jesus' and 'Fight the Good Fight' until Miss Chass realised what we were doing and chose a very gentle one like 'Jesu, Lover of my Soul', something at which Mr Callow couldn't thump away.

We had a visiting master called Mr Kerr-Davis. He was a bearded man and always seemed to have gravy stains down his waistcoat. He used to take us for mathematics and a subject that was always a mystery to me – mensuration. I don't know to this day what it meant but I can remember awful problems being given us, such as working out the length of a shadow thrown by a ladder leaning against a wall. It didn't mean a thing to me, like algebra. I was more for geography and English. We also had a little French mistress, Mlle Lecerf. She was quite charming and used to teach us French songs.

We played tennis in Ellenborough Park as well as croquet. We played hockey on the sands and went to the Knightstone Baths to swim. Once a week we marched to the YMCA at the top of High Street where there was a gymnasium. We worked for exams for the College of Preceptors and then we moved on to Junior Cambridge and Senior Cambridge and took music exams for one of the big London exam boards. I got as far as the Higher.

I recall one occasion when Miss Chass said to us, 'If you go out in the hall and listen you'll hear Clara Butt singing'. Clara Butt was a well-known contralto of the day and was giving a concert at Knightstone. Her accompanist was normally Kennerley Rumford. Clara herself was a great big woman, nearly six feet tall. Kennerley Rumford was a tiny chap and when you saw her concert, she would bring him on just like a little toy poodle. She had come down to Burton House and was rehearsing with Miss Tilly.

We used to have painting lessons and I never ventured very far with my painting but those who were good at it had great big canvasses about three feet high and they always seemed to paint the same picture, which was our old friend 'The Monarch of the Glen'.

There was a passageway at Burton House with a shelf along it and I can see all these Monarchs of the Glen stuck along there. My work never rose to those heights I'm afraid.

Mrs Weir used to sit and read to us whilst we had our sewing lessons – usually one of the classics such as Jane Eyre. I also remember John Halifax, Gentleman, a dull old book. We were given pieces of white calico cut out in the shape of knickers. I understand those knickers were sent to a missionary society in Africa. I don't know whether the recipients appreciated all the work that went into them, but on these pieces of calico we were taught the basics of sewing. We would learn hemming and feather stitching and run-and-fell. I don't suppose anyone would know what that is today. We learnt how to make a buttonhole and how to sew on a button. I remember some of the things Mrs Weir taught us. She said, 'Now girls, when you are turning over the pages of a book you must never lick your fingers and when you blow your nose you must never use two hands.' I often think today, when I'm dunking a biscuit in my cup of tea, that she would have had a fit if she could see me! Another thing she would say is you must say February and Government. She was most particular about all these things.

Those were our happy school-days and I've still got a few school friends left. One is Kay Elliott who lives in a penthouse in the Tivoli Flats. She was Kathleen Watts at that time. Another one who was ahead of me, and she died a couple of years ago, was Elsie Beaton. She lived until she was a day short of 100, which was a great pity. She worked at the Great Western Railway, and from there she moved and went to Transport House and became secretary to George Thomas who was the speaker of the House of Commons. She worked at Speaker's House and had a wonderful job there meeting all sorts of people. She was an interesting person to talk to. I remember George Thomas coming to speak at the Victoria Methodist Chapel in Weston and Elsie Beaton rang me up and said George Thomas is coming down. We went to the service and on the way out he was shaking hands at the door and I made a point of speaking to him and telling him that Elsie was an old school friend of mine. He was so pleased and shook me by the hand. He was a lovely man, and his sermon that day was absolutely brilliant.

Freda Warrilow was my friend from the very first day in school, and we have been friends ever since. I've still got several other friends who started school after me, such as Betty and Peggy. Peggy lives with her daughter Jane at Lympsham and Betty, who married Dick Bucknall whose father kept Kingsholme School, lives on the seafront. We have an Old Burtonians Association which is flourishing. We have a luncheon every March at Dauncey's Hotel and last year over 80 people attended. I don't know many of them now because I'm about the oldest I should think, but it's nice to think that the spirit goes on.

I remember our motto was 'To thine own self be true,

and it must follow, as the night the day, thou canst not then be false to any man.' That was printed and hung up in one of our classrooms. Of course the shamrock was our school emblem and when we have our luncheon we are all given a little piece of shamrock, which is rather nice, I think. Our school uniform used to be navy blue gymslips with green blouses in the winter, and in the summer, green and white dresses and a straw hat. Our winter hats were simply dreadful – great big thick navy blue bonnets, we looked like district nurses I always thought – not very pretty. Burton House has since been converted into flats.

Childhood

Before I go any further with my reminiscences. I feel I must make an apology for the way I jump about a bit. Because of my loss of sight I cannot refer to any notes and have to rely solely on memory.

Now I go back to my early days in Meadow Street. My friends then were Mary Bay and Olive White and our pleasures were so simple when we were young girls. We used to go and play up in the woods. I remember Bluebell Valley was one of our favourite spots in the spring. That was beautiful. We liked to walk up to the water tower in the centre then take the path to the British Encampment [Worlebury Iron Age hill-fort] and down to the Old [Birnbeck] Pier. We would then play on the rocks at Madeira Cove. I think I knew every

Right: Sailing bill for the Ravenswood paddle-steamer. Steamers sailed from Birnbeck Pier both up and down the coast as well as across to Barry and Cardiff. They were used as much for transport as pleasure.

inch of those rocks. We would climb along them and go round into Anchor Head. There was a rock in Anchor Head which we used to sit on and slide down. We wore out any amount of knickers doing this. Today it's just a little tiny rock but to our young eyes it was enormous! We could walk on round to the Old Pier and have our trips on the water chute and the charaplanes and buy fairy floss. I can remember on the way up to the top of the water chute you passed the two-headed giant. I never went in there; I was too frightened. I read in the newspaper not long ago that that the two-headed giant

Anchor Head, c.1903. A local fishing boat or flatner is boarding passengers for a trip around the bay. Anchor Head was a favourite spot for visitors as it is sheltered from any wind.

is still on display somewhere in California. Tram cars went along the seafront and on the beach there were people who did sand sculpture. We used to go to the Little Sands, which is now Marine Lake, when we were on holiday in the summer. On the sands there would be stalls selling nougat and rock – pineapple rock and peppermint rock – and great big carboys of highly-coloured lemonade, cherryade and orangeade. And there would be fish stalls and coffee stalls, the donkeys, the Merryfolk Concert Party as well as Punch and Judy. On Sunday evenings the Salvation Army Band would play and we would all go out and sing hymns. There was a little mission there and we would go out quite early and build up a heap of sand for the minister to stand on [see page 33]. He would come and hand out the hymn books and we would have lovely times together. We were quite safe on our own as youngsters. Life was much simpler and I'm sure we were happier, although, of course, we didn't have as much money as we have these days.

Beyond the Old [Birnbeck] Pier there was a bathing cove off the Kewstoke Toll Road. That was the venue for many picnics. As I say, my mother was a great one for picnics and we used to go out there quite frequently. There was a ladder there from which you could jump off into the sea and the swimming must have been quite safe. The Campbell's Steamers used to come in and we would have trips across to Cardiff and Barry and the boats went down to Ilfracombe and Lundy Island, but I don't think I ever did that; I wish I had now. We used to play in Grove Park and Ashcombe Park.

We started to have our boyfriends. Marwood Bailey and his cousin Cyril Harris were great friends of ours. As we grew older we had bicycles. That was the signal for picnics to be held further afield. We could go over to

Herr Julian Kandt's Band, photographed in the Grand Pier Pavilion, c.1904.

Brean Down and so on. Another thing we used to like to do was to go up to the Grove Park to the Concert Party. It's a car park now, but there was once a nice pavilion and every season there would be a Concert Party. I remember Carlton Fredericks had a group called The Sunbeams. They used to wear very pretty blue satin dresses and the men used to have full trousers in blue satin with bobbles all down the side. Clay Thomas, Emil Clare and Ronald Franko and his Cabaret Kittens were regulars. We used to have our bicycles and lean them on the railings outside so I'm afraid we never paid anything, but we would see all our friends there. Harry Burgess and his orchestra used to play every summer at the Rozel Bandstand. They used to call it the Dutch Oven. Opposite that was a big shelter on top of which was a promenade – we used to call it the 'Chicken Run', and that was another place where we used to meet

The Roof Gardens on top of the shelter at Madeira Cove, c.1909. This was nicknamed the 'Chicken Run' by Madge Frankpitt and her friends, and was a favourite place to meet their boyfriends.

The Grand Pier Pavilion at 11.45a.m. on 4 July 1905. The boy is selling programmes, probably for the concert by Kandt's Band advertised on the poster. Note the American flag flying to mark Independence Day. As well as giving concerts in the Pavilion itself, the bands also used to play in the bandstand, just in front of it.

The water chute on Birnbeck Pier. This was just one of the extremely popular fairground-style attractions on Birnbeck Pier. It was installed about 1905 and was still in use in 1931.

Glentworth Bay, or the Little Sands as it was sometimes called, 1920s.

our boyfriends. Sunday afternoons we would walk through Madeira Cove in our best clothes, and perhaps have a deck-chair! Life seemed to be all sun and fun.

The Grand Pier was another happy hunting ground. There was a bandstand outside and military bands used to play all through the summer. I remember Mother telling me there was a man called Herr Kandt who had a band (before the First World War). Companies touring the country would perform in the Pavilion; I remember No No Nanette, Wild Violets and Maid of the Mountains and on one occasion there was a matinee when Pavlova came to the Grand Pier Pavilion and Mother went out to see her because Mother was a great theatre fan. For sixpence you could go upstairs into the balcony and lean over and watch the shows – they were called 'Sixpenny Leanovers'. You can imagine, it was a real promenade and you'd see all your boyfriends up there!

All the dances and balls were held at Knightstone. The Hunt Ball, the Golf Ball and the Military Ball were held there. It seems strange that, for a small amount one could sit up there in the balcony and look down on

Evangelist Frank Farley preaching at the Sands Mission on Weston Beach, 1950. In the 1930s, Madge Frankpitt remembers going out early and helping to build up the 'pulpit' of sand whilst the minister handed out hymn books.

the dance floor and see all the people who had come to the ball. Mother used to take me. I must have been quite a little girl but the scene was simply lovely. The ladies were standing there in all their pretty dresses and they had little programmes with tiny pencils and the men would pencil in the dances they wanted to have with these ladies. Our own doctor was always there, Dr Marmaduke Alford. There was another very handsome man called Captain Wicksteed. I think Mother had an eye for him. I can't remember how we got out there or how we got home. It was quite a long way to go, but life on the streets was so much safer in those days.

Meadow Street

Now for a walk up Meadow Street and a talk about our neighbours. Most people lived over their shop in those days. Meadow Street was a jolly street. It was lit with gas lamps as I've said before. There were no boarded-up shops like we see today. Every shop was catering for all our needs. Supermarkets weren't heard of. We had to be careful of the prices in the shop. I can remember Father sending one of the boys up the street to see how much was being charged for bacon at David Greig's! However, we were at the bottom of Meadow Street. Before you came to our two shops, on the corner of Meadow Street and Alfred Street was the Star Coffee House. I imagine that they served coffee and tea to labourers and workmen around the place but I do remember that they sold lovely dripping cakes and ham sandwiches, long tin loaves of new bread and they would cut the ham off the bone – it was absolutely delicious. It was kept by a Mr Sibley and when he died the Star Coffee House was put up for sale and my father bought it. He had heard on the grapevine that Sainsbury's were contemplating moving into Weston and he was frightened that they were going to be opening up right next door to him, so he bought the Star

Meadow Street looking east from the corner of Palmer Street, c.1910. Farrows, the fruiterers, are at No.18, next to the New Inn.

The Dorothy Sweet Shop in Meadow Street, c.1910. Madge Frankpitt recalled this business making the most delicious ice-cream!

George Mason's grocer's shop, Meadow Street, c.1920.

Meadow Street, looking east, 1950s. Quick's Domestic Bazaar is on the corner of North Street.

Coffee House and in the contract for its subsequent sale, he put in a clause that it must never be used for a grocer's shop. He sold the premises to a Mr Tidball who had a shoe shop further down in Baker Street. Mr Tidball, when he moved in, knocked it down and rebuilt it as two shops with flats above. One he let to Pickfords, the removal people, and the other one he kept for his shoe shop. [In 2004 both shops belong to Peter Castell].

That was the bottom of Meadow Street. Then you came to our shops. Next to us was Mr Gambling who was a boot and shoe repairer. Next came Farrows, the fruiterers and vegetable shop. I remember Kate Farrow used to work in that shop. Recently I met Kevin Farrow who is a roof contractor and a descendant of Kate's. Next door to that shop were two small gentlemen's outfitters and they were kept by a Mr Olsen. He must have had a good voice because his nick-name was 'Toreador'. Next came the corner shop which was kept by Bill Trapnell as a newsagent. Bill himself was a barber next door to the newsagent – he was a proper barber with a barber's pole outside and Father used to go there for his haircut. They had three sons: Jim, who was in the Navy and I remember being told he had fought at the Battle of Jutland, Bert, who ran a coal business, and Cliff who worked in the shop. These lads also had a sister, Phyllis. I was bridesmaid at her wedding.

Then we come to Alma Street. On the corner was Mr Knott the grocer, a nice little grocer's shop. Next to him was Mr Watkins, the chemist. Only recently I met his son who is still living in Weston. I can remember Mr Watkins, commonly called Dr Watkins, and his little beard and all the lovely bottles of coloured water that used to fascinate me so. He also had lots of bottles of perfume and I used to love to take a little bottle up and buy two or three pennyworth of Heliotrope or Jockey Club. It must have smelt terrible but I always had a leaning for perfume and still have to this day. Next to Dr Watkins came The Dorothy Sweet Shop and they made particularly nice ice-cream. There was a shop next door, but I can't remember what it used to be. Certainly in later years it was a grocer's shop. Next door again was a man who mended clocks. Then we came to a fish shop. It was run by Mr Fisher, his son Harry and his daughter Winnie. Mother was always very disgusted because Mr Fisher would call her 'Ma' – that didn't go down very well with Mother.

Then we come to the corner of Orchard Street and there was Mr Bown, the butcher. I was despatched most Saturdays to go up with five shillings to buy a nice piece of topside of beef with a bit of fat on the top. I would like to have one of those joints for five shillings these days! Across Orchard Street was a pub on the corner which was called the Elm Tree. It was kept by a relative of ours, Bill Payne and his wife Daisy. Next to them was a dairy, then another butcher and then we came to John Baker's two gentlemen's outfitters shops. Next to John Baker we come to the Jacksons who kept a fruit shop. Next to North Lane was Mr Jelly who ran a

newsagent. Then there was the New Inn and that was kept by Mr Freeman, who used to play the flute in Burgess' Band. Next door was another fruit and vegetable shop kept by Mr Beeton and then on the corner of Orchard Place and Meadow Street was Mr Cattle, the butcher.

Across Orchard Place was Steel's, I think. It sold ladies' clothes as well as curtains, etc. Next to that was another pub called the Spread Eagle kept by the Merrick family. Then we came to another ladies' outfitting shop called Brecknells and that was quite a nice shop – in fact, I think he had two shops. Next to him was another pub kept by the Banwell family that was called the Cardiff Arms and then we came to Cooksley, Son & Forsey, house furnishers. The street cut back a bit at this point where there were a couple of ladies' outfitting shops and another newsagent. At the end of Meadow Street up by the Big Lamp was Lennards, the shoe shop.

Across Meadow Street and coming down the other side, there was a very nice butcher's shop subsequently kept by Mr Whitton. It's still there and it's a very busy spot. Next door to that was the Scotch Wool Shop and then we came to Poole's butcher's shop and then Stevens Restaurant, a popular venue for visiting Sunday-school outings. Behind the restaurant was a billiard saloon. Next was Quick's Domestic Bazaar. On the other side of North Street was Fred Thorn, the ironmonger, who was there for many years.

Next to him was Spencer Tyler, a very high-class grocer. I was very fond of Spencer Tyler. He was such a nice man. He was on the executive committee of the Town Advertising Association and I liked him very much. He was a friend of my father's. He had two handsome sons. One of them used to take the leading part in the local operatic shows. Next to Spencer Tyler was Burrows, the gentlemen's outfitters which stayed there for a long time, then came Frisby's, the shoe shop. Next was Mr Dale's chemist shop on the corner of Palmer Street. Opposite him on the other side of the road was Pfaffs, the gentlemen's outfitters. The Pfaffs were a German family and I've been told that when the

Burrow's menswear shop, Meadow Street, 1983. This photograph was taken just before a new shop front was installed. The tiled entrance was lifted and is now in North Somerset Museum.

First World War broke out they were interned, which was a shame because they were a very nice family. Next to them came Mr and Mrs Hazelton who had a very high-class sweetshop. They used to dress their windows at night so they could see the effect reflected in the gas-lit shop windows opposite. Next to them were the Roe Brothers who were picture framers. One of the daughters was at school with me. Then on the corner was Liptons. Across Hopkins Street and another corner shop which was a ladies' outfitters. Then came Rossiters' shop and Townsend's sweetshop followed by Mr Dennis with his boot and shoe shop on the corner of Orchard Street. I do remember that shop, for the side window facing Orchard Street was full of hobnailed boots. I suppose lots of workmen used to wear hobnailed boots but he used to dress his window with all the hobnails facing out and it looked so funny. He was our Sunday-school superintendent and a very upright gentlemen. He had two daughters, both of whom went to Burton House School.

So we've come back to Orchard Street, and on the other corner was an ironmongers kept by Mr Waddon, and his daughter went to Burton House too. Next to Mr Waddon, where Brown's is now, was Miss Longley, a maiden lady who kept this dreary shop, it was so dark inside with wooden floors and was so depressing. There was a sort of arcaded entrance where she would hang out all these directoire knickers [long-legged knickers with elastic round the waist and the bottom of the legs] and combinations and stockings, etc. I remember that if she had two customers, she would call in a very high-pitched voice, 'Counter', and from the cash desk on the next storey would come her brother to help serve the customers. If you had a farthing change Miss Longley would say, 'Would you like a packet of pins for the farthing?' It's a long way from the days of decimalisation isn't it?

Next to Miss Longley was Dewhurst, the butcher and then we came to Rowan Tabrett's, a beautiful pork butcher's shop. Mr and Mrs Tabrett served behind the counter and their daughter Edith was at the cash desk. They had three sons, Will, Horace and Wallace. They were at the rear preparing all the dripping and sausages, pork pies, faggots and peas and cold meats, etc. The side window was always full of joints of bacon, there wasn't a sign of any lean, it was all pure fat. I suppose people used to have it and frizzle it out to get the lard. They had shelves along the top and all these lovely sausages

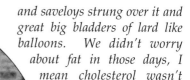

Mr and Mrs Dennis in their shoe shop. This was on the corner of Meadow Street and Orchard Street. Madge Frankpitt remembers the side window filled with a display of hobnailed boots – with all the hobnails facing upwards!

and saveloys strung over it and great big bladders of lard like balloons. We didn't worry about fat in those days, I mean cholesterol wasn't heard of. Mr and Mrs Tabrett were friends of ours. They were nice people and they lived over the shop, of course. Next door to them was a baker's shop and then came Mr Harding, the chimney sweep, and next to him a fish and chip shop. A fish and chip shop is still there to this day [Atlantic Fish Bar]. When I was little it was kept by a Mr and Mrs Sampson and their two daughters. Even now I can see Mr Sampson shovelling up the great big mounds of chips and taking them out of the fat and putting them on the draining board. For a penny we could go for a bag of 'scrumpies', which were all the bits of batter that used to come off the fish. It was lovely.

Next door to them was Stockers, the newsagent. That was the shop that my Uncle Walter had kept many years before. Next came Blannings Dairy and then an umbrella shop. Then we came to The Gem, a sweetshop kept by Mr and Mrs Parsons. I was sent over every Saturday with, I don't now how much, a couple of shillings I suppose, to buy the sweets for the rest of the week. I remember I always used to buy Turkish Delight and some caramels made by a firm called Murray's. They are not in existence anymore but they were nice, those caramels. Mrs Parsons was behind the counter. Mr Parsons was a rather fierce-looking gentleman with another of those big moustaches! Next to The Gem was Mr Wood, the butcher, who came from the Midlands and he ultimately served as a mayor of Weston at one time. His daughter, Mary, went to Burton House. Next to him was John Bathe. He was a tinsmith and ironmonger, but it was one of those dreary shops. There was a great big tank filled with oil. They also sold gas mantles and other household things. Mr Bathe himself was a Plymouth Brethren and he used to cycle out to Bleadon every Sunday and take a service. You went through his shop and through a passageway to the kitchen and beyond to a workshop where he used to give magic-lantern shows for us children. Mrs Bathe was a nice woman, very regal and quiet. They had a big family; there was Elsie and Jessie, then came Charlie and Arthur, two sons who worked with their father in his workshop. As soon as they became able to leave, they went off to London. After the boys came Mary, who was my friend, and Robert, the two youngest of the brood. Next door to the Bathes was Mrs Smith, the greengrocer, where Mother's friend, Mrs Warrilow lived with her husband and little girl, Freda, but they didn't stay there very long. They went to live in Dickenson Road and then moved to Moorland Road. Pete Warrilow had a motor parts shop and garage in Oxford Street but later he became the photographer for the Weston Gazette and was a well-known Weston character. Bill Tarr, the butcher, came next. He was one of Father's card-playing friends.

Then came The Princess Alexandra Hotel, which in those days was kept by a Mr and Mrs White. Mr White was a retired RSM, popularly called 'Dad'. They also had a big family and we were all very friendly. They were warm, lovely girls. The eldest was Hilda and she married a petty officer in the Navy and later became licensee of The Foresters in Alexandra Parade. Next came Lily, the prettiest of the lot, she married a very handsome retired Army officer called Frank Parker and they went to The Ashcombe pub in Ashcombe Road. Next came Gladys who married Jimmy Webb and they took The White Hart in Palmer Row, at the bottom of Hopkins Street. Olive was next. She was my friend and she married a policeman and went to live in Shepton Mallett. Oh, I've missed out Ivy. Ivy married Jimmy Wilde, who ran Wilde & White who were carters and did deliveries from Bristol to Weston. She went out to The Full Quart at Hewish. Then there were the two boys – Ernest, who married one of the Merrick girls from The Spread Eagle in Meadow Street, and they had the off licence in Orchard Street, and Wilfred who joined the Metropolitan Police.

Harry Mogg and his band pictured in The Silver Queen charabanc at Banwell on their annual outing. Mogg's Band was famous in Weston. It was founded in 1887 and won several prizes at the Crystal Palace Military Band Competitions.

I remember also, just across the way in Baker Street, there was a place where tramps would be taken in. These tramps could stay for a night and I think they had to do some work to earn their keep. I never saw any of them but I knew that they were there. I think it was called the Casual Ward and was run by a Mr and Mrs Bowden.

Well that's the end of my knowledge of Meadow Street. As I've said, we were all great friends and Father used to like to go to the lounge bar in The Alex of an evening with Bill Tarr, Albert Tabrett, Bill Trapnell and Mr Parsons where they'd play Solo. He also frequented The Hole in the Wall in Old Post Office

Big Lamp Corner, c.1903. It was so named after the splendid gas lamp in the centre of the road junction. Ahead to the left is Meadow Street, with Regent Street to the right. This area was the gathering point for many celebrations such as New Year's Eve.

Lane. He used to go up there most evenings and stand at the bar with some of his cronies – Mr Forsey, Charlie Walker, Cecil Walker and Fred Thorn, all businessmen in the town. There was another one in High Street, next to Margrate's Grill, that was No. 90. During the Second World War, I think Father had an unbroken record for getting a glass of Worthington most evenings! If he couldn't get one at The London he'd go up to The Hole In The Wall and from there to No. 90. Mother used to get so cross! She said, 'You're out beating the streets at night'. He was very limited in what he drank. He would only have a couple and then he'd walk down the Boulevard to Arundell Road to catch the bus back to Rode-Heath when we were living on Milton Hill. All the bus drivers knew him and they had to change gear outside Rode-Heath which was the name of our bungalow. They would always slow down and almost stop. Father would hop off the bus. That would save him having to go to the top of Worlebury and walk down. Mother was always frightened he was going to fall and that's what prompted her to leave Rode-Heath and go back to Walliscote Road.

At the top of Meadow Street, with Lennards and the butcher's shop, one came to the Midland Bank and that was what we called the Big Lamp Corner, in the centre of the town. There was always a policeman on point duty there and for any celebrations, we always went to the Big Lamp Corner, particularly New Year's Eve when Mogg's Band used to play. When midnight came, the trains would blow their whistles and the gasworks hooter would sound. It was great fun.

At Christmas time we had the Meat Show Night, when all the butchers displayed their prizewinning cuts of meat and poultry. An outstanding example of this was Wildridge's in St James Street when the whole frontage of their three-storeyed shop was filled with row upon row of turkeys, pheasants, chickens, rabbits, hares and pigeons, not forgetting the fresh fish counter with salmon, crabs, lobsters and anything else you can think of. This, along with the Christmas decorations, plus all the colourful rosettes, made a spectacle not to be missed. I can still close my eyes and be transported back to one of those nights, walking hand in hand with Mother and Father.

Regent Street

Regent Street was another busy street as it led up to Grand Pier. On the left-hand corner was The Queens Hotel and then there were restaurants, because Weston was very busy with people coming over from Wales on the Campbell's Steamers. Men would stand outside these places, I remember them, with a straw hat and a rolled-up newspaper calling out, '1s.6d. for lunch, joint and two veg'. One restaurant called The Commercial was kept by Mrs Harding. Next to St James Street was the Cavendish Hotel, then Arthur Wreford's restaurant. My cousin Douglas was very friendly with Arthur's son Bob and was able to report what went on in the kitchens. Douglas used to say that Mr Wreford made pork pies filled with bread soaked in pork fat and sold as Bank Holiday specials! This may or may not have been true. He used to let out rooms to Welshmen who had missed the last boat home. Finally he sold out to the Gaumont Film Company and retired. On the other side I can remember Glass's Restaurant and Salisbury's which sold lots of souvenirs, jewellery, purses and bags. Then you came to the Royal Arcade with all manner of shops. The Plough Hotel came next and so back to the Big Lamp and William C. Thomas on the corner.

Regent Street looking towards the Grand Pier, c.1904. Wreford's Restaurant is on the left, with the entrance to the Royal Arcade on the right immediately opposite. Other establishments in this picture, mentioned by Madge Frankpitt include Glass's Restaurant and the Salisbury Bazaar.

Regent Street looking east, c.1904. The Cavendish Hotel, in the centre, is on the corner of St James Street. The tower on the opposite side of St James Street had a spire on top and was once a Wesleyan chapel, built in 1846. It is now a branch of Barclay's Bank.

The Royal Arcade was a fascinating place. It left Regent Street and you could walk down and come to a sort of crossing. The left-hand route led you out onto the seafront by Salisbury Terrace and the other one led you down to Post Office Road just off High Street. The shops were fascinating. They used to sell nougat, rock and jewellery. There was another place called the Fun Palace where you went in and there were all those funny mirrors that made you look fat or tall. I remember we used to love to go in there. I think it cost sixpence to go in. And then there was the waxworks and book shops, paper shops, coffee shops, all sorts, and then down at the very end there were roundabouts and amusements of that type. As you took the one fork and came out by High Street, on the end were two jewellers and Cecil Walker's shop which is still there.

I think it is rather nice to think that some of the old Weston families still prosper. Cecil Walker's shop is now run by Cecil's grandson. Rossiter's, the jeweller, is still in High Street, as are Walker and Ling's, they were always there. Around the corner in Waterloo Street is Leavers. They used to be in High Street. Of course, before the Winter Gardens were built in 1927, it was Rogers' Field. Henry Butt bought this land and gave it to the town. He also gave it all the Italian statuary that's there now. The field had been owned by a family called Rogers who kept The Royal Hotel. When they sold the field, they included a clause whereby they had the right to run the bar at any events staged at the Winter Gardens. The Post Office was there as well. That had been moved from Old Post Office Lane at the top of High Street, up by Grove Park.

High Street and Local Characters

Looking back on those early days in Weston, it seems as though there was quite a community spirit abroad, quite a village atmosphere almost. In the old days we knew everybody. One could walk up to the top part of High Street leading to Grove Park and Doug Bailey would be standing outside his pub, The Britannia. He always stood there wearing a straw hat. Doug Bailey was a great friend of our family. He had three sons, Hubert, Marwood and Stan. Marwood was one of my early boyfriends. Hubert and Marwood were great swimmers.

Opposite the market, where the Playhouse now stands, was Margrate's Grill and that was kept by Mr and Mrs Pierce who were retired Savoyards. As young girls we would often go in there for a snack of an evening and Mr and Mrs Pierce would put on a kind of cabaret. My brother Jack has just reminded me that he used to go in with some of his friends and one of the Pierces' famous songs was the 'Spider & the Fly'. There was a spiral staircase in the middle of the restaurant and I went once to Hubert Bailey's twenty-first birthday party there. Mr and Mrs Pierce put on their cabaret act and I recall Mrs Pierce coming down this staircase in a flowered hat and gown, singing 'Valencia'. That was the first time I'd heard that song, but [the couple] really were quite well-known in the town.

Then there were the people who did so much for Weston such as Henry Butt. They called him the King of the Beggars because, apart from giving Rogers' Field to the town, he raised enough money to build the new hospital on the Boulevard and it was opened by the

Fox & Mackie's ironmongery shop in High Street, Weston. This later became Leavers first shop. It shows the balcony that Madge Frankpitt remembered was used by Mr Leaver senr when he fired off a volley of shots while the Duke and Duchess of York visited the town to open the new hospital in 1928.

The boating pool on the beach, c.1920. The funding for this pool was donated by Mr Leaver.

Duke and Duchess of York, later to become George VI and Queen Elizabeth. Ted Leaver used to tell a lovely story about his father. Leaver's shop was in the High Street in those days and over the shop there was a balcony, from which the family watched the royal procession. Leavers sold guns, revolvers and rifles and Mr Leaver senr was a great royalist and he was so excited about this royal visit that he got one of his rifles and fired off a volley of shots, much to the consternation of the people standing on the pavement outside his shop. He wouldn't have got away with it these days. Mr Leaver himself was a great Westonian. There is a boating pond at the end of West Street which he donated to the town. It seems that people were so generous, and we knew them all.

It was quite a common sight to see Mr Jackson Barstow, who lived on the Upper Bristol Road at The Lodge. You would see him in his motor car being driven through High Street by his chauffeur. As I remember it I think it was an Armstrong Sidley, but this grey-haired old gentleman used to sit up quite regally.

Another well-known Westonian was Paulo Radmilovic, or 'Raddy' as we knew him. He was an Olympic gold medallist swimmer and a great hero in the town. He had two sons and a daughter, and I was very friendly with the younger son, Peter, and his wife Hermione, until Peter died last year. Raddy played water polo for Weston. We had a very good water polo team and I used to go the gala every Monday evening at Knightstone Baths and on several occasions Raddy would give an exhibition of fancy swimming. We used to laugh at this because the MC was one of the committee of Weston-super-Mare Swimming Club called Stumpy Banwell – he used to announce the different things that Raddy would do. He would shout out 'Swimmin' like a duck' and the next thing was 'Swimmin' like a seal' and Raddy would lay on the side of the bath and flap his hands and then roll into the water and we all clapped. Weston's water-polo team was very successful in those days. I remember there was Ebby Payne, Doc Griffiths, Baggo Barnes and I think Pete Warrilow played sometimes. Harry Dommett played in goal.

So as I say we had these local businessmen who were so well-known to us all, and then of course we had our eccentrics. There was, as I have mentioned before, Noah Brown with his drunken forays all up and down the side streets. Another was Piggy Fry. He used to wander around Weston with a barrow selling rather indifferent-looking fruit. You could hear him coming as he used to shout out 'Ripe Bananas, Ripe Bananas'. My brother Jack has also reminded me of another personality called Jumbo Bennett; he used to frighten me to death. He was very thin and looked like one of the apostles with a beard and a yellow coat. He used to walk about Weston but he was perfectly harmless. Then there was Bennett, the newspaper boy, who used to run up and down the street shouting the odds with his newspapers and he was wont to have epileptic fits very often, and several times he ended up laid out on the floor of our shop. Uncle Sylv was good at opening his shirt and helping him to recover. There was also a town crier called Mr Comer, but he was commonly called Cold-Water Jack – I don't know why!

I realise I've forgotten Mercury John, a very short man, very brown-skinned. He worked for Pages, the leather people and used to walk up and down High Street with a trunk over his head. Mercury John always took part in the local carnival which we had every November. There was another man who always walked at the head of the carnival procession. I don't think he was part and parcel of it but he always managed to be number one and he used to wear a top hat and a frock coat and he had a habit of sniffing violently all the time – he was called Sniffer Ackland.

There was a very funny story I can tell about Arthur, Freddie, Jack and I suppose Father was there too. One Christmas, they did their usual stunt of going out after the tea on Christmas Day, allegedly to feed the cats at the shop, but it was really an excuse to go to the local and have a drink and on one occasion they met Sniffer Ackland. Arthur, who was a bit of a wag, said to

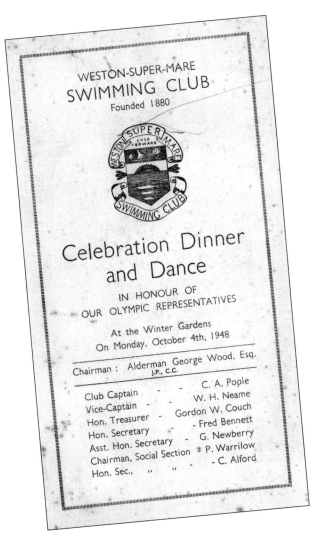

Souvenir programme for a Celebration Dinner Dance held by Weston-super-Mare Swimming Club, 1948.

Sniffer, 'Come back home Sniffer and have a bit of supper.' Well, the idea of Mother entertaining Sniffer Ackland, was something absolutely dire and poor Freddie, who was never on the best of terms with Mother, was so frightened that when they got back to Walliscote Road, he refused to go inside the house. He said, 'I'm not going in if Sniffer goes in because I know that I shall be blamed for it,' and Arthur had to send Sniffer on his way. Poor Freddie spent about half an hour out in Walliscote Road in the cold waiting for Sniffer to be despatched.

Weston nowadays seems to be rather faceless. We don't seem to have people of character running our town. I know times are different and people don't take the holidays that they used to take. No one comes for a fortnight these days and of course, when the railway came to Weston and the Campbell's Steamers used to come over from South Wales, Weston was awash with holiday-makers, and all the little streets like Alma Street, Alfred Street, Hopkins Street, Palmer Street, Severn Road, Clevedon Road, Clifton Road, all let lodgings. People would come and stay for a week or a fortnight and it brought trade into the town and a call for entertainment, of which we had plenty in those days, to say nothing of the hotels that we had all along the seafront and along Madeira Cove and Claremont Crescent. The town was alive.

From Meadow Street to Walliscote Road

Life is like a kaleidoscope isn't it? You sort of twist it around and new patterns form. Jack and I were growing up. Father and Mother thought it would be nice to move from Meadow Street so Father bought a house, Glenside, 64 Walliscote Road. I can't say how surprised we were to see this lovely house after our limited quarters in Meadow Street. There was a beautiful vestibule which led to the hall. Off the hall was the drawing-room, a dining-room, breakfast room and kitchen. Upstairs were four bedrooms and a bathroom. Mother had it beautifully furnished and we had many happy years there. When we moved I was about 16 so Jack would have been about 10. With our move to Walliscote Road I acquired a new circle of friends. Win Fear had been my great friend at school and she lived just below us in Moorland Road so I kept in contact with her. The Sleep girls were just around the corner in Whitecross Road. I became very friendly with Betty Harrison and Phyl Clark who were both at the local Grammar School with Marjorie Mason. I had left Burton House and went to Miss Brockhurst, who had the Commercial School in the Boulevard.

Miss Brockhurst was another character, a brisk little woman. 'Never let yourselves get in a rut girls', she used to say, with the result that we would go to the school one day and the chairs would be facing north, and then the next day we'd go and they would be facing south; you never knew what to expect. I had two very happy years there. When I was 18 it was time to look

for a job and my father approached a friend of his, Harold Pedrick, a member of the Town Advertising Association.

The Town Advertising Association

This organisation was composed of businessmen and professional men in the town and they had a franchise from the Urban District Council, as it was then, as this was before Weston had its Charter. This band of men were responsible for all the entertainments in the town, the deck-chair concessions and the advertising, which we did in tandem with the Great Western Railway. Harold Pedrick got a job for me at the Information Bureau, the head office. Walter Stray was the Secretary and Gertie Britten was the Chief Clerk. Both had been with the TAA since its inception. Mine was a temporary job for the summer. I started at Whitsun 1926 and the first job I was given was a great big pile of three-penny bits which I had to count from the deck-chair attendants who came into the Information Bureau. They were a nice set of men. They used to tramp up and down the sands. They always wore khaki-coloured coats. They would come in during the morning and we'd give them their ticket machines and a roll of tickets and take down the number of the last ticket. They would pay in their takings at lunchtime. We would deduct one set of numbers from the other and they would pay in the required amount. I can remember some of them now – Mr Griffin, Mr Mason, Mr Hale and Mr Arlotte. It was interesting work. I learnt to

One of the entrances of the new Winter Gardens, 1927.

Harry Leader and his band, one of many who played at the Winter Gardens.

read a Bradshaw [railway timetable] *and I learnt quite a lot about the town and helped with the production of the local Town Guide which brought me into contact with a lot of the boarding-house keepers and hoteliers. The job finished at the end of the summer season and Father, Mother, Jack and myself went to London on holiday. We used to stay at The Bonnington Hotel which was in Southampton Row. It was on that occasion I recall we went to see* On with the Dance, *one of C.B. Cochrane's shows at the London Pavilion with Jessie Matthews and Sonny Hale. One of the scenes was with Edith Baker, an American pianist. I recall her sitting at a white grand piano, and singing 'My Heart Stood Still'. At the interval, when the lights went up, a black man down in the orchestra pit played the piano. It was Hutch (Leslie Hutchinson). It was on that holiday that I had a telephone call from Frank or Arthur to say that the TAA had rung up and wanted me to go back and pick up my job again, so when I returned to Weston, I did just that.*

The following summer our office was moved from the Information Bureau to the Winter Gardens, which had just opened. I went with Mr Stray to that office and I stayed there for eight years. A Mr Cox took over the Information Bureau. I remember the night the Winter Gardens opened. I went with my brother Frank and his wife and several other people. We booked a table and I had a nice new black chiffon dress, I can recall it quite clearly. As I walked into the foyer, sitting at a table was Gordon Lane, who was Chairman of the Entertainments Committee. He had all the table bookings on a great big plan in front of him and he spotted me and called out, 'Miss Payne, I'm afraid you're going to have to work tonight. I've got in a bit of a state with these table bookings', so I had to sit down and help him sort them all out. I never did get a dance on that opening night, which was quite an event. The band was Hilda Ward and her Ladies' Dance Band.

Mr Stray was coming up to retirement age and a new man was appointed to take over the management – Fred Pickett from Lytham St Annes. He was a rather stern

sort of person to me; I was only 18 at the time and I suppose he was in his thirties. He moved the TAA office to a block at the end of the Winter Gardens, where he already had an office. Downstairs were two cashiers, George Henley and Isaac Davis.

This was the heyday of the Winter Gardens. When it opened it really was splendid. There were commissionaires in beautiful grey uniforms, a manageress in the café and a manager for the Pavilion. Many happy years passed there. The dance bands came and went – Tommy Kinsman was my favourite and he went on to London and became known as the Debs Delight. He used to play for all the debutante's dances. There was a variety of bands, all sorts and conditions, they were a bit of a raffish lot. Every Friday I would have to pay the musicians. Burgess' Band would come to my office from the Rozel Bandstand for their wages and were such fun, but they used to tease me terribly. However, it was a lovely job for a young girl to have and I thoroughly enjoyed it. Weston in those days was such a different place. Fred Pickett was a good boss because he always gave me full rein to do things. He would let me write articles for the guide. I would say, 'I can't do that', and he'd say, 'Yes you can', and he really gave me a lot of confidence. They were very happy days.

The four of us, Marjorie, Betty, Phyl and myself, used to go dancing – tea dances on Saturday afternoons and every Wednesday night. Marjorie's father bought her a little Austin 7 and Betty had the use of her father's car, which was a Clyno so we were mobile and able to get to Bristol to the Hippodrome and the Colston Hall for concerts. The Marine Lake opened in 1927 and that was a venue for us. We used to go out there on a Sunday when the weather was good and take a Columbia gramophone and the records and, oh, we had wonderful times – the picnics and all the boyfriends. Another place we used to go was the Elysee Café in Waterloo Street near the Congregational church. It was quite a luxurious café with couches all the way down either side and tables down the middle and there would be Len Godby playing the violin and Billy Doughty playing the piano. We would go there and have coffee of an evening. Sometimes we'd go to the Tivoli Cinema and then go on to the Elysee afterwards and there we would meet all our friends. I think it was there that I first met Freddie [Madge's husband]. I always recall one tea dance at the Winter Gardens – I can remember the actual dress and shoes I was wearing – when he asked me for the first dance!

And then somehow the picture changes again, the old kaleidoscope has another shake and Betty became engaged to Leonard England who worked for the Cable Company [the TransAtlantic Cable Office was in Richmond Street] and lived in South America, so she left Weston. Phyl Allen got married and went to live with her husband in March, Cambridgeshire. Marjorie Mason, along with her father and mother, moved to Bristol. My life changed quite a bit.

Moving On, Growing Up

However, to go back to Walliscote Road, we must have moved there in about 1925 or 1926 and there followed a very happy family life. At that time Jack was still at Lewisham School and I had started to go to Miss Brockhurst's school. We used to be taken to church every Sunday by Mother and Father. We would go to what was then the Congregational. It's now the United Reformed, but we had our own pew there and we used to be marched up there every Sunday. Jack would always go well equipped with cricket magazines which he would study during the sermon. It was quite a Sunday-morning ritual. My religious activities were varied. When we lived in Meadow Street, Olive White's family were Anglo Catholics and they worshiped at All Saints and we liked the choirboys up there so I used to go with

Olive to All Saints sometimes. Mary Bathe's family were Plymouth Brethren right at the other end of the scale and I used to go to the Gospel Hall with her. As for my own proclivities, I used to go to Clarence Park Baptist Church for my Sunday school – those were happy days with Sunday-school outings when we used to go on the Clevedon & Portishead Light Railway, or sometimes we would have a wagon of some sort take us into the country and have a picnic with races and games. At Whitsuntide, I was always given a nice white dress for the thanksgiving service. I remember reading the lesson at one of those services. I also used to go to Band of Hope meetings and sign the pledge every year!

When Jack left school he went to Austin Reed in Bristol and learnt the gentlemen's outfitting trade. It was an upmarket shop and he became a very smart lad. Of course all his friends were local boys. Derry Arch, Jack Rigby and Laurie Hawkins were among his special friends. They really had a hilarious time and I understand there were all sorts of parties being held to which we girls were not invited. Nevertheless it was a lovely light-hearted time for him and for me too with my friends.

At that time, Mother decided to let apartments for the holiday period and that would help to pay the rates. She let the front room and the back bedroom and we had a selection of interesting people who became quite friendly with us. They used to come back year after year, but much to Jack's chagrin, there was one dear old couple that came from Birmingham and the old man used to like to go out of an evening and lean on the front gate and smoke his last pipe of the day. Opposite us was a family with whom Jack was friendly and whom, we joked, were rather snobby. It didn't do Jack's pride any good to see this old man leaning on the gate, sometimes

Fred Frankpitt and Madge Payne with family and guests after their wedding at St Paul's Church, 1934.

in his shirtsleeves. He used to say, 'Can't you get him in?' but Mother would have none it.

We had magnificent Christmas parties enjoyed by all the family and Mother would work herself to a standstill. Every Christmas we used to have the Cowells, a family that had lived next door and then moved to Bristol Road. They used to come down with their two daughters and son after lunch on Christmas Day. The Wrefords would come and, of course, Uncle Sylv, Auntie Lil, Frank, Ethel, Arthur, Renee and Peter [Madge's nephew]. Every Christmas, after tea, Mother would have invented some sort of game which we would have to play. One year she had a fishing game. She put up one of the big screens which we used to keep the draughts out, because the rooms were very large and there was only a coal fire. Anyhow she had a screen put up and Frank was standing behind with a pile of parcels and we would be on the other side with fishing rods fishing for presents. Another time she had a treasure hunt and we were each given a little piece of wood with a string on it and we had to wind this string and follow it all over the house because she had wound it all in amongst the banisters and Mr Wreford got so fed up he got a pair of scissors and he cut all the strings so we never knew where our presents were! Once he invented a dreadful game. We all had to go in one at a time and he would sit in this room and we would be blindfolded and he would trace on our forehead and face with his finger and he would say, 'The moving finger writes and having writ moves on', and then he would go into some sort of poetry and we had to guess what he was talking about. However, when we came out we found that he had not been tracing all over our faces with his finger but, rather, had used black-lead; we all repaired to the bathroom to wash our faces!

Then Jack came to the time when he left Austin Reed and went to Plymouth. That was shortly before the Second World War. I had gone to work at the Winter Gardens and then I met Freddie. After a very happy engagement we married and went to live in a flat in Clevedon Road. Walliscote Road was now getting a bit too big for Mother and Father. Everyone had left the nest. Arthur was living in Wooler Road. Frank was in Moorland Road South before he emigrated to Australia, so Father bought a piece of land at Worlebury on Ern Wells Market Garden. It was a nice plot facing due south across to the airport. Freddie's father was a builder and mason and, with his partner, they built Rode-Heath, which was a lovely bungalow, well built. But looking back, it was still fairly primitive by today's standards. There was a triplex grate in the breakfast room, which I don't suppose you'd ever see these days. There was no central heating. Mother and Father let Glenside in Walliscote Road to a Mr and Mrs Higley and their son when they moved up to Rode-Heath.

Freddie served his apprenticeship at Cooksley, Son & Forsey and when that partnership broke up, he went with Mr Forsey who opened up on his own as an undertaker and cabinet maker. Freddie and I married on 20

September 1934. Unfortunately there was not much trade doing and very often the wages would not come in so Freddie decided to go on the road. The 1930s were difficult times. We bought a car and he got a job as a representative for Clapworthy's of Plymouth, bedding manufacturers. He also worked for another firm just outside London that sold china cabinets, which were popular at the time, and then a firm in Bridgwater that made basketwork. With those three firms he set out on the road. I went back to work – it was the norm in those days for women to give up their jobs when they got married – but I went to see Miss Brockhurst and asked if she could get me some work, which she did. I went to Wansborough, Robinson, Tayler & Taylor, a solicitor's in South Parade. I worked for them for a time and then I went to Lalonde Brothers & Parham. Then my old boss, who had left the Town Advertising Association and moved to Wookey Hole Caves, rang me up and said would I go out there and help him with a job, so I did that for one summer. I used to go out on the Wells bus every morning at eight o'clock. That road to Wells is very windy and I'm not a good traveller so I used to land up in the market-place at Wells feeling as sick as a dog, then get on another bus and go to Wookey Hole. Despite all that it was worth doing as it was a great help to our finances. Then Freddie decided, after I suppose about 18 months, that it was no go and he went back in the retail trade and took a job with White's of Boscombe. He found a nice little bungalow at Christchurch and I moved down there. I suppose, looking back, they were the two happiest years of our married life. Once a week on Thursdays, which was half day, we would go into Boscombe and have a drink at The Salisbury Hotel and then see a show at the Boscombe Hippodrome – that was our weekly treat.

But all good things come to an end and the war came along. Freddie got his calling-up papers and I came back to Weston when Freddie joined the Air Force. Then our son Jonathan came along and of course he was the joy of my life. Mother brought Jonathan up to a great extent because during those war years I had to work at the shop. Our own staff were taken and that just left Arthur and Clifford Hawkins who was given a dispensation because of working in the food industry. I went to work in the office and finally landed up behind the counter and it was jolly hard work. We were short staffed and rationing came in and I remember the day after Jonathan was born, I was sitting up in bed counting points and coupons and there was no let up at all. Mother came to the fore and she used to have lovely birthday parties for Jonathan and we had friends that came year after year. Of course, keeping a grocer's shop meant we weren't really short of sugar and fruit so mothers used to like to come to the parties as well because the tea was always delicious. Many of the boys and girls are still around today. David Martin was a little boy who used to come with his mother Mary, while Sybil Wreford used to come with Judith, and Erica Spalding with Gillian and Jane. Jo Hunt used to bring her daughter Ann, son Nick and the twins, Ian and David. Jonathan is still in touch with so many of these same friends today.

At that time Mother thought that it would be nice if we had a little car so she encouraged me to learn to drive. She arranged for me to have lessons and we bought a little green Austin 7, ADV 8. I passed my test and we used to go off on her famous outings. I was able to take Jonathan to the Pony Club meetings on the hill where there was a little school with ponies kept by the Tonkin sisters and when Jonathan was quite small he went up there and learnt to ride. He used to ride a little pony called Sooty. Then he started school at The College, the prep school there, which was held in the Albert Memorial Hall. Later it was moved back to The College proper in Walliscote Road and he stayed there until he took his 11+. He passed, which meant he was admitted to the Grammar School, which was a great relief; there were no private schools left of any note in Weston and I wouldn't have wanted him to go to one of the state schools. Around that time we had the tragedy of losing Arthur [Madge's brother] which broke all our hearts. It was dreadful, he was so lovely, but he was a chain smoker and I suppose it took its toll. When he died, it left Father with the burden of the business, and he was getting old. Mother had the feeling that it was getting a bit too much for Father to get up to Rode-Heath and down to the shop, so she decided we would go back to Walliscote Road. She got the tenancy back from the Higleys. They in turn got the tenancy of their old house in Clevedon Road back and we moved down to Glenside again. There was quite a bit to be done. We had a new bathroom suite and various alterations but we went back there happily. That was in 1951.

In 1952 Mother was taken ill. She went into hospital on the Monday and she died on the Sunday. My goodness, that didn't half bring us up with a jolt. I was left with Father, who was then 80, and Jonathan who was aged nine. It was big age gap to cope with as well as a big house and the business.

Jonathan, Father and I lived together quite happily at Walliscote Road but as I say it was a big house and I found it was too much for me, so we turned the top floor into a flat and let the bottom floor. That worked quite well. I was able to cope with that and get to the shop and look after Father and Jonathan as well as I could. This went on from 1952 until 1957 when Father died. He was 87 and had a lifetime of good health; it was only at the very end that he had a little prostrate trouble and then as a secondary his lungs gave out. When one realises that he was a chain smoker all his life he was a very fortunate man. So, what was I to do? The whole estate had to be settled up. There was Rode-Heath and Walliscote Road and the business, of course. So I sold Rode-Heath and Glenside in Walliscote Road, and I bought a little bungalow out at St Georges – Jonathan and I moved out there. It was a nice little bungalow with a big garden but we kept it going and we managed to grow all our own vegetables and flowers and we kept

a little car going. I sold the business to Clifford Hawkins who had a share in it anyway. This was a time when trade was getting a bit difficult and the supermarkets were coming along and I was advised to sell.

By that time Jonathan was coming up to school-leaving age and it was decided that he should go to John Hodge and take up the law. I had to earn some money somehow and I was offered a job by Mr Stephen, at Stephen & Co., the estate agents, helping in the cash office. After working all those years as my own boss in Meadow Street it was a bit of a blow to my pride to make the tea and coffee for all the staff at Stephens but I stayed there for 25 years. I loved the work. I made friends and the bosses always treated me with great respect because they had known my father and I was held in good esteem. I had only been there about three weeks when I was offered a job in the front office on the telephone. I was happy to get out of that dreary old cash office. Joan Squire was the receptionist there and then, when she became ill, I stepped into her shoes and that became my job for the rest of my time there. Joan and I have stayed friends ever since, and I am still friends with lots of the other staff that were there at the same time.

Jonathan, meanwhile, did well at John Hodge and passed his finals with honours – I think that was the most wonderful day of my life. Some 40 years on, Jonathan is now the senior partner of the business. We left the little bungalow at St Georges and moved into Shaftsbury Road. When Jonathan got married I decided I would move into town, on the level near the shops, with a view to old age. I sold the Shaftsbury Road house and bought my little house in the centre of town and I have been there ever since. And that brings me right up to date.

Charles Bidwell

Like Madge Frankpitt, Charles Bidwell knew a very different world from that of today. He was born in 1905 at 3 Jubilee Path, Milton. In the 1970s he wrote the following short account of his memories of life in those days for his granddaughter's school project. Unlike Madge, his life was not so comfortable and carefree. Summers were spent barefoot to save on shoes and children often went without food at lunchtimes. The school to which he refers is now Hillside First School.

I was born 22 December 1905 in Milton near Worle and completed all my schooling at Worle, having moved there when very young. My old school still stands next to the church on the hillside and I have very fond memories of a kindly old gentleman schoolmaster and his sister, who very often gave us poorer children a midday meal of bread and cheese, it being wartime. Nevertheless, they never spared us a good thrashing when it was warranted. I think the discipline they taught me and my brothers has stood us in good stead all our lives. My thanks to Mr Bennett and his sister, Molly, who of course have long since died.

Not Charles Bidwell, but other Worle children, c.1925. Ann and Alf Bishop on the doorstep of their rented home, the Thatched Cottage, Church Road, Worle. Like Charles Bidwell, their childhood years were often hard but happy. Note their lovely toy train and wicker dolls' pram. Alf's maternal grandfather was a plasterer and worked on the interior of the dome in the Winter Gardens Pavilion.

Worle Laundry, 1964. Charles Bidwell's mother worked there in 1914 for one shilling a day.

I recollect that our classes in those days were roughly 35–40 pupils and for good behaviour, such perks as ringing the school bell and running errands for the schoolmaster were considered by us children to be a great honour.

The majority of the people of Worle in my young days were very poor and in consequence clothes were usually passed down from older brothers after being altered to size by Mother. Worle village of 1906–16 was a real gem of old Somerset. I well remember the white dusty roads. No gas or electricity. Candles and paraffin lamps were the only means of light in the cottages. All water was fetched from the village pump and we enjoyed the beautiful sight of the horse-drawn carriages of holiday-makers from Bristol on their way to Weston-super-Mare. Motor cars were almost a nine-day wonder then.

There were six boys and one girl in my family and regular attendance at church on Sundays was a must. I can well remember having holidays from school in the summer and that all our boots and shoes were taken away and most of the boys and girls ran around barefoot to save shoe leather! Mother used to bake good wholesome bread in the kitchen oven and Father, being a farm hand, used to supply the potatoes. It was not unusual to find a huge piece of bacon hanging in our cottage kitchen...

The only holiday in my memory was a Sunday-school outing from Weston to Clevedon on the Light Railway, all in a coal truck. The journey to and from Weston to Worle had to be walked as there was no other form of transport then.

I left the old school on my twelfth birthday and started to earn my living as a butcher's boy... 8a.m.–8p.m. all week except Saturdays, which was 9a.m.–9.30p.m. We had a bath in the big wooden tub in front of the kitchen fire on Saturday nights. I can still smell that huge cake of Sunlight soap even now. All water, of course, had to be carried a goodly distance from the village pump.

After several jobs and some unemployment Charles joined the Somerset Light Infantry and served all over the world. After the Second World War, he joined the GPO, from which he was retired when he wrote the above account. He died in 1978.

Leonard Portch

Leonard Portch wrote down his reminiscences for his four sons. Born in Bristol in 1908, Leonard became a tram driver and bus conductor for the Bristol Tramways & Carriage Co. This is a brief extract taken from his account of a holiday to Weston in 1919, when he was 11 years old.

The year after the war ended something happened that had never happened before. We had a week at Weston-super-Mare. All firms were bound to give employees one week's paid holiday and Frys Factory closed during the last week of July. I remember my dad saying they had £5 and that would cover the cost quite well. I've an idea it was part of his war gratuity.

It turned out that there was quite a party of us on Bedminster Railway Station that Saturday. Uncle Ern's brother Syd, his wife and son Len, a niece and her husband Bert Fielding and Billy Morgan, were all going.

We stayed in several little cottages at the foot of the hill at Uphill. Weston looked good, and like nothing I had seen before, with the sands, donkeys and rows of stalls selling ice-cream, cockles, teas, windmills, buckets and spades and the rest. There were morning tides and we were out every morning on the sands with a ball. Billy Morgan performed at concerts locally in which he dressed up and did a Charlie Chaplin act, and when we went out in the mornings he dressed up with his bowler, cane, baggy pants and small moustache and played the fool.

We had swimming-costumes and splashed about in the water. There wasn't a bathing pool then, or the Winter Gardens. Any amusements were on the Old [Birnbeck] Pier – there weren't any on the New [Grand] Pier. When we got to the beach, the men and women changed into their bathing suits in the bathing huts on wheels which were lined up along the sands. The women wore mob caps lined with elastic over their hair, and a bathing dress which reached from their neck over pantaloons with frills stretching below the knees.

We all had donkey rides; adults, even fat men and women, were allowed. The donkey rides cost a penny each and if you had a party of a dozen the donkey man would knock a penny off. The Marine Lake had not been constructed then but Knightstone Pavilion was there.

On the sands, not far from the New Pier was a small canvas stage with rows of deck-chairs and wooden seats, where concert parties gave entertainment. They charged one penny for the wooden seats and tuppence for a deck-chair.

There were tram cars running along the front from the Sanatorium to the Old Pier. Some were open-top double-deckers and some of the single deck 'toast-rack' variety. I didn't notice many motor taxis, but the horse carriages did quite a trade trotting along the prom. The drinking-water at Weston in those days had a strong tang of salt. I suppose it was something to do with the ways used for cleansing it.

Nancy Williams

Nancy Davis (née Williams) remembers her holidays in Weston as a child growing up in South Wales. Her mother was a teacher and her father a mine inspector. They travelled to Weston every year for their two weeks' holiday. It cost sixpence to come over from Cardiff on the paddle-steamer and then they took a tram into town. As was normal at that time, they didn't book anywhere in advance but looked for lodgings when they arrived. Some places wouldn't accept children but they found a place in Ashcombe Road. Nancy's mother would buy the meat and let the landlady cook it – bacon for breakfast and chops for dinner. There was no bathroom for them, just a jug and basin in their bedroom. Nancy recalls:

The Williams family on holiday in Weston from South Wales, c.1913. Nancy is on the left with her father, a mine inspector, her mother, who was a teacher, and her brother and sister.

The first thing mother would do was to book a deck-chair for the fortnight, join Boots' Library and watch the Pierrots and Punch and Judy. Mother would always sit in front of The Grand Central Hotel so we children could run about and always know where to find her.

Every morning they watched tennis and bowls in Ashcombe Park. Sometimes they took a picnic to Sand Bay or went with their father to watch the water polo in Knightstone Baths. The first Sunday morning they always walked to the water tower in Weston Woods.

The family still holidayed here during the Second World War. By then Nancy's husband was in the RAF in Bristol and came down to be with her. During the 1942 blitz in Weston he heard the planes coming and ordered her to get under the bed. Their lace curtains were blown to shreds. They stayed one more night and then Nancy went back home to Wales and her husband to Bristol. Her sister was in a Welsh tuberculosis hospital at that time and saw the glow of the fires over Weston and was very frightened for her sister. Not surprisingly she was relieved to see her safe and well when the family returned to Wales.

⊕

Chapter 4

Trade and Industry

Like many women I love shopping, but my fascination with old shops probably began in childhood. I can just about remember the grocery stores of old, many of which survived well into the 1960s when supermarkets began to replace them. I remember sitting on tall bentwood stools beside long wooden counters while my mother read off a list to the shop assistant who would go from shelf to shelf gathering up the items. Rows of glass biscuit containers were lined along the front of the counter, from which you could choose a selection. Tall shelves behind were filled with tins and packets in

Osmond's grocery shop, 100 Locking Road, Weston, c.1911. Master grocer Harold Osmond with his wife Bessie are outside their shop with their horse, Kitty, who pulled the delivery cart.

bright colours and the shops had names that seemed to reflect Britain's Imperial past – stores such as The Maypole, International Stores and Home & Colonial. Then there were the wonderful fish shops, open to the street at the front, with sloping marble slabs glistening with silvery fish laid out on crushed ice and decorated with bunches of parsley.

In 1970, Weston was still full of small individual family-run shops. Coulstings is one shop that will forever remain etched on my memory. It was a very long shop stretching all the way from High Street back to North Street. It was also very narrow, giving you the feeling of an explorer as you worked your way ever backwards through high shelves of goodies. It was a bazaar in the old meaning of the word, selling all manner of things from coffee sets to Christmas decorations, with a wonderful toy department upstairs, where dolls' clothes were kept in little drawers which you drew out to choose an outfit. Because these shops had been in business for decades, you never knew what might still be lurking in their storerooms, which then reappeared in their closing-down sales.

Sue Ryall remembers with affection the shops of Worle and Weston just after the Second World War:

Most women shopped daily; with no fridges or freezers to keep food fresh it was a case of having to. There were no supermarkets so buying the weekly food took a long time and a visit to many different shops. There were still ration books in use when I was a child, and I can remember going to a shop called Korks at the bottom of Spring Hill in Worle to buy sweets. The owner had a small pair of scissors tied to a piece of string and hung from the counter. She cut out the coupons from your book and popped them into a shoe box with a slot cut into the lid. Korks also sold bottles of Corona which had wired stoppers on them. It was a treat to get a bottle of real fizzy lemonade because Mum usually made our own from Eiffel Tower Lemonade Crystals, which wasn't fizzy but it saved money. On days when we wanted ice-cream for tea I was sent to this shop with a pudding basin to get three or four scoops of ice-cream. I had to run like mad to get home quickly before it melted.

I often went into Weston with Mum to do the shopping. If we needed meat she would go to Whitton's,

Left: Miss Eileen Beach's greengrocer's shop in Clifton Road, Weston. Eileen bought the shop in 1928 with a loan from her parents.

Above: *This man is advertising the forthcoming film* The Magnet *to be shown at the Odeon Cinema, pictured in Oxford Street, c.1949. The boxes are a delivery for Betteridge Bros.*

A wet day in the High Street showing WH Smith's, Macfisheries and Hiltons shoe shop. The strangely-dressed figure is advertising a forthcoming film to be shown at the Odeon Cinema.

a butcher's shop at the top of High Street, now called Palmers. There were huge animal carcasses hanging from the ceiling on hooks, which you bumped into if you turned around quickly without looking first. The floor was covered in clean sawdust swirled into patterns. The counter was wooden and the joint you wanted was cut straight from the carcass; nothing was pre-cut. An assistant sat by the till, to whom we handed the money and a thick blue pencil line was marked through that week's meat ration coupon.

There were many different shops to visit in town in order to get everything on your list. Lipton's for loose tea in packets – there were no teabags then. They also sold sugar and dried fruit and so on. David Greig's on the corner of Meadow and Orchard Street for ham cut from the bone, cheese from a large cylinder-shaped piece and butter patted into shape with wooden butter pats. Then on to any shop that had the best bargains of the week. You could only get fruit and vegetables in season and we all looked forward to having lettuce, cucumber and tomatoes in the summer.

Dad sometimes liked a quart of winkles for his tea, bought from Macfisheries in High Street, and he and Mum sometimes had jellied pig's trotters for their supper. I can't say I ever fancied this. The only way to eat them was with your fingers because if you used a knife and fork they were so slippery they tended to shoot around the plate.

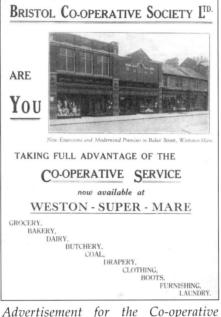

Advertisement for the Co-operative Stores in Baker Street, 1934.

Mum and Dad also liked tripe and onions which was cow's stomach, well cleaned and cooked slowly in milk with onions and eaten with lots of pepper – horrible!

Mum went into Worle village most days as there was always something that was needed. We bought bread daily from Neathways at the far end of Worle. My walk home was slower because I spent the time breaking off the corner crusts and eating them. Skidmores had a tiny little shop around the corner from their big one in Worle High Street. Old Mrs Skidmore would serve glasses of cherryade for tuppence. In the 'Jug and Bottle', at the Golden Lion pub you could buy penny bags of broken crisps so, for very little, a child could stave off hunger until it was time to go home.

Even in the late 1940s and early '50s Worle Post Office was old fashioned. I found it a fascinating shop, like walking into a time warp. It had a dusty wooden plank floor and was very dimly lit. There was a long brown wooden counter each side of the door. One side was the Post Office which was housed behind a metal grill, while the other side was haberdashery, but the things for sale were so out of date that I never saw anyone buy anything from that side of the shop. Faded

old-fashioned aprons were hung on hooks, along with tea towels and roller towels, black and white elastic and dull ribbon wound onto cards, ladies' lisle stockings and hand-knitted bed socks. The whole of that side of the shop had an air of 'time stood still'.

Next door to the Post Office was a wet fish shop run by Mr and Mrs Porter. I remember that the fish was beautifully laid out on a large sloping marble slab with plastic greenery placed around it.

I think I liked visiting the Co-op most of all. There were bentwood chairs to sit on while your order was being attended to and a huge, wide, shiny, dark wooden counter behind which the assistant would stand. She listened while you read out each item then would go off and get it, one thing at a time, placing each item on the counter and then writing it down on a duplicate pad. This was then added up and the top page of the pad and the money put into a small brass cylinder which was fixed to an overhead wire. The cylinder was sent whizzing across the room to a high office at the back of the shop which had white painted glass around it. The assistant who sat hidden inside sent any change back using the same method.

There was a big laundry at the end of Worle High Street that washed, dried and ironed clothes; there was no dry-cleaning then. I remember there was a shoe shop called Smiths, a bicycle shop which mended bicycles rather than sold them, two butcher's shops, two or three grocer's shops, a paint shop, a bread and cake shop, a bank, Skidmores furniture shop and a fish and chip shop. There was one other shop that we used very rarely, but only because it was at the top of the hill close to The Old King's Head pub. It was called Gunning's Stores and, as far as I can remember, it sold hardware and household goods. In later years there was the Manor Dairy at the bottom of Spring Hill which sold bottled milk. This was after Tripp's Farm had stopped selling it, although they still had a small dairy shop attached to the farmhouse which sold cream and butter. Just about everything that was needed in the home could be bought in Worle village when I was a child.

Sue's first job was in a Worle grocery shop:

Mrs Jones' grocer's shop was situated halfway up Coronation Road in Worle... Apart from bottles and tins, most goods were sold loose. The only thing frozen was ice-cream and that was mainly a summer item, so things like potatoes, vegetables, dried fruit and bacon were weighed or cut as needed. The bacon came in as half a pig, which I soon learned to bone and divide into

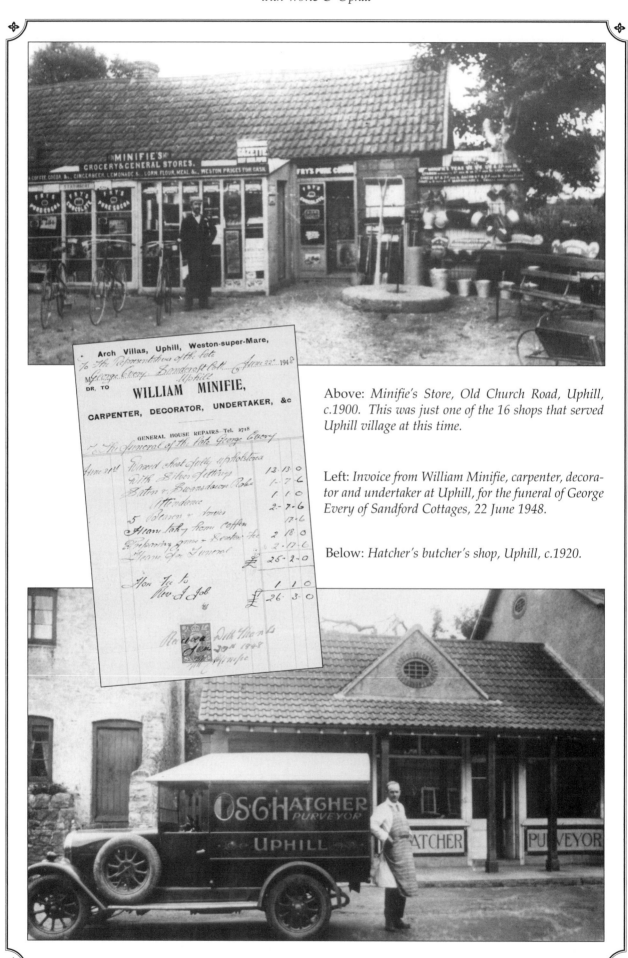

Above: *Minifie's Store, Old Church Road, Uphill, c.1900. This was just one of the 16 shops that served Uphill village at this time.*

Left: *Invoice from William Minifie, carpenter, decorator and undertaker at Uphill, for the funeral of George Every of Sandford Cottages, 22 June 1948.*

Below: *Hatcher's butcher's shop, Uphill, c.1920.*

the various cuts, long back, short back, gammon and streaky. We sliced the bacon on a hand slicer into the thickness the customer wanted, turning a handle with one hand and moving the piece of bacon back and forth across the revolving blade.

At Christmas time dried fruit came in flat wooden boxes which we levered open to get at the fruit. During a quiet time this was weighed out into 1lb portions and packed into thick, dark-blue paper bags. Tangerines came in sixes, each one wrapped in tissue paper in little wooden boxes. All around the front of the counter there were large square tins full of biscuits which were sold loose. Crisps were sold in waxed bags in those days and they went soft very quickly, even though they were in tins as well, so we had to be careful not to over order in case we were left with a lot of damp crisps!

Potatoes, carrots and other dirty vegetables had big floor-standing scales with a large brass open-ended scoop with a handle at one end. The weights were iron and went from 1lb up to 20lbs. For dried goods and biscuits we had smaller chrome scales which didn't have weights but had a pointer scale so that you could read off the price per pound. Sweets came loose in large glass jars and had their own little scales with weights from ½oz up to 1lb.

The first washing-up liquid had just come on the market. It was called 'Squeezy'. Before that there were only soda crystals to get rid of grease, which were very hard on the hands. The first ready-made shampoo was in a little plastic sachet, instead of having a packet of powder that had to be mixed with warm water in a cup. We also sold bundles of sticks, candles and paraffin, which were kept outside in the shed. Behind the counter was a barrel of vinegar and customers brought in their own bottle to be filled.

I loved working there, it wasn't hard work as some days were very busy and others quiet, customers came in to gossip as well as buy, and I became very good at adding up bills on paper. Fridays were rush days because people brought in their orders for the weekend which had to be delivered. We had a delivery boy and I also did some deliveries on my bike. There was such a lovely mixture of smells in there, soap powder, cheese, bacon and tobacco. They all bring back memories of the little corner shop.

The villages of Worle and Uphill were self-sufficient in all daily needs. There were 15 shops in Uphill at one time, including two butcher's, a bakery, a sweet-shop, the Post Office, a grocer's, a chemist, a coal merchant, a dairy and an undertaker. You could also buy milk and dairy products straight from the farms that surrounded both villages.

Betteridge Brothers

The Castle Stores were founded about 1907 by W.R. Milner and sold fancy goods and toys, gramophones, phonographs and records. Bicycles were later added to their stock. During the First World War business

declined, as luxury goods could either not be obtained or were prohibitively expensive. When the war ended in 1918 the shop was sold to W.G. Betteridge, who was visiting Weston from London. With Weston now entering a new phase of development he saw great possibilities for expanding the business. For the first few weeks, Mr Betteridge worked alone until, in March 1919, his brother was demobilised from the Army and joined him; the firm then became known as Betteridge Brothers. Sales grew rapidly and they were soon having to employ staff. The decision was taken to drop fancy goods and concentrate on the cycle and gramophone departments. In 1919 their first consignment of prams arrived! At a retail cost of £8 each, these were most definitely luxury goods. Cycles, too, were expensive at £10–£20 each and many people chose to have their bicycle renovated to as-new condition, saving them quite a lot of money.

The year 1922 heard the first radio broadcasts and Betteridges were in the forefront of this new technology, stocking three crystal sets even before the Cardiff Broadcasting Station was opened. The sets sold out within days and a valve set was bought and installed in the shop. A radio required four or five valves at this time to receive any station from Cardiff. Every evening the shop was crowded to the doors with people who would come to hear the first concerts broadcast on radio. Mr Betteridge also took this radio out once a week to village halls and set it up so that people could hear these early live concerts. The halls would be packed as spellbound villagers listened to the programmes.

The Castle Stores, Magdala Buildings, Walliscote Road. This picture was taken just after Mr Milner sold the shop to W. G. Betteridge in 1918.

Right: *Window display of Echo, Pye and Ferranti radios at Betteridge Bros, 1934.*

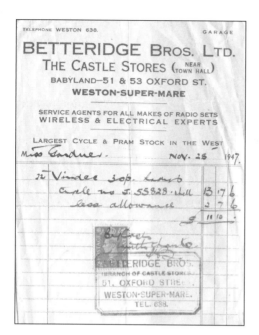

Above: *Invoice for a lady's cycle bought from Betteridge Bros, 1947.*

Right: *The interior of the cycle department of Betteridge Bros, 1934.*

The frontage of Betteridges, 1950s.

In 1924 the shop expanded to a second floor where the record and gramophone department was relocated. A stock of 5,000 records were available, including such gems as 'The Flies Crawled up the Wall', 'I Want to Cling to the Ivy' and 'A Four Ale Bar Concert'! Two years later the business opened a second showroom in Oxford Street for prams and cycles, whilst the shop next door, in Magdala Buildings, was also acquired so that the record and gramophone department could add sheet music to its ever-growing list of items for sale.

Every year, exhibitions were held at the Town Hall to display the latest equipment. Each day a different machine was used to play recorded music:

Tuesday 15 November 1932: Programme
10.30a.m. *Exhibition opens*
11a.m. *Programme of records of light instrumental music*
12 noon *Radio programme from London Regional Station*
1p.m. *Interval...*
3p.m. *One-act play:* The Love Nest...
5.15p.m. *The Children's Hour from Cardiff...*
Entertainment of Radio and Gramophone Music is today provided by HMV Radio Gramophone Model 532.

By 1933, the Betteridges decided to rebuild the Oxford Street shop, making it three times larger. A total of 20 staff were employed and it became one of Weston's largest retailers with 2,000 square feet of showrooms, plus stores and a service department. As well as being on sale, radios, prams and even vacuum cleaners could be rented and accumulator batteries recharged. In 1934 a booklet was published listing the brothers' achievements. The statistics make interesting reading. In 1934 the number of wireless licence holders in Weston was 7,765. Over 800 wireless sets and radiograms were sold by Betteridges in 1934. The firm even wired and supplied radios to the Wincanton Workhouse Infirmary. Their vans travelled 30,000 miles every year in service calls and deliveries. The first radio on Lundy Island was supplied by Betteridge Bros.

During the Second World War the shop was requisitioned by the WVS as a clothing store. The firm managed to survive and reopened in 1946 but closed in the late 1960s.

Lalonde Brothers & Parham

Emille and Mary Lalonde emigrated from France to England in the 1870s, sailing in one of their family's

---

TOY DEPT.

Fairy Cycles.

These toys increase in popularity. They are sturdily constructed of best cycle tubing. All are fitted with adjustable saddles and brakes. Blue or black finish.

Prices: **29/6 49/6 55/- 59/6**

Model No. 2 (*Illustrated*). A very popular model with thick rubber tyres, ball-bearing pedals, two-coil spring saddle, rim brake.
Price **39/6**

Juvenile Cycles.

We have a big stock of these machines, suitable for all ages up to 14—15 years. A visit to our Oxford Street Showrooms will convince you that the value cannot be beaten anywhere.

PRICES from **£3 19 6**

THE FAMOUS "RALEIGH JUNIOR."

Boy's or Girl's Model **£4 7 6**   Frame size, 18" & 20"   Wheels, 24"

Tricycles.

Specially designed for young children from 3 to 7 years of age. Low built to prevent overturning. Adjustable saddle and thick rubber tyres.

TRI-ANG TRICYCLES
ARE SAFE AND STRONG, AND WONDERFUL VALUE.

Tricycle No. 5. A splendidly made Tricycle with sponge rubber tyres and rim brake on front wheel. Free wheel and roller chain. Chrome fittings. Finished in blue or black.
Price **59/6**

Other Models: **29/6 39/6 45/-**

TRIUMPH CYCLES

Model.	£	s.	d.		Model.	£	s.	d.
Gent's Popular Roadster ...	4	19	6		Lady's Sports Club (Enamelled Black)	5	2	6
Lady's Popular Roadster ...	5	5	0		Gent's Speed Club (Enamelled Cream) (Maroon, Blue or Black optional)	6	17	6
Gent's PopularLight Roadster	4	19	6					
Gent's Standard Roadster...	5	15	6					
Lady's Standard Roadster	6	3	0		Lady's Sports Club (Enamelled Blue or Maroon ...	5	5	6
Gent's Standard Light Do.	5	15	6					
Lady's Standard Light Do.	5	18	6		Lady's Sports Club (Enamelled Ivory)	5	7	6
Lady's or Gent's Tourist ...	6	7	6		Gent's " Flyweight " ...	8	17	6
Gent's Sports Club (Enamelled Black)	4	19	6		Lady's or Gent's Club Tourist	6	7	6
Gent's Sports Club (Enamelled Blue or Maroon)...	5	2	6		Gent's Light Tourist (Enamelled Black)	7	12	6
Gent's Sport's Club (Enamelled Ivory)	5	4	6		Boy's Juvenile	4	4	0
					Girl's Juvenile	4	6	0

3-Speed Gear **£1** extra.
CASH OR EASY TERMS FROM 10/- DEPOSIT.

SUNBEAM CYCLES

"*PRODUCTS — of — SPECIALIZATION.*"

	£	s.	d.
Silver Sunbeam Light Roadster	6	19	6
Silver Sunbeam Road Racer	7	10	0
Golden Sunbeam Road Racer	9	15	0
Golden Sunbeam Light Roadster	10	15	0
The Golden Sunbeam Cycle, Lady's or Gent's	10	10	0

3-Speed Gear **£1** extra.

We suggest that your New Machine should be a " SUNBEAM "—and you will be proud of it!

THE CHEAPEST ARTICLE MAY PROVE THE DEAREST IN THE END.

Advertisements for cycles, from Betteridge Bros, Oxford Street.

own ships. When they arrived in Southampton they sold the ship and used the money to travel to Weston-super-Mare where they settled. One of their six children, also called Emille, started work for Samuel Norton, an auctioneer and valuer with premises in West Street. In 1886, Emille junr married Samuel Norton's daughter Kitty, and was made a partner in the firm which was renamed Norton, Son & Lalonde. When Samuel died in 1894, Emille brought one of his brothers, Septimus, into the firm and so renamed it Lalonde Brothers. Another of Emille's brothers, William, had opened a furniture shop in Weston, for which he owned a horse-drawn delivery van. It was this van which became Lalonde's first furniture-removal vehicle. When Septimus married he discovered his new brother-in-law was Ernest Parham, who worked for an estate agency in Salisbury. The family realised that between them they had the related businesses of auctioneers, furniture removers, valuers and estate agents. In 1898 Ernest Parham was asked to join the firm and run the first Bristol office of the company, by this time called Lalonde Brothers & Parham. By 1908 the company had abandoned horse-drawn vehicles in favour of a new 'Patent Steam Road Locomotive', to draw the removal vans. Its advert stated, 'As many as 5 vans can be conveyed by road in one journey by each locomotive.' An early brochure printed a number of testimonials in the back:

From W.A.T. Esq, I beg to say I am quite satisfied with the manner in which you conducted the Removal of our furniture from Weston-super-Mare to Stoke Bishop, and am of the opinion that your method of removing with an engine is certainly preferable for long journeys as compared with horses. (This removal consisted of EIGHT van loads.)

Nancy Davis of Weston, in her nineties at the time of writing, remembers a man moving from South Wales into a house in South Road. All the furniture was brought in large vans drawn by traction engines via

Lalonde Bros & Parham's horse-drawn wagon and trailer, pictured outside the Summer & Winter Gardens in the Boulevard, 1905. This venue later became the Palace Theatre and then the Tivoli Cinema, before being destroyed by incendiaries in 1942.

Gloucester. In South Road the drives are very long and steep and the men were not amused to find they had to park in the road and carry everything up to the house. The driver then went down to Norman's the grocer's to buy bacon and eggs so that the women would cook for them! G. Ritchie also had reason to remember the firm:

We left Weston and went back to London in 1923. The removal firm was Lalonde & Parham. The move was memorable because they came a day early which caused consternation. We went into The Grand Atlantic Hotel for a day. While there we got stuck in the lift between two floors. The removal van was pulled by a traction engine, and took two or three days to get to London. We were all sorry to leave and a flat in London was a poor exchange. We left behind friends and a lot of happy memories – the sea, Miss Burt's toy shop in Whitecross Road...

In 1905 Lalondes had a new purpose-built warehouse and saleroom built on the corner of Station Road and Graham Road. With its distinctive red-tile turreted roof, it is still in the hands of a removal firm – Nightingales.

In 1938 Richard Pool joined the partnership, the first person to do so from outside the family since its inception. As house building gathered momentum in the postwar years, the firm prospered. In 1955 they opened a separate commercial department for shops and businesses. They also moved into property management which covered anything from looking after a client's home whilst he or she was away on holiday, to managing a multi-floor office block in the centre of Bristol. In 1967 the estate agency business was separated from the removals, warehousing and auction rooms. Whilst the former continued as Lalonde Brothers & Parham, with offices in Waterloo Street and Bristol, the latter became just Lalondes, run from the repositories in Station Road, Weston and Oakfield Road, Bristol. In 1973 the firm celebrated its 125th anniversary with a dinner at The Grand Hotel in Bristol. In 2004 the name is no more. A series of consolidations of estate agencies and buy-outs by other firms has resulted in the closure of all the businesses.

The Royal Pottery

The Royal Pottery in Weston began in the 1840s and closed in 1961. They employed many hundreds of people in the town over the years and were one of Weston's longest surviving industries before the introduction of the plastic flowerpot, among other issues, put them out of business. They alternated between making building materials such as bricks and roof tiles, and elaborate garden statuary, whichever was the more profitable at the time. In the late-nineteenth century the firm was exporting wares worldwide and was known for producing the very

Horse-drawn furniture-removal wagons used by Lalonde Bros, 1888.

Lalonde Bros & Parham's Patent Steam Road Locomotive with one trailer, 1916.

Smart new removal vans, used by Lalonde Bros & Parham in 1945.

Right: *Top part of Betteridges calendar for 1966.*

Female worker trimming the top of a flowerpot at the Royal Pottery in the 1950s.

Derelict buildings at the Royal Pottery in Winterstoke Road, late 1960s.

The old Royal Pottery clay pits, off Winterstoke Road, late 1960s. The pits have become overgrown with reeds. The clay was extracted using a Stothert & Pitt multi-bucket excavator which delivered the clay into side-tipping wagons, which were then hauled to the works along this railway line by a small Hudson diesel locomotive. The length of the clay face worked required the track to be set back once a week, usually on a Sunday.

best garden pottery. Kew Gardens and the royal palaces bought Royal Pottery pieces and the firm supplied all the flowerpots for the coronation displays in London in 1937 and 1953. Sue Ryall worked there in the 1950s after she left Mrs Jones' grocer's shop in Worle:

My next job was at the Royal Pottery in Langford Road. I didn't have an urge to work there, it was just the first job that was offered me, so I took it. It was very different from the grocer's. I was paid piece work, in other words, I was paid by how much work I did; in my case how many flowerpots I could make in a week.

The clay was dug from the clay pits further down Winterstoke Road. It wasn't a wide road then, just a narrow country lane with hedges each side. The clay pits were about where the Hutton Moor Leisure Centre is [in 2004]. The clay was treated after it was dug out of the ground but I don't know how. It was delivered on a flat wooden handcart to the workers at the beginning of each morning.

We worked in long wooden sheds and each operator stood at a motorised spinning-wheel with a stop/start button at knee level. The wheel held a white plaster mould which would be the size of whatever flowerpot you were making that day. You pressed the start button with your knee and threw a fair-sized lump of clay into the spinning mould. You then had to pull down a wedge-shaped knife into the mould, which was held on a fixed handle above the wheel. The knife cut the shape of the pot out in the mould, the stop button was pressed with the knee and before the wheel had stopped spinning, the pot was removed and placed on a long wooden plank which rested on two trestles next to the wheel. Another lump of clay was then thrown into the mould, the start button was pressed and you carried on cutting out pot after pot.

When the plank was full of pots it was carried above the head to a drying cupboard with sliding doors and the plank carefully slotted in. When your cupboard was full, the next stage began. By this time the pots were slightly dryer but still the same grey clay colour. Each one was again dropped into a spinning mould, this time smaller than the pot so that the pot poked up over the edge. As it spun around, the edge of the pot was shaved smooth with an L-shaped knife and a hole was poked in the bottom of the pot by pressing another button. The pots were stacked ready to be counted and collected by the men who then took them to the kilns ready for firing. The most pots I ever made in a day was 200 but a couple of the girls were very fast and regularly turned out 300 or more each day.

There were two kilns still being used when I worked there, one was gas-fired and the other used coke. They were huge walk-in kilns with tunnels around the bottom leading to the outside where the gas or coke flame was fired into them. After being filled with the 'raw' bricks and pots the kiln was sealed and fired up. It took days to get to the right temperature and days to cool down before the men could get inside to empty it.

The firm employed a night watchman when the firing was on in order to keep it going at the right temperature. I can remember calling back at work one evening and found the night watchman sitting on an old upholstered chair, very cosily by the kiln fire. He took me up a long wooden staircase to the top of the kiln and draped all over the top were old blankets and coats. 'That's where the tramps sleep when its cold', he said, 'It's lovely and warm for them up here.'

I didn't mind working at the Royal Pottery but Mum thought it was a bit rough so I left and went to work in Woolworths.

Aircraft Manufacture

Aircraft manufacture began in Weston during the Second World War. American Tomahawk aircraft were assembled in a building off Locking Road whilst operating at the airport since 1933 were Western Airways, which offered passenger flights to Cardiff and other UK destinations. When war broke out, they were chartered by the Air Ministry for a variety of work, including running a flying school for the RAF based at Weston Airport. To facilitate the work, a new 1,000 yard runway was built to meet Air Ministry guidelines. In addition, a new 60,000 square feet hangar was built. On 5 September 1939 an air navigation training school was set up at the airport, using Avro Anson aircraft. Having the Avro aircraft on site allowed the maintenance staff to build up valuable skills, which were put to use when the Ministry of Supply granted the company a contract for the repair and reconditioning of Avro Anson aircraft. A new railway link was built from the main GWR line to the assembly hall doors to aid this work. In 1939 approximately half the 760 Avro aircraft in service with the RAF were used as training aeroplanes, while the remainder were used in Coastal Command for reconnaissance duties, with a few constructed as air ambulances.

The war forced firms to disperse production around an area. In 1940, the Bristol Aeroplane Company (BAC), based at Filton near Bristol, built a 'shadow' factory at Oldmixon close to Weston Airport, with another built on the outskirts of Banwell. As the factories provided an inviting target for enemy action, a decoy 'Q' site was set up at Bleadon. If a night raid was expected, the decoy site was lit up to draw fire away from the factories – a plan that proved successful. Other efforts were also made to hide the factory from spying eyes. Stan Terrell remembered that:

We had near us in Weston an aircraft factory at Oldmixon producing Beaufighters. This factory was camouflaged. What I found interesting is a corner of one of the buildings was so well hidden it looked like a 'cottage in the woods' from the air.

The main work at the BAC factory at Oldmixon was assembling and flight-testing Bristol Beaufighters. The Beaufighter was a twin-engined, two-seater fighter aircraft that had evolved from the Bristol Blenheim. As well as the four 20mm cannons and up to six Browning machine-guns that they were fitted with, they could also carry rockets, a torpedo or a 1,000lb bomb load. It was also one of the first aircraft to be fitted with radar. At one time 87 aircraft a month were being turned out with the total wartime production at Weston numbering 3,345. The first batch of 500 of these aircraft went to Fighter Command, who used them as night-fighters, and to Coastal Command, who used them as long-range strike aircraft. Others went to the Australian, Canadian and South African Air Forces; the Japanese began to call the aeroplane 'The Whispering Death' because of the speed with which it would appear, fire and disappear. At the start it took 18 months to make one Beaufighter. Maurice Pitman was a flight engineer in the RAF and was released to BAC to try to reduce this length of time. He managed to get it down to 12 months per aircraft.

At the end of the war, the main production at Weston switched to prefabricated housing in order to meet the severe shortage of homes caused by the bombing. These were the famous AIROH houses (Aircraft Industries Research Organisation for Housing), of which very few now remain. By 1948 whole schools and hospitals were also being made and distributed worldwide.

In 1952, the factory again switched to aircraft manufacture or assembly, building, among others, Bristol Britannia aeroplanes and Sycamore helicopters. Four years later all the helicopter production was moved to Oldmixon, including design, development and servicing. The design office at Weston also worked on some subcontracted work on the supersonic airliner, Concorde. In 1960 the firm became Westland Aircraft Ltd and so Weston's long association with helicopter production began. In the 1970s some 1,500 people were employed at the Oldmixon factory.

In 2001, with orders declining, Westland merged with the Italian company Agusta. A year later the shock announcement of the closure of the Weston works resulted in the loss of 350 skilled jobs. At the time of writing, the future of the site is still to be decided although the airfield has been bought by a developer.

Above: *Interior of the Western Airways Oldmixon factory with work taking place on Avro Anson aircraft, 1942.*

Below: *Reconditioned engines arriving at Weston Airport to be installed in Avro Anson aircraft, 1942.*

Right: *Dismantling an Avro Anson aircraft before taking it in for reconditioning, 1942.*

Left: *View looking east over what was then farm land to Westlands Factory, c.1959.*

Chapter 5

✤

Weston's Sons and Daughters

Quite a few well-known people have had links with Weston-super-Mare. As the town grew and fashionable crescents and detached villas became available to rent and purchase, many chose to retire here – a trend that has continued into present times. Others were born here and achieved fame and renown elsewhere. I have picked out a few of the less well-known or more interesting to comment on further here. They are listed alphabetically as far as possible.

Albert Alexander

The son of a blacksmith, Albert Alexander was born in George Street, Weston-super-Mare, in 1883. At the age of 13 he joined the Bristol School Board where he stayed for the next 20 years (broken only by his service in the Artists' Rifles during the First World War), becoming chief clerk of the Somerset County Council Higher Education Department in 1919. He developed an avid interest in the Co-operative Society and its aims and in 1920 Albert left Somerset County Council to become secretary of the Parliamentary Committee of the Co-operative Congress. He was elected Labour MP for Sheffield Hillsborough two years later. He became a passionate and intelligent debater, particularly on trade and industry matters, and in the 1924 Labour Government he served as Parliamentary Secretary to the Board of Trade. In 1929 he was named First Lord of the Admiralty, a post he held again during the Second World War and for which he was awarded the Freedom of the Borough of Weston-super-Mare in 1943.

Albert had a square jaw and a wide mouth and often appeared gruff but he was a genial man. A good speaker, spontaneous and never at a loss for words, he is reported as having had a warm, resonant voice with a slight Somerset accent. Outside of politics he was a Baptist lay preacher and a fan of football. A plaque commemorates his birthplace at 33 George Street.

Jeffrey Archer

Politician and author Jeffrey Archer will probably need little introduction. Controversy has followed him throughout his life. Jeffrey's mother, Lola Cook, met William Robert Archer whilst working as a nurse in Weston. They married in 1939 in Glasgow and Jeffrey was born 15 months later. He was Lola's third child, the previous two having been illegitimate and given up for adoption. William changed his name to Archibald William Archer and in 1942 the family moved to Mark, a village a few miles south of Weston. At this time, Lola began writing articles for a women's magazine and working occasional shifts at Weston General Hospital. Two years later they moved back to Weston living in a variety of rented properties. In 1946 William and Lola set up a publishing business, *West Country Publicity – What's On in Weston-super-Mare*, which later became the official *Entertainments & Holiday Journal*. The family moved to 51 Locking Road where the business was based and for the next three years Jeffrey became a weekly boarder at 7 Gerard Road, a home for children run by Ellen Lever, while he attended Christchurch Primary School.

In May 1949, Lola became the first woman journalist for one of the local newspapers, the *Weston Mercury*. Her column, entitled 'Over the Tea Cups', which she wrote for nine years, included interviews with local personalities, bargains in fashion shops, dress patterns and recipes. Jeffrey made frequent appearances in the column, which often involved Lola recounting in an exasperated or amusing way his most recent scrapes or his latest craze. He was always referred to as Tuppence in the newspaper, apparently because of his habit of going into a sweetshop and asking, 'Anything for tuppence?' One article, written in 1949, recounts how Lola gave Jeffrey his pocket money which he spent immediately. She wonders how he will manage his money when he is older!

Jeffrey's father seems to have inspired his love of cricket. William Archer was vice-president of the local club and often took Jeffrey to matches. In 1952 Jeffrey won a scholarship to Wellington School in Somerset. The children at Christchurch School were given a half-day holiday to mark the occasion.

William Archer died in 1956 and is buried in Ashcombe Cemetery. Lola moved to Eastern Mansions in Atlantic Road and continued to write for the paper until the 1970s. Jeffrey's story, meanwhile, became the stuff of legend. He went to university, became the youngest ever MP in Parliament at the age of 28, was made bankrupt after some unwise investments, and started to write best-selling novels. In 1993 he became Lord Archer of Weston-super-Mare and Mark. He worked tirelessly for the Conservative Party until expelled over a perjury case for which he went to prison. Lola remarried twice and outlived all her husbands. After a bout of ill-health in 1997, Jeffrey moved his mother to a nursing home near his home in Cambridgeshire. She died there in 2001 at the age of 87.

Brian Austin

Brian Austin is a local man born and bred, best known for his columns in the local newspapers and his extensive knowledge of family and local history. In his own words he recalls:

Thanks to the skill of Dr Richard Alford, I was born by caesarean section at Weston General Hospital on the Boulevard, on 3 September 1942. My mother had played tennis that morning and, years later, my godmother told me that mother always held it against me because she had been winning!

My father was an Army man, later becoming Councillor Brigadier Ronald Austin CBE (I didn't take after him) and dying in 1976 aged only 64. He had been a violinist/tenor for Burgess' Band at the Rozel Bandstand in the 1930s, together with his brother Eric, whilst his father looked after the horses of the Weston Urban District Council. We lived at 123 Locking Road, nearly opposite St Saviours Church, with my grandparents, Bert and Nelly Hook. Bert had managed local theatres for the council and Nelly was a Trapnell, the only daughter of the eldest of 12 brothers. The fact that I took after the Trapnell family so strongly was a constant source of wonder to my father, whose brothers, sister and father were very distinctive and easily recognisable.

I clearly recall sitting in the back room for hours on end, listening to music and comedy from the radio and then, when we had the evening 'quiet' period, listening to Bert whisper all the news to himself as he read the paper.

I arrived at the kindergarten of Burton House School in 1946 with a basic grounding of songs, jokes and up-to-date news. I would add that my mother had taught me the alphabet and basic maths tables by not allowing me to leave the bathroom until I had shouted them out loud through the door. In 1948 I moved to The College in Walliscote Road, where I spent eight years learning cricket, football and little else until a classmate brought in a gramophone and we had rock-and-roll sessions in the science lab. Ah! The evocative sound of Bill Haley and Little Richard, the sound of the Royal Pottery hooter and the foghorns in the Bristol Channel, the smell of steam trains and of fresh-made coffee in Fortes Coffee Bar. Most of all, and oddly enough, the 'weather

'plane', a lone aeroplane that droned slowly across the sky after dark in my childhood years, which became a trusted signal that it was time to sleep. Fond memories!

William Lisle Bowles

The poet William Lisle Bowles was born in Northamptonshire at King's Sutton in 1762. He moved to Uphill in May 1769 when his clergyman father was presented with the living of Uphill and Brean. Bowles was moved by his first sight of the village and the sound of the sea and loved to take long walks in the countryside. 'The long waves, breaking slow with such a sound as Silence, in her dreaming mood might love.' At the age of 14 William went to Winchester School and thence to Trinity College, Oxford. His first book of poetry, *Fourteen Sonnets* was published in 1789 to great acclaim by Coleridge and other well-known poets of the time. Bowles revisited the Uphill coastline in later years and was inspired to write 'Banwell Hill', which vividly describes the landscape of the area. His last poem was written in and about Weston-super-Mare:

Was it but yesterday I heard the roar
Of these white coursing waves, and trod the shore,
A young and playful child – but yesterday?
Now I return with locks of scattered grey.

In 1828 Bowles was made Canon of Salisbury and died there in 1850. He is buried in the cathedral.

John Cleese

Actor John Cleese was born in Weston in October 1935. His parents were Reginald Cleese, an insurance agent living in Uphill, and Muriel Cross, daughter of local estate agent, Marwood Cross. In fact Reginald's family name was Cheese, but he changed it by deed poll just before joining the Army in 1915. After a somewhat secretive courtship, the couple married at Bristol in 1926. It was to be 13 years before John, their only child, was born. The family were then living at 6 Ellesmere Road, Uphill.

In 1940, after the first bombs fell on Weston, the family moved to the safety of Brent Knoll. The restless Cleeses seemed unable to stay in one place for any length of time, however, and soon moved again. John started his first schooling in Burnham-on-Sea before being enrolled at St Peter's School in Shrubbery Road, Weston in 1948. The family had by then moved to Clarence Road North. Details of his school years are recounted in the section on St Peter's School in Chapter 7. John was a day pupil and his spare time was spent playing in Clarence Park with his friends, perhaps visiting Knightstone Theatre or the cinema. Weston, its people and its middle-class values and emphasis on respectability were to provide inspiration for much of his later comedy.

John Cleese at St Peter's School, Weston, c.1949.

After several more moves, his mother came back to Weston and remained in the town until her death at the age of 101 in 2000. Her ashes are buried at the cemetery at Worle.

Wilkie Collins

The Victorian writer Wilkie Collins was a frequent visitor to Weston during the mid-nineteenth century. Collins was friends with Edward Smyth-Pigott of Grove House and used to stay with Dr J. Stringfield of Verandah House, which stood approximately where the Sovereign Centre is located in 2004, opposite The Royal Hotel. During September 1855, Wilkie Collins and Edward Smyth-Pigott went on a cruise from Weston to the Scilly Islands in the boat *The Sisters*, with local boatman Aaron Fisher. The trip was written up as *The Cruise of the Tomtit*. Collins was also great friends with Charles Dickens, who published some of his stories. Collins is best known today for the novels *The Woman in White* and *The Moonstone*, but on his death in 1889, he had written 24 other novels, over 50 short stories and up to 15 plays.

Jill Dando

The late television presenter Jill Dando was born in Weston in 1961. She attended Broadoak School and on leaving in 1979, followed her brother Nigel into journalism by becoming a reporter on the *Weston Mercury* newspaper. She stayed with the paper for five years before moving into television and radio. She soon became a household name reading the 'Breakfast News' and 'Six O'clock News' for the BBC. She then moved to television reporting for shows such as 'Crimewatch' and 'Holiday'.

In 1999 she was murdered on the doorstep of her London home by Barry George. Not since the death of Diana, Princess of Wales, was the nation so moved by an untimely and tragic end. She will be best remembered locally for her charity work, especially for Weston Hospicecare. On her death a fund was set up in her memory. Remembering her work for 'Crimewatch', the decision was taken to establish the Jill Dando Institute of Crime Science. It is the first of its kind in the world and is devoted to reducing crime through teaching, research and public policy analysis. In July 2001 the Jill Dando Memorial Garden was built in Grove Park in Weston. It was designed by Alan Titchmarsh and constructed by the BBC 'Ground Force' television team in just three days.

Captain George Day

Captain George Day retired to Weston with his wife and daughter in 1875. He had a little less than a year to enjoy the delights of the Victorian resort before he died in December 1876. George Day had enjoyed a long and successful career in the Navy, joining as a volunteer in 1833. It was as a Lieutenant during the Crimean War in 1855 that George Day won the Victoria Cross. The *London Gazette* published his actions in full and it makes fascinating reading:

With great enterprise and Gallantry, landed and successfully carried out a reconnaissance within the enemy's lines at Genitchi. This service was performed by Lieutenant Day with the view to ascertaining the practicality of reaching the enemy's gun-vessels, which lay within the Straits of Genitchi, close to the town. It was performed by Lieutenant Day alone on a dark but fine night, with the assistance of a pocket compass. After traversing four or five miles of low, swampy ground, occasionally up to his knees in water, he at length advanced to within about 200 yards of the vessel. From the perfect silence on board it was his conviction that they were without crews, and when he returned it was with the full conviction that the expedition was a feasible one. This opinion, however, he was forced to change, on the following day in consequence of the increasing activity which was apparent in the direction of the enemy vessels, and therefore he determined on making a second visit to the spot.

On this occasion the night was squally, and the journey longer and more difficult than before. On reaching the spot and finding the enemy vessels manned, and their crews apparently on the alert, he decided the effort to surprise them was out of the question. Lieutenant Day was so long on shore that the seamen stationed to pick him up gave him up for lost and returned without him. Mr Parker, however, came to look again and found Day lying exhausted on the shore and took him back to the ship where he eventually recovered from his exposure.

Day's naval career ended in 1867 when ill health forced his retirement. He was buried in Ashcombe Cemetery in an unmarked grave. It was not until May 2002, that a headstone was unveiled by the Mayor of Weston to mark his last resting place. A plaque commemorates George Day on the wall of his home in Claremont Crescent. His medals, which beside the VC, include the Companion of the Most Honourable Order of the Bath, the Naval General Service Medal, the Baltic Medal and eight others, are in the Sheesh Mahal Collection in India.

Harry Day

There have been many locally well-known personalities. Between the wars one such was William Henry 'Harry' Day. Harry was a son of William Day of Swiss Road, who was one of the last survivors of the original fishermen who fought the lord of the manor so vigorously for their austere tenement rights. In his youth he played for Christchurch Old Boys' Football Club and later was a member of the First Gloucestershire Artillery Volunteers. During the

First World War he joined the Royal Army Service Corps, in the motor boat section, and took part in the Dardanelles landing. Toward the end of the war Harry transferred from the RASC to the Labour Corps and on demobilisation was employed at the gasworks in Weston-super-Mare. In 1924 he had an accident in the coke-screening plant at the gasworks – his leg was caught up between a chain and a revolving shaft, which meant his whole body was twisted and stuck. He was extricated with difficulty and taken to Weston Hospital where his left leg was amputated above the knee. In addition, his right ankle was fractured. The accident engendered more profound sympathy as he had a wife and eight children to support.

When he recovered, Harry was granted permission by the council to operate a weighing-machine at Anchor Head, where he remained for several years before he transferred to another pitch outside the West Street shelter on the promenade. Thousands of holiday-makers made a point of visiting him on the first and last days of their holiday. 'Nine out of ten are delighted to find that they have put on weight,' he once said.

He loved sport and was an expert trainer. For several years before his accident he trained the

Harry Day with his weighing machine at Anchor Head, c.1926.

Harry Day meeting the Duchess of York on her visit to open the new hospital in Weston, 1928. He is pictured in his self-propelled wheelchair donated to him by the players and supporters of the Weston Association Football Club, for whom he was trainer before he lost his leg.

Weston-super-Mare Swimming Club and its water-polo team as well as the Weston-super-Mare Association Football Club. The players and supporters of the AFC thought so much of Harry that they presented him with a self-propelling wheelchair, in which he was a familiar sight about the town.

He was proud of having had several chats with royalty. King George VI and Queen Elizabeth, when as Duke and Duchess of York, they opened the Queen Alexandra Memorial Hospital in 1928, had quite a long talk with him. In addition, the Duke of Kent, when he visited Weston to launch the new lifeboat *Fifi & Charles*, also had a friendly word for him.

Two of William Day's brothers were members of the first local lifeboat crew while one of Harry Day's brothers was killed while serving in the Navy just after the First World War. Another brother also saw service in the war and was later killed in a road accident. Yet another brother – a well-known member of Mogg's Band and the Territorial unit of the local Wessex Royal Engineers – died through an accidental fall from a bus. Harry died suddenly at his home, 26 Coronation Terrace, Drove Road, in 1942 at the age of 60.

Jacob Dillenius

Long before Weston had a tourist industry, the town was known further afield for its interesting botany and geology. People such as Jacob Dillenius, the first Professor of Botany at Oxford University, travelled on foot or by horse to 'discover' this tiny village of 100 people on the road to nowhere. Worlebury's Iron Age hill-fort also attracted antiquarians (the forerunners of archaeologists) who marvelled at its ancient walls.

Diana Dors

Diana Fluck was born in Swindon in 1931. It had been a difficult birth in which she and her mother nearly died. Afterwards, her parents lavished every care on their daughter. She was taken to watch her first film at the age of three and thus began her love of Hollywood and movie stars.

In 1944 the country was flooded with American soldiers as they prepared for D-Day and the family had a Californian GI billeted with them. Diana was thrilled to meet a real American and vowed to get to the US any way she could. She always looked and acted older than her real age, wearing make-up from the age of 12. It was therefore no problem to her when, on holiday in Weston in 1945, she pretended to be 17 and entered her first beauty competition. The Modern Venus competitions, held at the Open Air Pool at Weston, were started to find pin-up girls for soldiers' magazines. At the real age of 14, Diana came third. The picture was published and led to modelling contracts and acting lessons. Her career began from that moment.

General Dwight Eisenhower

In 1944 General Dwight Eisenhower visited the US troops stationed at Weston during the build-up to the Normandy landings. It was part of a morale-boosting tour throughout southern Britain in his role as Supreme Commander of Allied Expeditionary Forces in western Europe. He stayed the night in a caravan on Worle Hill, near the water tower.

Frank Castle Froest

In 1910 the murderer, Dr Crippen, was the first criminal captured by the use of radio. As he attempted to escape to Canada with his lover, Ethel le Neve, the captain of the ship recognised him and radioed back to London with the information. Bristol-born Frank Castle Froest was superintendent of the Criminal Investigation Department of Scotland Yard, and authorised Crippen's arrest, sending Chief Inspector Walter Dew to board a faster liner, so he could be waiting at Quebec to arrest the pair. Froest retired to Yatton near Bristol. After the death of his wife he moved to Charlton Road, Weston-super-Mare, taking the post of honorary superintendent of the Sanatorium. On his death in 1930 he was buried in the churchyard of the Old Church of St Nicholas at Uphill, close to where Marconi's first ever broadcast across water had been received.

Vernon Goold

The last ever Mayor of Weston-super-Mare Borough was Councillor Vernon Goold, whose term of office ran from 15 May 1974 until 31 March 1975, when the new District Council of Woodspring took over. Vernon Goold was born in Bristol. He worked for the Bristol Aeroplane Company during the Second World War as well as serving in the National Fire Service. When he and his wife, Hilda, came to Weston in 1946, Vernon opened an estate agency in Orchard Street, specialising in business transfer. He became president of the Western Counties branch of the Valuers' Institution in 1958, and was a Fellow of the Incorporated Society of Valuers and Auctioneers and a Fellow of the Institution of Business Agents.

Councillor Goold, a Conservative, was first elected to the Borough Council in a three-cornered contest in central ward triggered by the death of Councillor Richard Ivens. In 1964 he lost his seat by a narrow margin to the Liberals, but won an Ellenborough ward seat in 1965 when he topped the poll. He repeated this success with the distinction of recording the highest number of votes in the 1968 Borough Council elections, and so established a record of contesting four municipal elections in only four and a half years.

He took a very active role in the town and became vice-chairman of the Parks Committee and a member of the Works, Catering and Entertainments and

Libraries Committees. He was a member of the Accident Prevention Advisory Panel and served as a governor of Weston Technical College and Bournville School. Vernon Goold died in 1983. His wife still lives in the town.

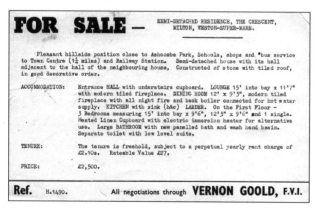

Cllr Vernon Goold hauling down the borough flag of Weston-super-Mare on the Town Hall roof for the last time on Friday 29 March 1974, following the dissolution of the borough through local government reorganisation. Mr Jackson was the bugler.

FOR SALE — SEMI-DETACHED RESIDENCE, THE CRESCENT, MILTON, WESTON-SUPER-MARE.

Pleasant hillside position close to Ashcombe Park, Schools, shops and 'bus service to Town Centre (1¼ miles) and Railway Station. Semi-detached house with its hall adjacent to the hall of the neighbouring house, Constructed of stone with tiled roof, in good decorative order.

ACCOMMODATION: Entrance HALL with understairs cupboard. LOUNGE 15' into bay x 11'7" with modern tiled fireplace. DINING ROOM 12' x 9'3", modern tiled fireplace with all night fire and back boiler connected for hot water supply. KITCHEN with sink (h&c) LARDER. On the First Floor – 3 Bedrooms measuring 15' into bay x 9'6", 12'3" x 9'6" and 1 single. Heated Linen Cupboard with electric immersion heater for alternative use. Large BATHROOM with new panelled bath and wash hand basin. Separate toilet with low level suite.

TENURE: The tenure is freehold, subject to a perpetual yearly rent charge of £2.10s. Rateable Value £27.

PRICE: £2,500.

Ref. H.1490. All negotiations through **VERNON GOOLD, F.V.I.**

Card from the window of Vernon Goold's estate agency, c.1953.

Rupert Graves

Actor Rupert Graves was born in Weston in 1963. He went on to star in films including *The Madness of King George*, as well as stage productions such as *Torch Song Trilogy* and *The Importance of Being Earnest*. More recently he played Young Jolyon in the recent television remake of the *Forsyte Saga*. In the summer of 1996 he returned to Weston to make a short feature on the plight of Birnbeck Pier for the BBC2 programme 'One Foot in the Past'.

Thomas Alfred Harding

Explorer Thomas Alfred Harding died at 187 Moorland Road, Weston, in 1936. Harding was a survivor of the *Challenger* scientific expedition to the Atlantic, Pacific and Antarctic Oceans. HMS *Challenger*, a converted 18-gun corvette, embarked from Portsmouth in December 1872 on a four-year oceanographic expedition under the direction of the Scottish professor Charles Thompson and the British naturalist Sir John Murray. This was the first totally scientific journey of exploration. Physicists, chemists, and biologists collaborated with expert navigators to map the sea, gathering data on temperature, currents, water chemistry and marine organisms, over 14 million square miles of ocean. It resulted in a 50-volume report that took 23 years to compile.

Bentfield Charles Hucks

Bentfield Charles Hucks was an early aviation pioneer. He was originally a motoring enthusiast, but after a speeding offence, which resulted in a £50 fine and the loss of his licence for three years, he moved on to aeroplanes. He learnt to fly in 1910 and travelled to the USA. On his return he joined the Blackburn Company, test-flying their new mono-plane. In 1913 Hucks became the first British aviator to fly upside down and loop the loop. After this he toured the country giving aerobatic displays. On at least one occasion he performed at Weston, landing and taking off from the sands near Uphill or a field in Locking Road. Hucks became the first person to fly across the Bristol Channel as he took off from Weston, circled over Cardiff and returned. When the First World War broke out Hucks joined the Royal Flying Corps. He died of pneumonia a week before the Armistice.

B.C. Hucks, in his Blackburn monoplane, at Weston-super-Mare, 6 September 1911.

Children's postcard artist, Ivy Millicent James, photographed c.1900.

Ivy Millicent James

Ivy Millicent James lived in Weston for most of her life, from her birth in 1879 until her death in 1965. She was an artist and illustrator of children's postcards. Her family moved to Weston from Wales in about 1868. It was in 1 Atlantic Villas that Ivy was born, the youngest of four children. Ivy was a delicate child and prone to headaches. She attended Miss Astle's school in Holywell House, South Road, before entering the new School of Art in Lower Church Road in 1895. Both her mother and her older sister, Maud, were also artistic and the family frequently went to exhibitions in London, where Maud studied at the Slade School of Art.

By 1901 Maud and Ivy had work published as Christmas cards and calendars and in 1907 Ivy's first postcards were published. At this time postcard collecting was extremely popular and millions of cards were sold every year. Her designs, usually signed IMJ, often featured children in Dutch-style costume.

The two sisters travelled extensively in western Europe, which influenced the subject matter and settings of the cards. Ivy was also a keen suffragette, designing the banner for the Weston-super-Mare branch of the Women's Social and Political Union.

After the First World War, Maud and Ivy let their home and moved to London, doing good works for St Cyprian's Church. Neither Ivy nor Maud married and when the latter died in 1930, Ivy was heartbroken and moved back to Weston. Her last cards were published in 1919 but she had a comfortable income from her father's investments and lived quietly at 9 Grove Park Road. Although childless herself she was a great supporter of the Holy Family children's home of St Margaret's in Queen's Road and enjoyed the children's visits to their 'Auntie Ivy'. She died in Weston in 1965.

Valery Larbaud

French writer Valery Larbaud wrote 'Weston-super-Mare Midi', a poem about Weston on a rainy day. Larbaud was born in the town of Vichy in 1881. His father was a chemist and built a fortune on the local mineral waters. As an only child Valery was somewhat of a dreamer. He knew from the age of 15 that he wanted to write and began with translations of English and Spanish literature, making them accessible to the French. He published his first poems in 1908. Over the years he received numerous honours, notably the Prix National des Lettres in 1952, five years before his death. He was inspired by the work of James Joyce and wrote three short stories of his own, using Joyce's stream-of-consciousness technique. He also agreed to undertake a translation of Joyce's influential work, *Ulysses*.

Sadly Larbaud was struck down by a brain disease in his fifties and could no longer write. His library, including original manuscripts and correspondence, was acquired by the town of Vichy as a memorial to the writer and at the time of writing is open to the public. Copyright to all his works was bequeathed to the town; this funds exhibitions and an annual literary prize. His fame is such that an International Association of Friends of Valery Larbaud was founded in 1957 on his death. It promotes his work and decides the recipient of the annual award.

Dr Langhorne and Hannah More

As Weston developed as a tourist destination, the rich and famous made their way here. Two such people were Dr Langhorne, and the reformer and writer Hannah More. Dr Langhorne was the rector of Blagdon and well known as a translator of Plutarch's *Lives*. He met Hannah while she was convalescing at Uphill. It is said that when he failed to meet her on one of her morning rides on the beach he wrote the following verse in the sand, 'Upon the shore walked Hannah More, Waves let this record last! Sooner shall ye, proud earth and sea, than what she writes, be past.' As Hannah rode along shortly afterwards she replied in the wet sand, 'Some firmer basis, polished Langhorne choose, to write the dictates of thy charming muse; Her strains in solid characters rehearse, and be that tablet lasting as thy verse.'

Alfred Leete

Cartoonist Alfred Leete was born in 1882 in Northamptonshire to a farming family. His father's ill health forced them to give up farming and move to a warmer climate; in 1893 they came to Weston-super-Mare. Here Alfred attended Kingsholme School in Arundell Road while his parents ran Sutherland House and Addington House as hotels.

Alfred Leete, pictured with one of his cartoons of a British workman on the wall behind him.

On leaving school Alfred was apprenticed to a Bristol architect. While he hated the work, he discovered a love of drawing and before long was supplying cartoons and drawings to the *Bristol Magpie* magazine. His success led him to leave Bristol for London. It was a long hard struggle but soon he was designing advertisements for firms such as Connolly Leather, as well as cartoons for magazines such as *Punch* and *London Opinion*. He is most well known today for his First World War recruiting poster 'Your Country Needs You', featuring Lord Kitchener pointing a finger at the viewer.

Leete continued to visit Weston and loved the town and its people and it was here he met Edith Webb whom he later married. In June 1933 he was taken ill on holiday in Italy. He returned home but died in London a few days later. He is buried in Ashcombe Cemetery, where his tombstone features his distinctive signature on an artist's palette.

Guglielmo Marconi

The arrival of Guglielmo Marconi in the area in 1898 left Weston with one of the most significant events in its history. In May that year Marconi, along with Post Office engineers, including Sir William Preece, Engineer in Chief, sent the first ever wireless signals across water. They were transmitted from Lavernock Point near Cardiff in Wales to Brean Down near Weston-super-Mare, via Flat Holm.

Marconi first began experimenting at his home near Bologna in Italy in 1894. His aim was to achieve wireless telegraphy using radio waves. Marconi gradually improved existing techniques until he eventually achieved a range of over two kilometres. At that stage he decided he was ready to approach prospective users in the hope they would finance further research. The Italian Ministry of Post and Telegraphs declined, so Marconi came to England, the birthplace of his mother. In June 1896 he filed the first radio patent. The following month he gave a demonstration to Post Office engineers. They were very impressed but wanted further demonstrations of its potential uses. One obvious application for wireless telegraphy was across water. The existing method of laying submarine cables was expensive and unreliable as they were prone to damage. Sir William Preece therefore arranged for the experiment to be made across the Bristol Channel. Marconi and his assistant, George Kemp, first arrived in Wales on 6 May 1897. For the next month they experimented over various distances and in varying weather conditions. For at least some of the time, Marconi is believed to have stayed at Coastguard Cottages, Uphill. Masts were erected at Lavernock and Brean Down and at 2.50p.m. on 18 May, Morse code messages were received at Brean Down. Later trials were conducted by the Post Office between Lavernock and a site in Weston-super-Mare itself, probably Knightstone, but we do not know whether Marconi himself was involved in these. Marconi's work laid the foundation for the development of radio communications and broadcasting throughout the world. Marconi died in Rome in 1937 aged 63. The following day every radio transmitter in the world was closed for two minutes as a tribute.

Dan Maskell

On 15 May 1941, Dan Maskell, the famous Wimbledon tennis coach, gave an exhibition tennis match on the courts of the County School in Weston. All schools in the area were invited to watch, including private ones and the schools evacuated to the area. The admission fees were collected in aid of the Red Cross.

Emmeline Pethick-Lawrence

Emmeline Pethick-Lawrence achieved fame in the Suffrage Movement. Henry Pethick, along with his wife and family, moved from Bristol to Trewartha House, Montpelier, Weston-super-Mare in 1877. Emmeline was the second of 13 children. As she grew older she left Weston for London, working with the West London Methodist Mission for five years from 1891. There she was shocked by the poverty she found and became a socialist. She founded the Esperance Club which helped young women to form a dressmaking co-operative. In 1901 she married Fred Lawrence, a lawyer studying social conditions and taking on cases for the poor. In an action ahead of her time, she asked her husband to adopt her maiden name in addition to his, and they became the Pethick-Lawrences. In 1906, together with the Pankhursts, Emmeline became a founder member of the London Committee of the Women's Social and Political Union. She was a successful fund-raiser and became national treasurer; she was a major inspiration to the suffragette movement.

Emmeline played her part in militant action and was imprisoned and force-fed on six occasions. Her husband, too, became involved in the fight for women's suffrage and launched the magazine *Votes for Women*. However, the couple became unhappy at the increasingly violent tactics employed by the Pankhursts. In 1912, when the women began the wholesale smashing of shop windows, both Frederick and Emmeline were arrested, together with the other leaders of the Union, and all sentenced to nine months in prison. After their release, the Pethick-Lawrences spoke out about their unhappiness over the tactics used and they were expelled from the Union. Nevertheless Emmeline and her husband continued campaigning, speaking across America and Europe on women's rights.

The outbreak of the First World War brought the campaigning to an end. During the war women had to take over many jobs traditionally performed by men and as such, by the end of the war, their status had changed for ever. In 1918, women were given the right to vote, although initially only those over the age of 30 were allowed to do so. Emmeline was one of the 16 women candidates who stood for election that year, all of whom were unsuccessful. Fred Pethick-Lawrence went on to became a Labour MP and, in 1945, Secretary of State for India and Burma. Emmeline died in 1954. Her husband died in 1961.

Paulo Radmilovic

Paulo Radmilovic was one of Britain's greatest swimming and water-polo stars. Raddy, as he was popularly known, was born in Cardiff. By the age of 16 he had become one of Britain's best swimmers and by the time he was 45 he had swum in six consecutive Olympic Games – an achievement never

surpassed. He represented Britain in a world-class competition for the first time at the unofficial Olympic Games in Athens in 1906. In 1908 he was one of the gold-medal winning 800m relay team at the London Olympics. He also won a gold medal as a member of the water-polo team. After that he concentrated solely on water polo, winning gold medals in 1912 and 1920, making him the holder of the largest number of gold medals in Britain.

In his time he was 'the world's quickest human being in water'. He also won nine Amateur Swimming Association titles and became the first British sportsman to be given a place in the Swimming Hall of Fame in Florida. Even after his Olympic career ended he was able to take part in the Empire Games in Canada in 1930 at the age of 44. His sporting talents ran to more than just swimming. By the age of 18 he had won over 20 prizes for track events and was a talented amateur boxer.

After retirement from swimming he became a hotelier and restaurateur in Weston. He continued to play water polo locally and gave special displays of swimming at Knightstone Baths. He died in Weston in 1968 at the age of 82.

Paulo Radmilovic, wearing just a few of the swimming medals he attained during his career spanning over 30 years. He took part in six consecutive Olympic Games and was the first Briton to be included in the Sporting Hall of Fame in Florida during his lifetime.

Haille Selassie

Emperor of Ethiopia, Haille Selassie, made a number of visits to Weston and the surrounding area in about 1937 when he was living in Britain in exile during the Italian occupation of Ethiopia. At one time it was reputed he was looking for a property in Weston to purchase.

George Joseph Smith

The 'Brides in the Bath' murderer, George Joseph Smith, was a frequent visitor to Weston in the years prior to 1915. It seems that seaside towns were a good place to pick up the wealthy single women who were his prey. One of his 'wives', Beatrice Munday, lodged at Norwood House, Weston-super-Mare in the year and a half between her 'marriage' to Smith and her murder by him.

Charles Summers

Sculptor Charles Summers was better known and appreciated on the other side of the world than in his home county of Somerset. Born in Charlton Mackerell in 1825, Summers began his career as a stonemason's lad working for his father. His father was not good with money and Charles had to help support his large family. Their search for work led them to Street, Wells and Bristol before they heard of the need for labourers to help build the Bristol & Exeter Railway in 1841. Consequently they moved to Weston.

This was a time of expansion for the town and the family were able to stay on, building the new villas and terraces then being constructed in Weston. Charles was developing a skill in wood and stone carving and this was noted by the foreman of Henry Weekes, a well-known sculptor. Weeks had just completed a marble monument for the late Emily Smyth-Pigott and Charles was chosen to help mount it in the chancel of Weston Parish Church.

By 1848, Charles had moved to London and was a member of the Royal Academy. He exhibited there for some years, mainly statues of classical subjects in plaster and marble. In 1851 he was awarded a silver medal for the 'best model from life'. His health, however, was not good and, although he won a scholarship to study in Rome, he decided to follow his family to the warm climes of Australia where they were working in the gold-fields. There he saw an advertisement asking for sculptors to work on the new Houses of Parliament in Melbourne. He was awarded a contract and from that point on, his fame was assured. He began to receive commissions for marble portrait busts and won the competition to design a monument commemorating Burke and Wills, who both died trying to explore the interior of the continent.

In 1867, he returned to Weston briefly, before travelling to Rome where he settled for the rest of his life. He made one more visit to Australia before his death in 1878 at the age of 53. Several pieces of his work can be seen in North Somerset Museum in Weston, including marble busts of Thomas Tutton Knyfton of Uphill Manor and Joseph Edgar of Swiss Villa.

Mary Webb

Author and poet Mary Webb (née Meredith) lived at Landemann Circus, Weston, between 1913 and 1914. Born in Shropshire in 1881, she was strongly influenced by the legends and landscape of her surroundings. After her marriage to Cambridge graduate Henry Webb, the couple moved to Weston-super-Mare where Henry's family lived, and where he had taken a job teaching English. Whilst here she was deeply homesick and began work on her first novel, *The Golden Arrow*, set among the rolling hills of her beloved Shropshire. Mary Webb went on to write five further novels as well as articles and reviews for *The Spectator* and *The Bookman*. Her book *Precious Bane*, written in 1924, won a prestigious literary prize and her work was acclaimed by other writers, including Rebecca West and John Buchan.

Henry, meanwhile, had become involved with a younger woman and left Mary, who died in 1927 at the age of 46 after suffering from Graves' Disease for many years. After her death, Henry married his new love, Kathleen Wilson, and became very wealthy on the royalties of Mary's work. In 1939, however, whilst on a solo walking holiday in the Lake District, he went missing and his body was later found at the foot of a deep precipice. It is believed he may have committed suicide. Henry Webb is buried in Ashcombe Cemetery in a family plot with his parents. Mary lies alone in a double grave in Shrewsbury. A plaque marks the house in Landemann Circus where she lived with her husband whilst in Weston.

Chapter 6

✤

Entertainments

Over the years Weston has been filled with entertainment, from bands and pierrots to orchestras and opera. Both professional and amateur productions received huge audiences and music of all kinds formed a large part of the life of the town.

On the beach were small groups or concert parties, of perhaps five to seven men and women. They gave themselves catchy names, strange to our ears today, such as Roy Cowl's Queeries and The Drolls. Many of the jokes would be understood only by residents as the names of local personalities were incorporated into part of the acts. In the early 1920s two who suffered in this way were Dr Geoffrey Prance, a local GP and Henry Butt, coal merchant, entrepreneur and later Weston's first Mayor. The joke went, 'What made Dr Geoffrey Prance? Because he felt Mr Henry Butt!'

Bands and orchestras were particularly popular from the 1870s onwards. Several local ones were formed, the most famous probably being Mogg's Band. This was founded by local postman, Harry Mogg, in 1887. Other well-known local bands included those of Herr Julian Kandt, who played mainly on the Grand Pier and Corelli Windeatt, an extremely talented violinist who studied at the Royal Academy of Music.

In 1937, F. Taylor wrote a fascinating article on some of the street entertainers that once filled Weston:

The Plantation, where the Floral Clock now stands, was a favourite pitch for all kinds of itinerant musicians. It was there that a portly middle-aged man played tunes and ditties with small wooden hammers on a row of pudding basins screwed to a board and suspended on two wooden uprights. Often in the gutter opposite was a one-man band – Old Johnnie Patchback we called him, tousled grey and grizzled...

Out on the Esplanade, long before the Grand Pier was built, was pitched an old man with a model of Canterbury Cathedral made in sea shells, and inside the model was a set of working figures of a wedding party... He would always finish his talk by instructing his son Henry to 'show the ladies the wedding party...'

Once you might find Harry Jones Blue Cord Rescue Band marching up Meadow Street in a maze of dancing lights, each player having a lighted oil lamp strapped to his left shoulder. Then came the White Ribbon Army Melodeon Band with Mrs Colonel Babbage in command.

G. Ritchie remembered being taken to a concert at Knightstone Theatre in 1919. He recalled seeing one sketch set in a First World War trench with two soldiers, one of whom shook Keatings insect powder down the back of his neck. A lady in the row behind commented that it was all in very bad taste. At the time Mr Ritchie was aged about five and didn't understand her feelings, but the war was still a recent and raw memory and he later came to understand that it may have been somewhat unfeeling to those who lost so many loved ones.

Playbill for the pantomime The Scarlet Goblin, *performed at the Winter Gardens, 1950s.*

Autographed programme for the show No Medals *performed at Knightstone Theatre, 1930s.*

Entertainment in wartime was very important for morale. Barbara Adams remembered her teenage years during the Second World War:

I came to Weston with my parents from Bristol in 1941. I was then 15. My father was working for the Bristol Aeroplane Company and I found a job in Lennards shoe shop, which was on the corner of Meadow Street and Regent Street (now demolished). I joined new friends at the YWCA and we spent our time playing table tennis, having debates, or a singsong around the piano. Later, some of the boys formed a dance band, calling themselves the YMCA Merrymakers, and the Meritors Swing Four. We held our dances in the gymnasium.

The cinema and little cafés, and the Winter Gardens were all popular with our age group, and there were Saturday dances and the balls, such as the Police Ball and the Arts Ball, also New Year's Eve. I have a programme for the 16th Arts Ball dated Friday 8 January 1943. The music on that occasion was provided by Felix Mendelssohn's Hawaiian Serenaders, but quite a few of the Big Bands came for these events.

Children, probably from the Winthorpe School of Dancing, performing at Knightstone Theatre, 1950s. The Winthorpe School was run by Greta Cousins, and her pupils regularly appeared either in their own shows, or as the chorus in pantomimes, etc.

Marina Coles remembers with affection the wonderful variety shows at Knightstone in the 1970s. Resident performer Vernon Adcock alternated with stars such as Terry Scott, Harry Secombe and Norman Wisdom. Vernon Adcock was born in Birmingham and worked with the Birmingham Symphony Orchestra. In 1945, he worked for BBC Radio with his own orchestra before coming to Weston. He then began a 30-year career here, playing

Above: *The Vernon Adcock show at Knightstone Theatre, starring Peter Lewis, Christine Campbell and Roger Green, 1980.*

Left: *Signed programme for the Vernon Adcock Show, 1980. This was one of the longest consecutively running entertainments in any seaside holiday resort in Britain.*

Below: *Vernon Adcock and his Aristocrats Show Band, c.1946.*

The Beatles, photographed whilst they were in Weston, 1963. They were playing for a week at the Odeon Cinema and stayed at the Royal Pier Hotel.

at the Winter Gardens, Knightstone Theatre and the Rozel Bandstand. On stage he played xylophone and vibraphone. He tapped the market for nostalgia, filling venues with holiday-makers and residents alike. Some of his orchestra, such as pianist Fred Kelly and trumpeter George Lakin, stayed with him from his first performance at the Rozel until his retirement in 1986.

Knightstone Theatre had a very chequered career. All its life there were complaints that it cost the ratepayers too much money and ever since its closure there have been complaints that nothing is being done to find a new use for the building. It opened in 1902 as a concert hall and opera house. Productions ranged from solo artists, such as Dame Clara Butt, to touring repertory companies with farces, musicals and comedies. It was the first place in Weston to show 'moving pictures' when, in 1911, short films

were put on between shows. As audiences for live shows dwindled, productions were cut to a pantomime in the winter and a summer show for visitors, but eventually, in the 1980s, the theatre was closed permanently. At the time of writing it is still shut and one wonders how long the building can survive before being beyond restoration or reuse.

In the 1960s and early 1970s, Weston played host to a myriad of well-known pop stars. Concerts at the Odeon Cinema and the Winter Gardens featured groups such as the Rolling Stones and Pink Floyd. In 1963 the Odeon booked The Beatles for a week. The person responsible for acts at the Winter Gardens seems to have had a great knack for booking groups just before they became really famous so that they were available, but by the time they performed in Weston they had become well known. Others that played in the Winter Gardens included Jethro Tull, Desmond Dekker & the Aces and Georgie Fame & the Blue Flames.

Local researcher and historian Chris Richards, himself a pianist, has had a long interest in the musical life of Weston. His painstaking research has uncovered many internationally-known musicians, singers and conductors who had links with Weston. He has written the following section, choosing a small selection from the many famous names to grace the stages and concert halls of Britain and who played in our town.

Sketches of Musical Life

The international music scene between the two world wars was graced by a group of well-known and much-loved women pianists who were English or at least resident in England. They were Irene Kohler, Myra Hess, Harriet Cohen, and Irene Scharrer. They all played in Weston several times.

Myra Hess

Myra Hess performed at Westcliffe School in 1921 and on a number of occasions afterwards. She inaugurated the National Gallery Concerts in London

ODEON THEATRE
WESTON-SUPER-MARE

THE ROLLING STONES SHOW

1st Performance at 6-0 p.m.

TUESDAY
AUGUST **25**

FRONT STALLS 12/6

B 9

No ticket exchanged nor money refunded
THIS PORTION TO BE RETAINED

Ticket for the Rolling Stones concert at the Odeon Cinema, Weston-super-Mare, c.1963.

Family photograph of Myra Hess holding her nephew, Alan Hess, outside her brother's flat in The Shrubbery, Weston, March 1941.

Portrait photograph, taken in New York, of Dame Myra Hess at the piano.

Peter Hess and the other is chiropodist John Hess, whose son is composer and conductor Nigel Hess. Nigel grew up in Weston. He was taught piano by, among others, Evelyn Porter of Weston, and was once a member of Weston Youth Orchestra. He went on to study music at Cambridge University, during which time he became Musical Director of the Footlights Revue Company. In 1981 he became Company Music Director and House Composer for the Royal Shakespeare Company, where he stayed for five years. He then left to concentrate on his commissions for film and television, which include themes for such programmes as 'Wycliffe', 'Dangerfield' and 'Hetty Wainthropp Investigates'. In 2003 he conducted the Youth Orchestra in a performance of his own film music at the Playhouse.

Irene Scharrer

Irene Scharrer performed Schumann's Piano Concerto at the Winter Gardens Pavilion on 23 November 1943 with Lemuel Kinsey conducting the Weston United Orchestra, followed by solo items from the pianist. Scharrer is remembered today for a beautifully sensitive and even touch, showing great refinement in phrasing. It was particularly noticeable in her performance in Weston that night in her performance of Bach's 'Jesu – Joy of Man's Desiring', arranged by her great friend, Myra Hess.

Photograph of Irene Scharrer holding Alan Hess, nephew of Myra Hess, outside the Hess family home in The Shrubbery, Weston, March 1941.

Irene Kohler

Irene Kohler was a regular visitor to Weston and her strong technique was always commented upon. Indeed, she is remembered for her power that allowed her to successfully perform works usually played by men. Imagine the scene as Kohler stormed through Balakirev's formidable 'Islamy' at the Winter Gardens Pavilion on 24 August 1947 after having played Rachmaninov's Second Piano Concerto with the Weston Light Orchestra conducted by Lemuel Kinsey, or perhaps her performance of Beethoven's 'Waldstein Sonata' on 14 February 1949 in the ballroom of The Grand Atlantic Hotel at a recital organised by the Weston Music Club. At a Winter Garden Celebrity Concert on 15 June 1943 Irene Kohler came to play Beethoven's Fourth Piano Concerto with Lemuel Kinsey conducting the Weston Combined Orchestra. Of this concert, in which Kohler also played some solo pieces, a *Weston Mercury* reviewer wrote:

Most music-lovers, one imagines, carried away with

during the dark days of the Blitz playing with other brave musicians even when bombs were falling. She became a national symbol of fortitude for keeping afloat an appreciation of music under difficult circumstances and won a special place in the hearts of many people. At the time of writing Myra's nephews live in Weston. One is retired accountant *them an indelible mind-picture of a charming figure in a golden gown seated at a grand piano on the stage. There was something appealingly beautiful appertaining to the performance of Miss Irene Kohler, and the audience went into raptures at her playing.*

The *Weston Gazette* published a photograph showing an elegant Miss Kohler about to play those famous soft chords on the piano, that revolutionarily open the concerto, with Lemuel Kinsey, baton poised, looking adoringly at the pianist waiting to bring in the orchestra's equally soft reply.

Harriet Cohen

Harriet Cohen was unconventional in her concert programming. She played Bach and early keyboard composers such as Arne and was an advocate of English music championing, for example, the piano music of her lover Arnold Bax. This choice is well shown in her Weston concerts. At the Winter Gardens Pavilion on 25 October 1941 she included two arrangements of chorales by Bach and on 12 January 1943 at the Winter Gardens Pavilion she played Bach's D minor Piano Concerto with the Weston United Orchestra conducted, as usual, by Lemuel Kinsey. On this occasion the *Weston Gazette* commented on her 'slim striking figure in a full-skirted gown of gold silk.'

Cohen gave a recital at the Town Hall in November 1952 put on by the Weston Society of Arts at which there was standing room only. This was the first time Cohen had performed in the provinces for four years. In 1948 she had cut her right hand badly on a wine glass and it was many months before she had full use of it again. She introduced the items in the programme herself. As usual there was Bach, Arne and Bax on the programme, the obligatory Chopin, works by De Falla and Turina who were personally known to her and who had written works specially dedicated to her and, most amazingly of all, one of the late pieces by Liszt called 'La Lugubre Gondola'. This was probably the first time Liszt's enigmatic and puzzling late piano works had ever been performed in Weston.

Jelly D'Aranyi

Many world-class violinists once appeared in Weston, among them Fritz Kreisler, Marie Hall, Milan Bratza, Daniel Melsa, Albert Sammons, Alfredo Campoli and Jelly D'Aranyi.

Jelly D'Aranyi, a fiery female Hungarian violinist to whom Bartók dedicated two violin sonatas, came to the Winter Gardens on 14 September 1943. With Lemuel Kinsey conducting the Weston United Orchestra, they performed the Bruch violin concerto followed by some solos by D'Aranyi including Bazzani's 'Dance of the Elves', which almost brought the audience to its feet. A special request was for the 'Andantino' by Martini-Kreisler which was played by D'Aranyi on a 200-year-old violin belonging to Mr R.W. Hunter, a viola player in the orchestra. It is interesting to note that D'Aranyi actually stayed at Mr Hunter's house in Clarence Road East for her Weston visit where she played another old violin in Mr Hunter's collection. A few years ago a TV film called *Elgars Tenth Muse* explored the bittersweet encounter between Edward Elgar and Jelly D'Aranyi in 1919, which was put forward as a source of inspiration behind the composition of Elgar's Cello Concerto.

Benjamin Britten and Peter Pears

Benjamin Britten was one of Britain's greatest composers and Peter Pears was one of the great tenors of the twentieth century. Their musical partnership is of inestimable value in the history of music. They came to Weston to give a song recital on the 31 March 1948, with Britten accompanying Pears on the piano. The recital, performed to a packed auditorium, prompted an enthusiastic review in both the town's newspapers. The *Weston Gazette* reported:

No finer climax than Wednesday evening's superb recital in the Winter Gardens Pavilion could have been chosen to end the winter season of mid-week programmes jointly arranged by the Weston-super-Mare Society of Arts and the Council's Entertainments Department. The vivid flash of brilliance released by Mr Benjamin Britten and Mr Peter Pears made an impact on jaded senses not soon to be forgotten.

A central feature of the recital was Britten's own 'Seven Sonnets of Michelangelo' that he had composed for Peter Pears in 1940.

Clara Butt

For three decades the magnificent contralto Clara Butt astonished Weston audiences in the Knightstone Theatre. She was born near Brighton in 1872 but by 1881 she had moved to Bristol with her family.

Postcard advertisement for a concert by Dame Clara Butt and Kennerley Rumford at Knightstone Theatre.

Her glorious career began in 1895 and was based on the works of Bach and Handel, some German lieder and most of all, popular ballads. She married her accompanist, baritone Robert Kennerley Rumford at Bristol Cathedral in 1900. The couple would go on to tour the world. Elgar created his 'Sea Pictures' especially for Clara Butt, which she performed for the first time in 1899.

Clara stood six feet two inches high and possessed one of the biggest and most powerful of all contralto voices. It ranged from the C below middle C to high B flat. The low register was dark and resonant and described by composer Reynaldo Hahn as 'cavernous'. Her life was marked by tragedies. Her eldest son died of meningitis while still at school and the younger son committed suicide. During the 1920s she was seriously ill with cancer of the spine but continued giving concerts. Her farewell visit to Weston took place on 9 October 1930 at the Knightstone Theatre, as part of a farewell tour of the world culminating in recording sessions in Tokyo. On that night in Knightstone Theatre, statuesque Clara looked magnificent in a scarlet and gold dress and a turban set with diamonds. The programme was distinctly her own: Handel, some lieder and, most of all, English songs with the favourites being 'O Lovely Night' by Landon Ronald and 'There is no Death' by O'Hara. The climax of the concert was a duet, 'Keys of Heaven', sung by Clara and her husband.

Harry Arthur Dossor

Harry Arthur Dossor and his brother ran a jewellery business in Weston's High Street called the House of Dossor. Between the two world wars tenor Harry was nicknamed by the public Weston's 'King of Song' and called himself 'Seymour Dossor' after his wife's maiden name. He was also organist at Sunnyside Road Primitive Methodist Church and was conductor of the Weston Choral Society from 1922–29. In 1932 he left Weston for London to further his musical career.

Seymour had a son called Lancelot Dossor who, in Weston, developed into a remarkable pianist. Like his father, he greatly contributed to the musical life of the town. Lancelot won a scholarship to the Royal College of Music where he studied under composers Herbert Howells and Hubert Fryer from 1932–37. By the time of the outbreak of the Second World War he had taken part in the Liszt Competition in Vienna, the Chopin Competition in Warsaw and the Ysaye Competition in Brussels. Before, during and after the war he performed with many of the world's leading orchestras and under leading conductors. He was also well known to radio audiences on the BBC and as an outstanding performer of chamber music. After the war he became Professor of Piano at Adelaide University and was presented with the university's Distinguished Alumni Award in 2002.

Eric Gilbert

Eric Gilbert of Northfield, Birmingham, was inspired to compose 'A Picture of Weston-super-Mare' while visiting the town in 1946. He was the Director of Northfield Operatic Society and had composed two operas and other works. 'A Picture of Weston-super-Mare' for orchestra is a 15-minute-long piece that consists of three movements respectively entitled 'Sunrise over Brean Down', 'Anchor Head' and 'The Winter Gardens'. The piece was dedicated to Lemuel Kinsey and the Weston Concert Orchestra and was given its first performance in Weston on 24 August 1947 by the Weston Light Orchestra conducted by Lemuel Kinsey. The work met with thunderous applause and Eric Gilbert, in the audience, was asked to rise and make his presence known. Such was the reception of the work that it almost stole the show from the internationally acclaimed virtuoso pianist Irene Kohler who played Rachmaninov's Piano Concerto at the same concert!

Lillian Hosbons

Lillian Hosbons (née Hawkins) was born in Bristol in 1888 and studied harp at the Royal Academy of Music where she was a contemporary of pianists Harriet Cohen, Irene Scharrer and composer Eric Coates. During further music study in Germany she met the composer Richard Strauss who urged her to remain in that country. He wanted to write a piece for harp himself.

The idea of a full-blown performing career came to an end in 1914 when she married the Revd Rowland Hosbons, rector of Uphill 1920–40. However, she continued to be musically active, giving lessons and taking part in concerts and recitals, especially those for charities and for troops, wounded and otherwise, in both world wars. Her musical 'at homes' were a feature of village life in Uphill. She gave her last public performance in 1959 at the Royal Crescent in Bath.

Her memories of Weston went back to before she married, having played with the Edward Pavey Band on the Grand Pier. Lillian Hosbons was ballerina Anna Pavlova's harpist of choice for her performance of Saint-Saëns' 'The Swan'. Her daughter Beatrice, who had a reputation as a promising soprano died at the early age of 28 in 1951. Lillian Hosbons had a collection of harps that was said to have been the largest in the world. The family lived at Youghal Lodge in Moseley Grove, Uphill, at the time of her death at the age of 72 in 1960. She was remembered as a thoroughly Edwardian lady driving a Rolls Royce with a bulldog on the passenger seat!

Julius Isserlis

What stories the Russian pianist Julius Isserlis, born

in 1888, could have told the people of Weston about his illustrious musical past when he came to play at the Winter Gardens in June 1947! He had been a contemporary at the Moscow Conservatoire with Rachmaninov and Scriabin and his teachers were Vassily Safonov and Sergei Taneyev, the latter a disciple and friend of Tchaikovsky.

Albert Ketelbey

Albert Ketelbey was one of the most popular composers of the twentieth century. Millions loved his characteristic music with titles such as 'In a Monastery Garden', 'Bells across the Meadow' and 'Wedgwood Blue'. He became Britain's first million-aire composer! It is not generally known, however, that he wrote an orchestral piece inspired by a visit to the Iron Age hill-fort at Worlebury, in the woods above Weston-super-Mare.

Ketelbey came to Weston in August 1924 to conduct a concert of his own works at Knightstone Theatre with the Cove Orchestra. During the afternoon the resident conductor of the orchestra, Harry C. Burgess, took Ketelbey to see the hill-fort. He stayed there a long time to take in the atmosphere of the place, composing in his mind an orchestral 'tone picture' that came to be known as 'In a Camp of the Ancient Britons'. At the after-concert party held in The Grand Atlantic Hotel he could talk of nothing else but the hill-fort and was spotted early the next morning gazing up at Worlebury from Knightstone. By the time he caught the train later that day the main ideas for the piece had already been sketched out! 'In A Camp of the Ancient Britons' received its first Weston performance in June 1925 by Burgess and the Cove Orchestra.

Ketelbey came to Weston again on Easter Sunday 1939 to conduct his works at the Winter Gardens. This was at a time when he was hailed nationally as 'the King of Light Music'. He made a special point of including his Weston-inspired piece and received a standing ovation. The next day he and his wife were entertained at a luncheon at The Grand Atlantic Hotel by the Mayor and on leaving the composer said, 'I am taking with me memories of a very enjoy-able visit to Weston-super-Mare.'

Lemuel Kinsey at the piano, with Isaac Davies.

'In A Camp of the Ancient Britons' was played by the Municipal Orchestra on several occasions after it was published in 1925 but since the Second World War became somewhat forgotten. It was revived in the town by Dennis Cole and the Weston Youth Orchestra in February 1994 who played it to a large audience at the Playhouse to enthusiastic applause. The piece has since become a staple in the orchestra's repertoire.

Lemuel Kinsey

No account of the musical life of Weston at this time can omit Lemuel Kinsey, already referred to as conductor and accompanist. This remarkable musi-cian was born in Treherbert in the Rhondda Valley in 1890 and at the age of 13 started work as a coal miner. Music was his passion and he studied books on musical theory during spare moments underground. He attained a Royal College of Music Diploma and became a member of the College of Organists. He accumulated other accolades later in his life.

In 1920 he met Harry C. Burgess, then Director of the Municipal Orchestra in Weston. Kinsey had a spell in Torquay where he played for Pavlova during the winter of 1921/22 and was pianist on board the Cunard luxury liner *Scythia*, playing with an orches-tra of 12 players. He then became pianist for the Weston Municipal Orchestra. Some idea of his prowess as a musician can be gathered from a review in the *Weston Mercury* of a recital he gave in December 1947. This was two hours long and given entirely from memory. It included Scriabin's 'Prelude' and 'Nocturne for the Left Hand' and the titanic 'Appassionata' piano sonata by Beethoven.

He retired in 1961 after dominating the local music scene for 41 years as a solo pianist, accompanist, chamber-music player, conductor, organist, and composer. His special memories were of the occasions that he conducted the orchestra for performances by visiting celebrities, or accompanied on the piano their recitals at the Winter Gardens Pavilion. Kinsey also wrote an anthem for the choir at Holy Trinity Church where he was organist. He lived at 211 Locking Road. He died in 1976 and his ashes were scattered in his native Rhondda Valley.

Frederick Lamond

'His visit amongst us will ever be a very memorable one, and an honour to the town in welcoming this distinguished virtuoso.' Such was the accolade handed out by a local paper with every justification to Scottish pianist Frederick Lamond. He was Liszt's last pupil and he gave a recital in 1886 in St James' Hall, London, at which Liszt was present. Liszt was undoubtedly the greatest pianist who has ever lived and he revolutionised piano music in the nineteenth century. At the Winter Gardens on the 7 May 1947

Lamond played solo items including pieces by Beethoven, Brahms, Tchaikovsky, Schubert-Tausig, Liszt and Chopin followed by Beethoven's Piano Concerto No.5 with Basil Cameron conducting the Weston United Orchestra. Lamond was aged 78 by then and died the following year.

Anna Pavlova

On 22 July 1921 the legendary ballerina Anna Pavlova danced at the Grand Pier Pavilion. After leaving the Diaghilev Russian Ballet in 1913 she formed her own Russian ballet troupe that toured the world. Unfortunately the music and dance performed at Weston was not reported in the local newspapers and a programme does not appear to have survived.

Three of the five dancers appearing with her in Weston later went on to have prestigious careers. Hubert 'Jay' Stowitts, born in Nebraska, USA, in 1892, was the first American to star with a Russian ballet troupe. Pavlova discovered Stowitts dancing at the Greek Theatre in Berkeley, California, in 1915 and invited him to join her troupe; he spent six years with her. He then followed a solo career and retired at 32 to pursue a career in painting and film. The Russian Alexandre Volinine had been premier 'danseur noble' at Moscow's Bolshoi Ballet and partnered Yekaterina Geltzer in Diaghilev's *Les Orientales* in 1910. He left Diaghilev's Russian Ballet in 1912 and became Pavlova's most famous partner between 1914–25. Retiring at 44 he established one of the best schools in Paris. Muriel Stuart was born in South Norwood, London, in 1903. She was chosen by Pavlova to study the famous ballerina's steps and then in 1916 she joined the troupe. She left in 1926, teaching at the New York City Ballet from 1937–72. In 1952 she wrote a book with Lincoln Kirstein called *The Classic Ballet: Basic Technique and Terminology*.

Two local musicians accompanied Pavlova in their time, Lillian Hosbons and Lemuel Kinsey.

Lev Pouishnoff

Excitement was generated in the Weston newspapers about the appearance of the Ukrainian pianist Lev Pouishnoff on 26 October 1937 in the Winter Gardens. Adverts in the *Weston Gazette* reminded readers 'Don't Forget the Pouishnoff Concert' and 'Record Attendance Probable at Winter Gardens', together with stage gossip and biographical information about him. 'Everyman' for the *Weston Mercury* captured the atmosphere and excitement of the night itself:

The scene in and about Weston-super-Mare Winter Gardens Pavilion on Tuesday night might have graced London's famous Queen's Hall. Cars and taxis swept in quick succession to the doors to unload their parties of evening-dress clad concert-goers. The parking accommodation was quickly filled, and a long line of cars stretched along the opposite side of the road. At eight o'clock the interior of the Pavilion presented the most brilliantly dressed scene which has ever met the eye at a local classical concert.

Courtenay Edwards for the *Weston Gazette* described the scene inside the Pavilion 'the dress shirts of the men gleamed in the diffuse lighting... and the smart gowns of the ladies made the auditorium ripple with colour.'

The concert was to include Rachmaninov's Second Piano Concerto, played by the Municipal Orchestra and conducted by Harry Burgess, followed by a number of solos played by Pouishnoff. Part of the concert was to be broadcast by BBC West Region wireless. The tall, pale figure of Pouishnoff came on stage, moved towards the piano in a leisurely manner but an overwhelming, some have said demonic, power was sensed, a fact confirmed by his riveting performances at the keyboard. After congratulating the orchestra for their part in the concerto, Pouishnoff launched into his solos. These included pieces by Russian composers such as Scriabin's 'Etude' in C sharp minor and the 'Poeme Tragique' and two 'Fairy Tales' of his own composition. He then rose from the piano and said, 'I thank you warmly for the wonderful reception you have given me. I could play to you all night, but unfortunately have time for only one more item.' This was Saint-Saëns' 'The Swan' and, urged by the enthusiasm of the audience, was obliged to continue with a tango he wrote himself. He claimed 'It was inspired by a visit to Spain but not a recent one.' This comment was an oblique reference to the Spanish Civil War then raging.

After the concert the local papers reported that it had been 'The Greatest Concert in the History of the Winter Gardens' and 'Pouishnoff Concert Breaks Winter Gardens Revenue Record – And Delights Hundreds'.

Pouishnoff's return the following year was not so happy. He was due to give a Chopin recital on Good Friday 7 April 1938 at the Winter Gardens. A total of 800 people packed the auditorium. The great pianist seated himself at the piano, played one piece and then rose from the piano and left the building saying that the piano was no good! In fact, the piano was supplied by one of his agents! Local piano experts could find nothing wrong with the instrument.

Pouishnoff's wife Dorothy played Liszt's First Piano Concerto with the Municipal Orchestra under Harry Burgess on 8 June 1938 at the Winter Gardens and Pouishnoff himself came to the same venue for a recital of solo items on 14 September 1947 showing there were no hard feelings on either side after the 1938 incident! There were more Pouishnoff concerts to come, including the one in July 1949 when he held the Winter Gardens audience spellbound for two hours.

He was here again in August 1952 when ten-year year old Alison Nisbet, daughter of the famous doll maker, Peggy Nisbet, sent him a wired red rose as a buttonhole. He apologised for not wearing it. When he came to perform in Weston again an unwired red rose lay on the piano but he didn't wear that either! Alison went on to become a piano teacher in the town and, in the 1970s, conductor of St John's Church Choir. Today she lives in Canada.

Paul Robeson

On Easter Sunday 1 April 1934 the audience in the Knightstone Theatre was dominated by the majestic presence of Paul Robeson, the black singer, scholar, actor, activist and athlete. He was in Weston at the time when he had decided to give up the classical repertoire in order to concentrate on folk-songs. His performance at Knightstone, delivered in that bass-baritone voice of unforgettable resonance, therefore included Negro spirituals together with traditional airs from Wales and Somerset. From the enthusiastic response he gave many encores, some of which were requested by the audience. Robeson could not, of course, leave the stage without giving Weston a rendition of 'Ol' Man River' from *Show Boat*. Robeson was accompanied on the piano by Lawrence Brown, a well-known black pianist and singer from Bristol who also sang two duets with the star.

Elisabeth Schumann

The audience in the Winter Gardens Pavilion on 30 November 1937 was captivated by the infectious charming stage manner and silvery voice of the internationally-acclaimed German soprano Elisabeth Schumann. On her programme that night were songs by Mozart, Schubert, Hugo Wolf and Richard Strauss.

Her close connection with Richard Strauss was one of the most important artistic and personal relationships of her life. It began in 1917 and finished acrimoniously in 1933 when she married for a second time. One of the Strauss songs she sang at Weston was the beautiful setting of a poem by Mackay called 'Tomorrow'. The first verse, translated from the original German in which she sang it, reads:

> *And tomorrow the sun will shine again,*
> *and on the path I will take,*
> *it will unite us again, we happy ones*
> *upon this sun-breathing earth.*

During the course of their friendship, or as some have tried to imply, a romance, Strauss composed and dedicated to her his 'Brentano Songs Op.68'. Strauss was in London in 1949 and Elisabeth, who had not seen the composer since 1933 went to see him. Much to her dismay, he did not recognise her and asked who she was! Elisabeth wished she had never gone.

Cecil Sharp

One wonders if the traditional Somerset airs that Robeson used in his 1934 concert at Knightstone, came from Cecil Sharp's folk-song collection. Sharp was an indefatigable collector of folk music in Somerset in the years 1903–24, making him an English counterpart of Béla Bartók who was doing the same thing in Eastern Europe. Sharp's collecting carried him into other parts of England and even into the Appalachian Mountains of America. He was inspired to collect folk music by hearing a gardener at the vicarage at Hambridge in South Somerset singing the song 'Seeds of Love'.

Sharp was born at Hampstead and spent some years in the 1870s at High Cliff School in Weston-super-Mare. While in Weston he met Constance Dorothea Birch. She lived at The Wilderness, Clevedon. On 22 August 1893 he married Constance at All Saints' Church in Clevedon and the wedding breakfast at The Wilderness took place on a lawn within an amphitheatre of rock surrounded with flower-beds, holm oaks and pines. The Wilderness became Sharp's base for recording Somerset folk-songs – in all he collected over 1,500 melodies from 311 singers.

Oda Slobodskaya

The Russian soprano Oda Slobodskaya came to the Winter Gardens Pavilion on 21 March 1939 and again on 6 May 1945. At her first appearance in the town she confined herself, as was her custom, principally to Russian music, then still largely unknown in Britain at that time. She sang songs by Tchaikovsky and Mussorgsky and some Russian folk-songs accompanied by Lemuel Kinsey on the piano. Mussorgky's 'Hopak' was considered to be the gem of the evening. More music from her native country featured in her 1945 programme. She chose the Letter Scene from Tchaikovsky's 'Eugene Onegin' accompanied by the Weston United Orchestra conducted by Basil Cameron. She also sang a selection of Tchaikovsky's songs again accompanied by Kinsey on the piano. The *Weston Mercury* review of the concert praised Kinsey's playing of the difficult accompaniments to these songs.

Eva Turner

Eva Turner, one of the great operatic sopranos of her day, is remembered today as the possessor of a voice of immense power and range. Indeed, the *Weston Mercury* for 10 November 1945 observed:

Probably not since the far away days when the late

Clara Butt sang at Knightstone has the theatre known a voice of such range and volume as was Eva Turner's contribution to the programme.

Like Clara Butt she had Bristol connections attending St Anne's Infants School, a fact celebrated today by a blue plaque. She also had the same singing teacher in Bristol as Clara Butt – Daniel Rootham, who was organist at St Peter's Church. Her programme for her 1945 Knightstone recital included songs by Weber and Rachmaninov with Lemuel Kinsey accompanying her on the piano.

Evelyn Porter and Athol Renshaw

How many people in Weston had piano lessons in Weston-super-Mare with Evelyn Porter or Athol Renshaw at Gayton, a Tudor-style 1930s house at the top of Ashcombe Gardens?

Miss Porter taught in a room on the lower floor containing two grand pianos, whilst Mr Renshaw's studio was on the upper floor containing an upright piano, clavichord, and spinet. Miss Porter died in 1987 and Mr Renshaw in 1991 but their names live on; awards bearing their names are handed out to children for pianoforte playing every year at the Junior Arts Festival in Weston.

Miss Porter was born at Pill in 1899 and eventually moved to London where she became a music teacher, writer, and lecturer. In 1961 she took over a piano-teaching practice at the Ashcombe Gardens house with Mr Renshaw, who had been a former pupil and colleague of Miss Porter. Evelyn and Athol, both Licentiates of the Royal Academy of Music, were much-loved personalities deeply committed, not only to their pupils, but to establishing an appreciation of music throughout the community. What was particularly remarkable was that they initiated their dynasty of excellence at a time of life when most people are thinking about retiring!

To be a pupil of either teacher was to have contact with a rich musical past. Mr Renshaw was present when Rachmaninov himself introduced his Third Piano Concerto to the British public in London and actually saw the blind and paralysed Delius being carried into the auditorium on the occasion of the 1929 Delius Festival in London. Miss Porter was present at the first performance in Moscow of Prokofiev's *Peter and the Wolf* in 1936.

The urbane, cultured, and fastidiously dressed Mr Renshaw gave me (Chris Richards) piano lessons for periods in the 1960s and '70s. The works of J.S. Bach were important to him as teaching pieces and music of this period was studied on a period instrument – a rare privilege and a mark of Mr Renshaw's extraordinary teaching talents. He also enthusiastically taught works by modern composers, especially Bartók, and his knowledge of European languages allowed him to announce the titles of the pieces in the composer's native Hungarian! Many of Mr Renshaw's words stand unforgettably in my memory. One sunny evening he was standing in the bay window talking about the slow movements of Mozart's piano concertos; he said they expressed a sadness that captured 'smiling through tears'. To this he added wistfully after a pause 'like watching children playing and knowing you'll never have any yourself' – a reminder that he had never married.

Weston Girls' Choir, 1950.

Milton Singers, with one of their number holding their LP disc which they recorded, c.1975.

When Miss Porter died in 1987 aged 87 Mr Renshaw paid her the following tribute in the *Weston Mercury*, 'Her monument is the countless numbers of pupils who have profited by her wisdom.' A more tangible monument to her is the churchyard at Easton-in-Gordano.

Mr Renshaw continued to teach up until within a few weeks of his death in 1991 at the age of 86. He was cremated at Worle and his ashes buried there under trees and close to the fields on the moor below.

Weston Girls' Choir

Weston Girls' Choir made its debut appearance in March 1950. As the *Weston Mercury* put it:

Providing something quite new in light entertainment in Weston, the choir, distinctive in dresses of pale blue, received an enthusiastic send-off from an audience of nearly 700.

The choir was founded by local pianist James Gautier who commented that 'This choir has the potential for making Weston famous throughout the country'. The ages of the 30 or so singers ranged from 15–25. By May 1950, they had performed a quarter-of-an-hour live radio broadcast on the West Home Service and there were even suggestions that they be featured weekly with the BBC's West Light Orchestra. Unfortunately, 'artistic differences' meant the choir split up and almost half the girls formed a separate group called the Regency Girls' Choir.

Milton Singers

The Milton Singers were founded in 1965 by Eric Darling and Jean Agnew. It began after a Milton Baptist Church Sunday School anniversary event at which Eric's daughter, Ruth, played her recorder. Someone commented that it would be nice to have more such events and a recorder group of eight children was formed. The group soon grew, as Milton Church took over the Puxton Mission Sunday School, which had to close because of the development of the M5 motorway. Among these new members, mostly from St George's, were singers, of whom a few started to form a choir. The Milton Singers were born. Over the years some members went on to have successful professional careers in music. The group performed at music festivals, entertained the elderly and held charity concerts. They even released their own record. Sadly, after 32 years, the group disbanded as a result of falling membership. Their final event was a thanksgiving service at Milton Baptist Church on 6 July 1997.

The British Legion Pantomimes

The pantomimes put on in aid of the British Legion from 1930–55 have achieved almost legendary status in Weston-super-Mare. They involved huge numbers of people from the community.

The first 'Dimo' pantomimes were put on as private shows in the home of Rosina Dimoline in Weston before the First World War. The local vicar watched one such show, and said that it was much too good to be seen by just the few people who could fit in the room and suggested they use St Paul's Church Hall. In 1935 Wilfred Roe and Victor Dimoline, Rosina's son, were reminiscing about these old shows and thought they would like to produce one more. Alec Nicholls became business manager and approached the British Legion to see if they would like the profits of the show to be donated to

Programme for Babes in the Wood, *the last British Legion pantomime put on in Weston, 1958.*

These members of the Weston Branch of the Women's League of Health & Beauty were some of those who danced for the British Legion pantomimes.

The chorus in Mother Goose, *Knightstone Theatre, 1947/48.*

The cast of Sinbad the Sailor, *Knightstone Theatre, 1954.*

them. The pantomime opened in Knightstone Theatre and was such a success that the organisers were asked to produce one every year.

In 1939, the Second World War intervened and the shows were suspended for the duration. They began again in 1946, and St Dunstan's Homes for the Blind became a second recipient of the profits. That year the group produced their ninth pantomime – *Robinson Crusoe*. All the well-known

stories were produced over the years, *Babes in the Wood, Dick Whittington, Mother Goose, Cinderella, Jack and the Beanstalk, Sinbad* and so on, often with local references thrown into the stories. However, all scripts were censored and had to be approved by the Lord Chamberlain's office. Auditions were advertised in the local press and were open to anyone. They attracted a wide range of talent, from some who had been professionals to many who

Long Service Awards to staff of the Odeon and Regent Cinemas, early 1950s. Amongst the smartly-dressed staff is the music-hall character Old Mother Riley, *centre front.*

Odeon Cinema staff at their Christmas party, early 1950s. The man dressed as Long John Silver was the doorman of the cinema. He really did only have one leg as he lost one in the war.

went on to become professionals. Pantomime was the training ground for television, film and stage. Leslie Powell was the Dame in *Red Riding Hood* in 1950. He had toured during the war with the Stars in Battledress, a professional company who entertained the Forces. He stopped the show with his rendition of 'I've got a Lovely Bunch of Coconuts', taking encore after encore.

Rehearsals began each September and were frequent and exacting; only after everyone was word perfect was the cast judged good enough to perform. One cast member recalled being kept rehearsing until past midnight. When his father rang to find out where he was he was told by Wilfred Roe, the producer 'When the entrances and exits are perfected they will be allowed home!' For many years the rehearsals were held on the top floor of the Weston Gas Company Stores in Burlington Street, now North Somerset Museum. Costumes were looked after by a team of wardrobe mistresses and scenery was provided by the Fredericks' Studios of Weston. The Fredericks' name was well known in theatrical circles, providing props, costumes and scenery for amateur and professional productions alike. Dancers came from local schools, mainly the Mavdor Troupe prior to 1939 and, after the war, the Alexander School run by Joline Alexander.

The shows became so popular that people travelled from all around the area, including Bristol, and special coaches and buses were laid on to take people home. Originally there were three days of evening performances, but these grew to ten days with matinées thrown in as well. In 1949, police had to control the crowds and close Knightstone Causeway, because of the sheer number of people who had come to the theatre hoping for cancellations or available seats! Most had to be turned away. In 1950 *Red Riding Hood* was seen by 10,000 people over the ten days.

Odeon Cinema projector with projectionist, Dave Tyler, early 1950s.

In the summer months there was a Panto Club, who put on small productions in Weston's original Playhouse or in village halls. These were usually fund-raising events for various charities. For example, a Summer Showtime was performed to raise funds for Weston Cricket Club's new pavilion. Another raised money for the rebuilding of St Paul's Church, hit by a bomb during the Second World War.

By 1958, the regular producers, actors and directors were getting older and the younger performers wanted to appear in more modern plays rather than traditional pantomime. Television, too, was making an impact on audiences and there were fears that the huge profits could turn into losses. As such, *Babes in the Wood* was the last British Legion pantomime.

Saturday Morning Pictures

An easy way to keep children occupied was to send them to the Saturday Morning Picture Club at the Odeon Cinema. Sue Ryall remembers she took a bus ride into town and got off at Lances Corner, which is where Argos is located in 2004.

A walk down High Street calling into Woolies to spend my threepence on sweets, then on to the Odeon Cinema. It was one large cinema in those days. The kids who could afford sixpence went upstairs in the balcony and proceeded to stamp their feet and throw sweet papers and chewing-gum down onto the ones below. Weston had two other cinemas, the Central and the Regent but only the Odeon had a Saturday morning show.

There was a ticket booth just inside the main doors. The lady who sat inside took your money, pressed a button and your ticket shot out of a little brass slot in front of her. Then up the steps into the main foyer. If you went upstairs you passed framed photographs of all the famous stars of the day such as Clark Gable, David Niven and Doris Day. An usherette with a torch checked your ticket and showed you to your seat. Attached to the back of every seat was an ashtray and a square of rough metal to strike a match on.

There would be lots of noise and yelling, then the lights dimmed and the program began. Up from the floor rose the electric organ and we all sang as loudly as possible. First our Cinema Club song 'We come along on Saturday Morning Greeting Everybody With a Smile', then the usual songs that we sang every week 'She'll Be Coming Round The Mountain', and 'I Love To Go A Wandering'. After 20 minutes or so of singing we had the first film which was always a cartoon, this was followed by a full-length film and then the interval. Anyone with money to spend raced down to the front and bought a penny ice lolly or more chewing-gum.

Then it was the weekly serial, 'Zorro', or 'The Lone Ranger'. There was always a cliff-hanger ending so that you would want to come back the following week to see what happened next. At the end of the show the National Anthem was played and those of us in the Guides stood to attention and saluted. Then we trooped out blinking into the bright sunshine when the doorman would stop the traffic so we could all cross the road safely.

If I wanted to see a film during the week and it was one where you had to go in with an adult, Mum would take me into town and pick a family waiting outside and ask them to take me in with them. You could do that sort of thing then; can you imagine doing that now, handing your child over to total strangers? It didn't matter if you were late getting to the cinema and went in half way through a film because you just stayed in there until it came round again because once they started, the programs were continuous. I once watched Robin Hood and the supporting film on with it all the way through twice! Mum was so worried that I hadn't come home that she had my name put up onto the screen. I will always remember my embarrassment when 'Susan Simmons please go home' was flashed up in front of my friends.

Dave Tyler was projectionist at the Odeon at that time. He remembers:

I left school in 1949 and went to work at the Odeon in the projection room. Saturday morning pictures were great fun with Uncle Pearce on the organ, a cartoon, a main film and a serial. Uncle Pearce's father was the caretaker at Locking School. On the night of the general election we always had a free show (one featured Frankie Howerd) and then the election results were shown on screen.

Dancing the night away

In the 1950s and early '60s 'Teen and Twenty' dances were held on a Wednesday night at the Winter Gardens. Again, Sue Ryall recalls:

We danced to a live band; rock and roll was still popular, but the new dance crazes were the Twist and the Locomotion. The only drinks were the soft kind.

The dances used to be very popular with RAF cadets who were bussed in from Locking Camp. The trouble was they were only allowed to wear their uniforms so they didn't look exactly trendy and their hair was rather short!

At about this time my brother, who was living in Canada, sent me a petticoat. I think Helen his girlfriend must have chosen it because it was the latest thing, yards and yards of pink net, which I dipped in a strong solution of sugar water and when it was dry I spent hours ironing all the frills. It stuck out stiffly all around and I wore it under a white 'sun-pleated' skirt, it was great for rock and roll and no one else had one like it. Winkle-picker shoes with stiletto heels were in at that time and they made a terrible mess of the ballroom floor because they covered it with tiny holes.

The most popular place for rock and roll enthusiasts was The Star in North Street just behind Woolworth's. It was run by two men who were excellent at jiving. It was a wooden-and-brick building and was probably an old cart shed or stables. It had a loft above and this was where the dances were held. We went up a narrow staircase into a room with shiny lino on the floor and old tatty bus seats around the edge, the windows were blacked out and the only lights were fairy ones around the usual soft-drinks bar.

The records, which were 45s by this time, were played on an old record player by the door where there was enough light to see by. There were two tiny loos at the top of the stairs. This was the only way in or out. I dread to think now what would have happened if there had been a fire, but luckily we never gave it a thought then. You had to be at least 15 to get in, and I remember standing at the back of Woolies with my friend Ann desperate to join in, but we were only 14 so we had to listen to the music down on the pavement.

It was at The Star that I perfected my jiving and more importantly I danced with boys, and met my first serious boyfriend. The Star was unfortunately pulled down when the road was widened, but I have some lovely memories of the tatty old place.

Chapter 7

The Three Rs

Not surprisingly, many people vividly remember their school days. At one time Weston was filled with schools – not only the publicly funded ones such as the Grammar School, Walliscote School and St John's, but dozens of small private schools, both day and boarding, for boys and girls. Pupil numbers in these could be as low as 12 but most were around 50 or more. Local people still remember the inter-school sports that took place on the sands, and Sundays, when the long crocodiles of pupils weaved their way to their chosen churches.

Early education for the poor was supplied by churches or charitable trusts. The first school in Weston appears to have been set up in 1702 by the overseers of the poor when Elizabeth Barber was paid to teach some of the poor children of the parish. During the nineteenth century churches set up schools such as the National School in Lower Church Road and the British School in Hopkins Street. In the 1870s, the Education Act brought in Board Schools, such as Walliscote. Meanwhile children of wealthier families were normally educated, if not at home, then at small private establishments, often run by spinster ladies and their sisters. Several of these small schools

had opened in Weston and Worle as early as the 1820s. Such establishments included Mr Brickman's Academy in Worle, and Miss Oliver's School for Young Ladies in South Parade, Weston. With no national syllabus, the variety and quality of the subjects taught could be very variable but, apart from the essential arithmetic, English, geography and so on, subjects usually included music, dancing, drawing and languages. The sciences were less well catered for. The small classes of perhaps eight or ten children, however, instilled concentration in the pupils and meant they all received the teacher's individual attention.

Madge Frankpitt's memories of Burton House School are recounted in Chapter 3. This was just one of the many private schools in Weston. Ruth Coles went to Stanmore School in Royal Crescent from the age of five in 1920 until she left at the age of 18. One of the oldest of the private schools in Weston, it was run by two spinster sisters, the Misses Marion and Winifred Smith. There were about 60 pupils, both boarding and day pupils. Ruth particularly recalled that at meal times, you had to sit where you were told at one of the six large tables. At Miss Marion's

Uphill Primary School, c.1960.

Pupils of Miss Kathleen Addison's school, pictured in Grove Park, 1949. This must have been the smallest school in the town with approximately 12 pupils.

Walliscote Road Infant School, 1930s.

Uphill School pupils with headmaster, Mr Dyer, 1906.

School report for Alfred Bishop, Worle School, 1929.

School report for Pat Kirby of Winthorpe School, 1961.

and matron's tables you were only allowed to speak in French. The Smiths also had a property in Switzerland and every second year Miss Marion took those senior girls that could afford it to Switzerland for the summer term in order for them to perfect their French. In about 1933, Stanmore took over Beaurivage, another private girls' school in Uphill Road North near the Royal Hospital.

Another school was Winthorpe, in Wilton Gardens.

It was run by Greta Cousins, who also had a dance school, so ballet was taught to everyone. The majority of pupils were girls, although younger boys were admitted. Pat Jones (née Kirby) spent many happy years at Winthorpe School. As her mother worked, she spent much of her time with her grandmother at 12 Moorland Road and walked to and from school each day, going home for lunch. She remembers some of the classrooms were in wooden huts with

Pupils and staff of Winthorpe School, Wilton Gardens, 1962. The teachers in the back row, left to right: *Mrs Wordingham, Miss Harris and Greta Cousins. Pat Kirby is third from the left in the back row.*

Above: A Hundred Children Calling *show at Knightstone. These shows were put on by Greta Cousins and the pupils of Winthorpe School, Wilton Gardens. The proceeds were donated to charities, in this case the money was given to a charity for the blind.*

Above: *Pupils of Winthorpe School in* A Hundred Children Calling *show at the Playhouse, 1958. These shows were put on annually by the pupils, in aid of various charities. The headmistress, Greta Cousins, is in the centre.*

Left: *Programme for* A Hundred Children Calling, *at the Playhouse, 1958.*

THE PLAYHOUSE.

Thursday, Friday and Saturday,
APRIL 10th, 11th and 12th, 1958, at 7 p.m.
Matinee Saturday at 2.30 p.m.

100
Children Calling

Presented by
MISS GRETA COUSINS, F.I.S.T.D. (G.D.B. Hons.)

Programme.

1. **POLISH WEDDING.** Children : Nicola David, Carol Rowley.
Children : Nicola David, Carol Rowley, Barbara Madge, Angela
Deannis, Janet Thomas, Susanne O'Driscoll, Ann Eggleton.
Jennifer McIntyre, Christine Wilcox, Susan Payne.
Maidens : Jeanette Clark, Joan Hughes, Susan Walthew, Brenda
Payne, Sandra Parkin, Karen Booth, Hilary Ducker, Linda Bailey
Bride : Ann Wirdnam.
Bridegroom : Pauline Davis.

2. **THE CHILDREN'S FAVOURITES.**
Children : Lyn Johns, Jeanette and Virginia Irving, Lynda
Turner, Rosemary McNulty, Barbara Stephens, Danielle Hibbert.
Valerie Vickers.
Little Miss Muffet : Anne Scammell.
Jack and Jill : Sandra Ling and Wendy Austin.
Dick Whittington : Jane Howell.
Cinderella and Prince Charming : Lynne Charlton and Susan
Payne.
Donald Duck : Natalie Booth.
Ducklings : Theresa Scott, Caroline Pfaff, Alison Kelly, Annette
and Alison Brenner, Lyn Witchell, Judith Price.

PRICE   FOURPENCE

corrugated-iron roofs, which were very noisy when it rained. Winthorpe School became well known for the annual shows put on at the Playhouse or Knightstone Theatre. *A Hundred Children Calling* featured all the pupils in a performance to raise money for charity.

Wyncroft School in Charlton Road was just one of three private establishments left in Weston when it hit the headlines in 2003. It was announced that the school would have to close as a result of financial difficulties. The school had been set up by Enid Thorne, who was headmistress for 55 years, only retiring at the age of 89. At the time of writing, Ashbrooke House and Lancaster House Schools are the only schools in Weston that cater for private pupils in Weston-super-Mare.

La Retraite and Corpus Christi

The Order of La Retraite was founded in the 1600s in Brittany, France. The main purpose of the Order was retreat work. The Weston-super-Mare religious community of La Retraite was founded by five nuns of this Order on 21 September 1899. They came at the invitation of Canon Eustace Barron, the priest of St Joseph's Church in Camp Road. In June 1898 he wrote to the Mother Superior of the convent at Burnham-on-Sea asking the nuns to come to Weston and open 'an elementary school and a day-school'. The Supérieur Général, Mére St Césaire, was interested in forming what would have been the sisters' third foundation in England and came to Weston to meet Cannon Barron. It was not a success. Cannon Barron failed to arrive and the answers to the nuns' questions to his housekeeper about the town and its Catholic community were not encouraging. 'There were very few children, scarcely half a dozen, of very poor families... The town was very Protestant.' The matter lay unresolved for a year, but in 1899 the decision was taken that the school should be established. A house, Rossmore, was rented in Paragon Road and five nuns were chosen for the community. Mére St Ignace was the superior. Two French nuns, Mothers Mary-Angela and St Ethelburga, from the Burnham convent joined her, together with sisters St Zita and M. Francis, both French but, at the time, based at their London convent.

On their arrival they must have presented a strange sight for the locals. The nuns later wrote:

Each one burdened like a donkey, travel bags, baskets of food, potatoes, onions, we had all we could carry. To save the fare, we walked from the station to Rossmore in Paragon Road, and we have often laughed at the spectacle we must have provided. It was certainly new for residents of Weston-super-Mare, who had never seen a group of five Sisters. We must have drawn many looks, of which we were unaware. Not knowing the way, we went along by the sea on the promenade to make sure we didn't get lost.

In those days Roman Catholics were often regarded with suspicion and the nuns were no exception. One Colonel Whale took to riding up and down the road on a horse shouting insults such as 'The Bible is England's Glory', whilst the two local newspapers were filled with correspondence, much of it controversial!

Despite coping with an unfamiliar town and antagonistic locals, it was just ten days before the nuns opened a small school in Florence Villa, Quarry Road. The school was divided into two parts. A free school was set up in the basement – just one pupil arrived on the first day – while the upper rooms

The tennis-court, La Retraite School, c.1920.

The main buildings of La Retraite School, c.1918. These two houses were originally called Holywell and Woodlands and were built in 1859. Woodlands became Forest Hill School in 1871 and Holywell was turned into Coombe Ladies College a few years later. La Retraite bought the two houses in 1910.

Pupils of La Retraite School, c.1917.

formed the fee-paying establishment which, it was hoped, would help fund the free school. Meanwhile at their home in Rossmore, the sisters took in lady-boarders and summer visitors (in 1907 a Spanish Countess arrived for a stay with them).

Canon Barron was not making their life easy. He was often away or ill and they were frequently unable to have Mass because of his absence. In fact it was not uncommon for him to take off for months to India 'for his health'! The nuns were beginning to wonder why he had asked them to Weston at all.

We say among ourselves that perhaps he realises he had made a mistake in getting us here. We have had to ask Mrs Shaw (a local Catholic) to go and hunt up two non-practising Catholics. She went round with Doris (Hansen), but only got vague promises out of them. In each family there are children at the Board School.

In the meantime the sisters were looking for a larger house to open as a boarding-school but they were still confronted with anti-Catholic sentiments. By 1904 the day-school had closed and there were just three lady-boarders at Rossmore and the situation was desperate. The new Superior, Revd Mother St Pacome, helped to make ends meet by giving private lessons in French and painting. Gradually the work of the nuns became better known and locals began to lose their suspicions. The schools began to enjoy an

Teaching sisters of La Retraite, 1960s. In 1964 the sisters abandoned these nineteenth-century habits as, among other things, the hoods prevented them from being able to drive a car.

increase in pupil numbers. By 1907 there were 30 pupils in the elementary school although the day-school was still closed. By this time the school had moved to a house in South Road, Fortfield, next door to a boys' school run by Mr Ibbs. When he left in 1910, the sisters were able to acquire the property and open a secondary school for girls – La Retraite. Despite signs being posted all over Weston, 'Beware of the nuns', in April 1911 '... five children, from the

Pupils of La Retraite, pictured in 1971, the year the school was closed.

best families in Weston' started as day pupils. The boarding-school began to grow in numbers also.

The free school, St Joseph's, opened once more in Oxford Street. Over the years it moved to above Barclay's Bank in the High Street, to Connaught Place in 1916 and to 25 Beach Road in 1919. Eventually, in 1931, St Joseph's School became Corpus Christi and was moved to Ellenborough Park South where it remains to this day.

On the outbreak of the Second World War, Corpus Christi, like all other schools in the town, received its allocation of evacuee children from London. Meanwhile the pupils of La Retraite were themselves evacuated to Brinsop Court in Herefordshire and the South Road building was leased to the Red Cross as a war hospital for wounded soldiers. The Red Cross stayed in the building until 19 May 1946 and much work was needed before the pupils returned from Hereford. In addition, two further houses in South Road were purchased as dormitories, known as Pen Maria and Saltaire (renamed St Teresa's). In 1949 great celebrations were held for the golden jubilee of both schools.

In the postwar years Corpus Christi expanded, acquiring part of Ellenborough Park as a playing-field in 1958. In 1962 a brand-new school was built, next door to Corpus Christi Church.

In the 1960s La Retraite also saw some expansion with the purchase of Dunmarklyn for extra dormitory accommodation and the building of a dining hall annexe to the main building. There was also vigorous expansion in numbers and in academic and cultural achievement and a large sixth form saw more and more pupils going on to university. However, the growth of Church-affiliated comprehensive schools in the Bristol area meant Catholic secondary education was becoming more available, and the need for private Catholic schools was diminishing. In 1971 La Retraite closed the school in Weston, amalgamating it with their Burnham school. A small group of nuns remained in Weston, teaching at Corpus Christi School and working in the community as they still do at the time of writing.

St Peter's School

St Peter's School is probably best known for such illustrious old boys as Roald Dahl and John Cleese. However, it turned out many hundreds of pupils during the almost 90 years of its history, most of whom went on to become professional men such as solicitors, surgeons and businessmen.

St Peter's School was founded in 1882 in Highbury House by the Revd Duckworth as a boys' preparatory school. It attained such success that it soon outgrew the premises and in 1906 a new purpose-built school was opened. Designed by architects Ward & Cogswell of London, it was built by Robert Wilkins & Sons of Bristol in a large field at the end of Shrubbery Avenue. Commanding panoramic views across Weston, and surrounded by its own playing-fields, it was designed so that all the main rooms faced south, with only corridors, bathrooms and kitchens on the northern side. The main school room seated 150, but could be partitioned off into three classrooms. There were two further classrooms, a dining-room, reading-room, carpenter's shop, four dormitories, each with 31 beds, as well as masters' accommodation and sickrooms, etc. There was a separate gymnasium.

The opening ceremony of the new building merited a full page in each of the two local newspapers of the time – the *Weston Mercury* and the *Weston-super-Mare Gazette*. The opening was performed by the headmaster of Clifton College, the Revd A. David, at the invitation of R. Fagan Duckworth and R. Crawford, the joint owners and headmasters of St Peter's. The Revd David's address paid particular emphasis to the easy natural relationship between the staff and the pupils, teachers who gave 'their lives, labour and friendship' to the boys, as well as the effect this had on achievements and exam results.

The south frontage of St Peter's School, built in 1906.

The playing-fields of St Peter's School, c.1905. At this date the school was in Highbury House. The house in the background on the left is Holland House, used by the school as a dormitory, 1917–24. The man with the bicycle is the father of L.P. Kent, a pupil at the school.

The dining-room of St Peter's School, c.1906. Dining rules included such items as 'unfold your table napkin before commencing your meal', 'do not spread your bread in the air', 'cut your bread when eating a slice with butter or preserves', 'break your bread when eating it plain' and 'look after your neighbours wants and do not stretch'.

The pupils' bathroom at St Peter's School, c.1906.

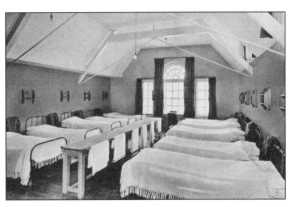

One of the dormitories at St Peter's School, c.1906.

One of the classrooms at St Peter's School, c.1906.

Holland House in South Road. This building was purchased in 1917 by St Peter's School for dormitory accommodation. It was sold in 1924 when the main building was enlarged. In 2004 the building is used as private flats.

Aerial view of St Peter's School, showing the tennis-courts, swimming pool and playing-fields.

Pupils and staff of St Peter's School, 1921.

It certainly appears to have been a popular school, both with parents and pupils, and most have fond memories of their time there and reunions are still held regularly.

In 1917 Holland House in South Road was acquired for expansion and remained part of the school until 1924 when the main building was enlarged and Holland House sold.

In a prospectus of the 1920s, St Peter's described itself as a 'Preparatory School for the Public Schools and the Royal Navy', taking boys between the ages of 7 and 14. Most boys then went on to such establishments as Charterhouse, Repton, Marlborough and Clifton College, many winning scholarships. At the time of the prospectus the headmaster was A. Francis, the fifth person to hold the office. Mrs Francis supervised the household arrangements assisted by two matrons. The syllabus then included scripture, English, mathematics, French, Latin, Greek, German, music, singing, drawing, physical drill and gymnastics, carpentry, boxing, shooting, swimming, dancing and riding. It boasted a five-acre playing-field and, from 1924, an open-air swimming pool. There was also a cinema projector for educational use. Fees included board, tuition, laundry, games, boxing, bathing, mending, hair cutting and sickroom, plus milk and biscuits. Parents had to pay extra for books, stationery, any medical fees, clothes and lessons in music, riding, dancing, shooting, carpentry and swimming. All jam, cake and biscuits brought back to school by the boys had to be handed in to matron and shared by all the pupils. Fruit also had to be handed in but not shared and sweets and chocolate were not allowed at all. Sunday mornings were divided into letter-writing and church (despite the proximity of Holy Trinity Church, the boys attended St John's Parish Church), with catechism, indoor games, reading or sailboats in the baths on Sunday afternoons.

St Peter's School cloakroom. Note the wooden tuck boxes under the seats. Roald Dahl refers to these in his autobiography Boy *as 'his own secret storehouse, as secret as a lady's handbag, and there is an unwritten law that no other boy, no teacher, not even the Headmaster himself has the right to pry into the contents of your tuck box.'*

In April 1920 a school magazine was started. There were then 95 pupils at the school. It was divided into two houses – Grasshoppers and Butterflies. The early magazine was mainly filled with sporting results – football, cricket, athletics, boxing – as well as something called the Ring Game. The latter originated at the Army Physical Training Centre during the First World War. It was played on a court and designed to promote rapid thinking and movement. It is not clear how long a match lasted or exactly how it was played. As well as inter-house matches, games were played against other local schools such as Etonhurst and Brynmelyn.

Like most private schools, there was a special day each year, in this case on St Peter's Day. This was celebrated with a church service and a wreath-laying ceremony at the war memorial in Grove Park in the morning, with fun and games, including a picnic, in the afternoon.

One old boy who apparently did not enjoy his time at school was author Roald Dahl. He wrote vividly of his time at St Peter's in his autobiography *Boy*. He joined the school in 1925 aged nine and stayed there for five years. His mother chose the school as it was within easy travelling distance of their home in South Wales. In those days regular paddle-steamer services ran between Cardiff and Birnbeck Pier, Weston. Dahl recalls his apprehensive arrival at the school, dressed in his new uniform and armed with his tuck box and trunk. He had never before spent a night away from home. He was terrified by the 'giant of a headmaster' and the stern matron and was desperately homesick.

When the Second World War began in 1939, preparations had to be made to protect the school and its pupils. Mr Geoffrey Tolson was then headmaster, with his wife Jean superintending the household arrangements. Mrs Tolson wrote an account of those years for her grandson. The following information is based on her account. Some boys returned to school early as Weston was thought a safer place than where they lived at home. They helped with the preparations for war, such as taping windows and covering them with chicken wire to stop glass fragments from flying into the room. The changing room was lined with sandbags and became the air-raid shelter. Boys had to carry gas masks when leaving the grounds and were lectured on first aid and fire-fighting. The school had its own fire-fighting squad equipped with stirrup pumps and buckets.

In August 1940 the headmaster wrote a letter to all parents concerned about the number of air-raid warnings they were getting at the school. He set out a number of points in favour of the school remaining in Weston 'I am aware of the fact that, although no bombs have fallen or are likely to fall on Weston... Weston is, I understand, in no sense a military objective.' The letter must have come back to haunt him in January 1941, when the Germans launched the first

Pupils and staff of St Peter's School, 1940. Because boys were always known by their surnames, even by their friends, their first names have not been recorded on the photograph. Where boys had brothers at the school, they were numbered, so the eldest boy would be Jones i and the next eldest would be Jones ii and so on. Back row, left to right: ?, Ash, T. Phipps ii, Fowle ii, George Francis, Alan Lowther, Singer, Rogers, Newton, Swift, Gale, Wreford, Hussey, ?, Fisher; fourth row: Mr Barlett, Mr Allen, Gordon Cotton, Holyoak i, Moffat i, Pain, Bird ii, Butcher, Higgs, Edwards, C. Ellis, Hugh Podger, Mills, Hubner, Ponsford, Meredith, ?, Mr J. Webb, Mendleson Browne (music teacher); third row: MacMichael, Brian Harris, John Lucas, Lowther i, Hammerton, John Phipps i, Andrew Hughes, Arthur Down, Lovibond, ?, Moore, Fowle, Atchley i, Sale ii, Kingsmith i, Winson, ?, ?; second row: Forbes, ?, Rowlands, Mrs Allen, Horton, Captain Lancaster (master), Birch, Jean Tolson, Geoffrey Tolson (headmaster), Arrowsmith, Mr Downing, Price, Miss Lovell, Hearn, Matron, Mann i; front row: Horton ii, Powell, ?, Whiting, Lowther iii, Dennis Mann, Carrington, Cowen ii, Hughes ii, Theo Bryan, Yates, ?, John Haines, Walter Huntley.

St Peter's School 1st XI cricket team, 1953. The tall pupil in the centre is John Cleese.

of two major blitzes on the town and for a year, all the pupils and staff slept in the changing room air-raid shelter rather than the dormitories. In 1942 they moved back to the dormitories but June that year saw the second of the two blitzes. Fortunately it was half term and many of the boys had gone home, but the 20 who remained in school (because they had mumps and were therefore in quarantine), were sleeping in tents on the playing-field as it was very hot. There was a mad scramble to get them into the shelter as the bombs began to fall. Luckily the school appears not to have been hit, although Jean Tolson remembers hearing incendiaries bounce off the roof. The main difficulty resulting from the raid was the fact that the laundry, where all the linen and boys' underwear was sent, was hit. This meant the hampers of clean school laundry were burnt to a cinder. Clothing was rationed so a long, complicated system of compensation had to be sorted out. Rationing also brought its own challenges in feeding the boys, but the school was lucky in that it grew its own soft fruit and vegetables.

In 1945 the war ended and life gradually returned to normal. The school continued to turn out boys for the public schools and was taking day boys as well as boarders. One pupil who joined in those years was John Cleese. By the time Mr and Mrs Reginald Cleese began looking for a school for their son, St Peter's had achieved its place as the pre-eminent prep school in the town. John started there in 1948 at the age of 8 years and 11 months. Unlike Roald Dahl, John appears to have enjoyed his time at the school, although, being a day boy, homesickness was never a problem as with Dahl. That said, being a day boy could bring its own problems, as in most such schools, day pupils tended to be regarded as an inferior species by the boarders. From about the age of 12, Cleese began to grow at an alarming rate and from then until he left he was the tallest boy in the school. Eileen Crews remembers a photograph being taken of her son Peter, then the smallest boy, and John, the tallest boy. His height, together with his rather unique and subtle sense of humour, led to Cleese being somewhat withdrawn. He eventually found his niche however, and in fact became something of a school star, especially in sports. He particularly excelled at cricket, becoming captain of the school team, with one of his best friends, Barney Butter, as vice-captain. By the time he left in 1953 to go to Clifton College in Bristol, Cleese was head librarian, prefect and deputy head boy. Not only did the 1953 edition of the school magazine note that 'Our Coronation Holiday was made all the more enjoyable by the news that Cleese had been successful in his examination at Clifton College...', but that he had been an able deputy head boy and was awarded the Whitting Cup for General Excellence. In the school sports day of that year Cleese came first in long jump and high jump and second in the quarter mile race, throwing the cricket ball, the hurdles and the 100 yards race.

John left Clifton College with the intention of going on to Cambridge to study Law. However, National Service had just ended and, due to the large numbers of entrants for universities at that time, he had to wait two years before starting higher education. He did this by returning to St Peter's as a teacher. At just 19 years old, he was responsible for imparting a knowledge of science, English, geography, history and Latin to boys just a few years younger than himself. His height, however, a newly grown beard and his acerbic wit, all helped him maintain an easy discipline. He also discovered that he loved teaching, something he has continued to use in his company Video Arts which produces training videos for business.

The Tolsons retired in 1968, and the school closed two years later, at a time when many of the old-established private schools were struggling to survive – La Retraite also closed in 1971.

Old boys, well known in the town, include Peter Nisbet, Michael Freedman, Paul Brenner, Roger Leaver, Gary Chapman, Ian and Peter Frampton and David Wright.

Barney Butter, best friend of John Cleese at St Peter's School, c.1949.

St Peter's School Library Committee, c.1964. Left to right, standing: *Geoff Pringle, Peter Lowell, Steven Chadwick, Chris Edwards, J.G. Baynton;* seated: *N. Hawkins, P. Burnett, C. Evans, A.C. Smith.*

Milton Infant and Junior Schools

When an infant school was opened by Miss E.M. Marigold in 1907 in Milton Park Road, Milton was very much still a distinct village with open fields between it and Weston and Worle. Miss Marigold began with 37 pupils aged from five upwards, although one three-year old, Victor Board, was admitted in 1913. A few days later Miss Marigold was joined by an additional teacher, Miss Pinton.

In 1980 George Gillingham wrote a brief account of the school from information extracted from the school logbooks. Milton and Worle are so urbanised today that it is almost a shock to realise just how countrified the area was in the early 1900s. For example, in 1909 two children were hurt when a bull that was being driven to slaughter, panicked and charged the children who were milling about as they left to go home.

The school year was punctuated with national occasions such as coronations and Empire Day, when the children marched to Grove Park to 'salute the flag', as well as traditional seasonal celebrations. In 1910 a maypole was erected so the children could dance around it. At Christmas, all the children were each given an orange as well as a toy or comic donated by well-wishers. It is interesting to note that at Christmas 1922 the school Christmas tree was <u>lent</u> by the father of one of the children!

When war broke out in 1914, the children were encouraged to do their bit. Money was donated to purchase blankets to send to the Red Cross for forwarding to the battlefront. In 1917 the War Savings Committee held a special meeting in Knightstone Theatre, for all the children in the town. All the schools were given a half-day holiday and the children gathered to form a huge procession headed by Mogg's Band, as they marched to Knightstone. When the war ended all the schools in the area gave the pupils an extra week on the summer holiday as a victory celebration.

At various times epidemics swept through the school. These were usually the normal childhood diseases of the period – whooping cough, scarlet fever and so on. The 1918 flu epidemic closed the school altogether, although whether it was the children or the staff who were affected is not clear. In 1927 diphtheria killed one pupil and caused others to be taken to the Isolation Hospital in Drove Road, Weston.

The teachers taught their young charges well, but it was an increasing source of dismay to Miss Marigold that there was no junior school to which they could progress; instead they were dispersed to other schools in Weston and Worle. For years Miss Marigold campaigned to remedy this situation, a campaign taken on by successive teachers until in 1930 a junior school for those aged 7–11 was finally established on the same site as the infant school. On the first day 114 children applied for admission!

These pupils were taught by one qualified teacher, assisted by one certified and two uncertified assistants in just two classes. From the very first day the school remained full and, with demand so great, a purpose-built school was obviously needed.

Six years later Milton Junior School was ready for pupils. Built next door to the Milton Infant School, there was a large assembly hall and eight classrooms, which meant that lessons could be taught to smaller groups of children. The following year, two commemorative rowan trees were planted either side of the girls' entrance, one to mark the coronation of George VI and the other in celebration of the opening of the school. In fact 1937 was a year of celebrations. Not only was the coronation marked by an extra two days' holiday, as well as gifts of a coronation mug, a new shiny silver sixpence and a free cinema ticket, but the Granting of the Borough Charter to Weston-super-Mare also fell that year. The school again closed for celebration.

On the outbreak of the Second World War many London children were evacuated to Weston. Milton Junior School was initially closed while special arrangements were put in place. When they reopened on 15 September 1939, they, like all the affected schools, worked in double shifts with the Weston pupils attending in the mornings and the evacuated ones in the afternoons. Milton Junior School took in two London schools, the Junior Girls' and Junior Boys' of Lathom Road, East Ham.

Stan Terrell went to Milton Junior School during the war years:

We had moved from Bristol as a family and I was nine years old. That was in June 1939. Milton Junior School was my school. All pupils were given the address of a safe house, usually one with a cellar, which was near to the school. When the siren sounded warning us of a raid, we would then make for this refuge as quickly as possible. My safe house was in The Crescent, just above Milton Park Road. I remember the lady. She was very kind and would get comics for us to read. I suppose it was to take our minds off what was going on outside.

I remember one occasion when making my way to this house, looking up into the sky and seeing many aircraft in formation. It was really scary. I learnt later that these were German 'planes on a mission to destroy the aircraft factory at Filton. A lot of lives were lost in Bristol on that raid.

With so many evacuees arriving from London for shelter during the war, the school very quickly became overcrowded. One of my lessons was taken in the Milton Baptist Church. As a family we had two evacuees, Dennis O'Neil and his brother Pat. They came from East Ham. Looking back I believe we all got on very well. Sometimes their mother came down to visit them.

By early 1940, nothing had really happened with

regard to major bombing and so many of the evacuees decided to go back home. The ones who stayed were amalgamated into the main school and classes went back to normal, albeit briefly. In June a second evacuation took place and Milton Junior School took in children from Willesden. However, the numbers were not so great as before and the school operated as one unit, although it used the Baptist Hall as an extra classroom. The teachers were shocked, however, by how little schooling some of the children had had, and some pupils were clearly very traumatised by being bombed back home.

By 1943 life was getting very hard. After the two major blitzes on Weston in 1941 and 1942, parents began to call for school air-raid shelters to be built. This was spurred on by the fact that some children had been killed in a London school. A one-day strike was organised but nothing was done, beyond the school losing its iron railings to the salvage effort. This, of course, had the additional effect of reducing the amount of shrapnel should the school have been hit. The winter of 1944–45 was very cold. The Government banned central heating and the temperatures in the classrooms were all below 40 degrees, with the toilets frozen and unusable. However, in May the Germans surrendered and there was a two-day national holiday to celebrate VE Day, an event repeated in September for VJ Day when Japan surrendered.

School life began to get back to normal. Milton Infant and Junior Schools were amalgamated and renamed Milton County Primary School, men began to return from active service and staffing levels were improved. The school returned to its natural rhythm, briefly interrupted by problems with the building, which was suffering from the neglect of the war years. Inspections also affected the smooth running of the school, as did, most memorably, the coronation of Queen Elizabeth II in 1953. The latter fell on 2 June 1953 and it was noted that the ceremony was 'watched by many children through the Television Service'. Some 16 days later the whole school – 360 pupils, plus their teachers – went to the Odeon Cinema to see the film *A Queen is Crowned*.

The cold winters of the 1950s tested the dilapidated heating system to the limit until finally on 8 November 1954 the following entry appeared in the logbook, 'The boiler job is 99.9 per cent successful – leak now only half a bucket a day.' Well into the 1960s, children endured conditions that would see them sent home or the school closed in more modern times. In the memorably severe winter of 1963, boys helped the headmaster thaw all the toilets using buckets of hot water and the temperature in the classrooms the following day was only 10 degrees above freezing!

Sue Ryall attended school in Milton and Worle in the late 1940s and early '50s. She remembers:

At four years old I was taken to Worle Infant School. There was a playground with a large Horse Chestnut tree in one corner, and Janet and John reading books. For some reason I also went to Milton Infant School as well, I can't think why. We had tiny blue chairs and tables to sit at and rested in the afternoon on little coconut mats and were each given a sweet from a silver tin.

I then went to Milton Junior School which was next door to the infants, everyone wore a school uniform – a brown gymslip and cardigan and a white blouse. The tie was brown and orange, as was the scarf. My school mac was always bought to grow in to. It was about a foot too long and turned up with a giant hem and was taken down inch by inch as I grew. I always had a turn-up mark around the hem of my mac.

The classrooms were built around the playground on two sides with a hall at one short end. The toilets were outside in a corner by the gate, they had no roof so when it rained you not only got wet going to them but also while you were inside! While at Milton School I left to go to Locking Camp School and then came back again when we moved back to Mayfield Avenue. Because I had suffered from TB my Mum was very careful to keep me warm, so I wore a pad of red cotton wool called Thermogene sewn to the front and back of my vest, I was so embarrassed when we had PE because we all had to undress down to our vest and knickers, and there was me with red cotton wool sticking out of my vest!

Advertisement for Couch & Sons, the main retailer in Weston of local school uniforms.

Annette Porter dressed as Queen Anne for the Worle Junior School pageant, early 1950s.

I took my 11+ at Milton Junior School. I was desperate to go to boarding-school if I passed. I had read so many school books, mostly by Enid Blyton, that I honestly thought boarding-school was all midnight feasts and games of hockey. But having lost so much schooling while I was in Egypt, on Locking Camp and when I had TB, I had no chance of passing so I went to Spring Hill Secondary School, Worle.

The school survived and indeed thrived, and celebrated its golden jubilee in 1980. Displays were mounted about the school, a maple tree planted and commemorative mugs given to all the pupils. It will be interesting to see how things change in the next 50 years.

A School Pageant

Annette Gibson (née Porter) remembers her school pageant in the early 1950s at Worle Junior School, now Hillside School:

Every time I pass by St Martin's Church on Church Road, Worle, and glance at the row of modern houses opposite it and the school my thoughts go back to the time when it was a large green field. There were lovely oak and other trees round the edge of it and the old manor-house to the right-hand side of it – where my friend Val once lived in the ground-floor flat.

Mr Bull, our headmaster then, had written the words for a pageant and this field was the perfect setting for it! For months the pageant was the main talking point. Every child in the school was to have a part to play, be it Saxon warrior, a country dancer, or a king or queen, etc. – my part was Queen Anne.

Mrs Bull was in charge of making all the costumes, and she and an army of helpers – namely teachers and parents I suppose – were sewing for months. Materials, beads and wigs, shields and bows and arrows were everywhere and sometimes during lessons, one or other of us had to go for a fitting when our costumes were being made. There were, I think, about four classes in the school, with about 25–30 children in each, so this must have been an enormous task.

Eventually the day of the pageant arrived and providence was indeed kind to us. The weather was perfect, our open-air theatre was all set, the children assembled fully-dressed, parents duly seated and the pageant began. It lasted almost two hours in total, which was a long time for the children, the eldest of which were only about ten years old, to be kept under control. While we were waiting for our turn, we were shielded behind screens and had to sing songs and provide background noises for the players out front.

Finally my turn came and I walked slowly and majestically, as befits a queen, out to centre stage and recited a verse about Queen Anne and her friend Sarah Churchill. And so ended my moment of glory, waiting so long for it and then over in barely three minutes!

The finale came all too soon and ended with the whole school parading round the field to the 'Pomp and Circumstance' march by Elgar played on a gramophone. A rousing and fitting end to the whole production.

A little later in the year, when the Worle carnival was being held, Mr Bull entered a float from the school. All the kings and queens from the pageant took part and we were all very excited as it gave us another chance to dress up in our costumes. We began in the quarry at the top of Kewstoke Road and had to stand very still while we were driven all along the top road, past the church and the school, down Coronation Road, left through the village High Street and right into Station Road and then to the recreation-ground where the procession ended. I don't remember much more about the carnival Day except that our float won and each child got 2s.6d., which was a fortune to us then.

Secondary Education

Until the 1970s, the main secondary schools for the town were the Grammar School (or the County School as it was previous to 1945) and the school at Worle.

Worle County Secondary School was established in 1940 in Spring Hill, in what is now St Martin's

Teachers at Worle County Secondary School, 1948. Left to right, back row: ?, Mr Stevens, ?, Mr Atkinson, Miss Smith, Mr Holly, Mr Johns; front row: Mr Matthews, Miss Snelgrove, Mr Prosser, Mr Bisgrove (headmaster), Miss Baker, Mr Finney, Miss Rossiter.

Worle County Secondary School pantomime. Among the cast are: *Diane Tabrett, Dermot O'Connell, John Andow, Micky Hurst, Ann Gillett, Virginia Waring, Valerie Gibbings, Jackie Moore, Margaret Wilcox, Judith Lane, Pat Corfield, Derek Parker, Sam Edwards, Jennifer Moxey, Annette Porter, Margaret Hastings, Judy Bouditch, Penny Pickering, Pat Ivy, Malcolm Venn, Terry Allen, Linda Day, Sylvia Whittle, Roger Lovell, Brenda Ellison, Margaret Sims.*

Junior School. The school opened with 133 pupils and the first headmaster was Mr Bisgrove. His initial task was to organise lessons to cope with the three London schools evacuated to Worle to escape the expected wartime bombings. As with everywhere else, this was achieved with a rota system.

In all schools at that time there was strict discipline and punishment for those who dared to rebel. Mrs Beckett recalls:

At the front door of the old school used to be the head-master's office and the offices of assistant head Mrs Baker and the school secretary. The floor was tiled and there was a line right along it. If you were naughty the chances were you would be sent down to 'the line'. So you would go down and stand outside the offices on this line with your feet apart, hands behind your back and you wouldn't dare move. The door at both ends would probably be open so you'd get cold; you'd get children coming through, with the teachers changing class-rooms, and they'd all look at you and ask what you were there for, and you felt like a criminal. You were on show; you really were punished.

Mrs Sandy said that she only remembered one boy getting the cane and that was for swearing in the playground. The headmaster would not tolerate that. On the rare occasions fights broke out, the two combatants would be given boxing gloves and told to fight it out in the gym. This often resulted in firm friendships being forged!

Sue Ryall went to Worle County Secondary School in the early 1950s and remembers her years there with fondness:

Worle was an excellent school, there were lots of new subjects I had never tried before such as PE in a proper gym, domestic science, history, geography and art. We used to have yearly exams and from the results were streamed into different classes.

When we arrived in the morning we had assembly. There were a couple of hymns, accompanied by Mrs Whittle, our music teacher, on the piano. She played standing up so that she could keep an eye on us. Then we had prayers and the headmaster, Mr Bisgrove, read the lesson and told us which House was top that week. We had four Houses named after the surrounding hills, Brendon, Blackdown, Mendip and Quantock which I was in. The school song was always sung when term started and ended.

Our school pantomimes were very good, and we did one every year. I was in every one while I was there. There was a large stage and the art class painted the scenery and we sold tickets to friends and family. Everyone wanted to be in the panto because it meant that you could skip lessons to go to the rehearsal, and on the three days when the panto was on we were allowed to rest in the afternoon in the gym.

Every year we had a school dance. At last we could dress up and wear make-up and hopefully impress some boys! They were very tame affairs though. The only dances were the Gay Gordons, Moonlight Sonata and the Valeta, all of which we had learnt during the school year. The last year I had a black circular felt skirt on which mum had sewn different coloured felt hearts all around the bottom, worn with a shocking pink cardigan and flat black pumps – now that was up to date! During that dance someone put on a record called 'Bobby's in Love', it was a hit song of the time, and some

Worle County Secondary School netball team, 1956. Left to right, back row: Anita Bowering, Diane Tabrett, Valerie Gibbings, Susan Walters; front row: Maria Jones, Susan Wright, Jean Barnes.

Worle County Secondary School under 13 Rugby XV, 1953/54. Left to right, back row: Ronald Gill, John Riden, Peter Robinson; middle row: Roy Wilmot, Richard Burgess, Alan Smithen, ?, Malcolm Venn, Mike Bubear, Peter Fry, Dermot O'Connel; front row: ?, Tony Counsell, ?, David Moxey, Peter Hoddinot, Graham Hunt, Terry Widlake.

Class 4A, Worle County Secondary School, 1957. Left to right, back row: Susan Wright, Alan Denny, Alison Hammond, Christopher Ashmore, Malcolm Venn, Terry Alan, Brian Bond, Marion Jones; middle row: Vicky Venn, Jean Barnes, Margaret Wilcox, Susan Walters, Tony Bowerman, Edwina Sorbie, Diane Cooper, Elizabeth Vowles, Anita Bowering, Annette Porter; front row: Margaret Smith, Gillian Palmer, Gillian Stabbins, Isobel Hooper, Mr Brown (teacher), Trevor Jarvis, Raymond Munden, John Hodgson, Paul Bishop.

Staff at Worle County Secondary School, c.1957. Left to right, back row: *Mr Ruskin, ?, Mr Cawsey, ?, Mr John, Mr Galvin;* middle row: *Mr Stevens, Mr Pym, Mr Edwards, Miss Perkins, Mr Russell, ?, ?, Mr Brown, Mr Finney;* front row: *Mrs Whittle, Mr Holly, Mrs Snelgrove, Mr Prosser, Mr Bisgrove (headmaster), Miss Baker, Mr Brown, Miss Rossiter, ?.*

of the Sixth Form danced to it, or 'smooched' as it was known then.

Once a week during the summer we travelled by bus to the local swimming baths at Knightstone for lessons. All the girls wore white rubber bathing hats with a strap under the chin; they left a red mark on your forehead when you took them off.

Worle School had what was known as The Flat. When the school was built it was thought that girls needed to learn how to look after a home, so during their time in school, two girls at a time spent a week in The Flat. It had a bedroom, bathroom, lounge and kitchen. It was fully equipped and although they didn't actually sleep there, the girls were expected to clean the flat, cook all their meals and have friends to tea, including the headmaster. I got invited to tea but unfortunately never got a chance to look after it. I did think it a bit silly cleaning a clean bath, dusting a tidy lounge and unmaking and then making the beds. The school was growing so quickly that the rooms were needed, so The Flat got turned into classrooms and studies.

Girls did cookery and sewing and the first thing we all had to make were our cookery aprons in our house colours – mine was green check – and it had to have four pleats, a pocket and some cross-stitch embroidery across the top of it. During the four years at the school I also made a baby's dress, a toy donkey and a thing called a dirndl skirt (just a skirt with a waistband – very ugly).

Domestic science or cookery was a bit behind the times as well. The ovens were old-fashioned gas ones and when we had to clean them there were loads of different bits to put back together. We learnt to wash clothes by hand – they didn't have washing machines, anymore

than our homes had them – and we used the old flat-irons which were placed on the top of a flat square hob to get hot. We were also taught how to wash up using two bowls of water, one to wash and one to rinse. When we did cooking the teacher would hand out the ingredients to us and we weighed them and followed the recipe which was on the board. The whole of a morning was spent cooking, it was one of my favourite lessons.

The boys, of course, didn't do cookery, they had metal work, woodwork and in those days, gardening, which sounds a bit silly but it was another lesson left over from the war years. The bottom piece of the school grounds was the garden, and there boys learnt to dig a trench and plant potatoes and other vegetables. I think the school kitchen used the things they grew. The boys also had a separate entrance to the girls at the other end of the school, and they played in a different part of the playground.

Worle County Secondary School pupils at their reunion in March 2003. Left to right: *?, Jean Venn, ?, Marion Spanner, Susan Townsend, Valerie Gwynne, Jackie Moore.*

Boys also got the cane as a punishment. If it was a major offence then the caning was done in front of the whole school at assembly. The girls didn't get the cane, thank goodness. Instant punishment for both boys and girls was a rap over the knuckles with a ruler, a clip round the ear or having the blackboard rubber thrown at you from across the classroom. Alternatively boys and girls had to stand 'on the line' outside the headmaster's study – everyone could see you standing there and it was so embarrassing.

It was a great school and I was genuinely sorry to leave at 15 and go out into the big wide world to earn my living. Mr Matthews, our lovely fourth-year class teacher, Mr Causey our brilliant art teacher, Mrs Baker who ruled with a rod of iron, Mrs Whittle our eccentric music teacher, and many others, all gave their time and knowledge generously to try to install in me something, anything, of what I would need to face the future.

In 1971 the whole country's education was reorganised along comprehensive lines. Worle County Secondary School became Worle Comprehensive and was moved into a brand-new building in Redwing Drive where it remains at the time of writing. It was the first purpose-built comprehensive school in Somerset, with places for 800 pupils. Since then, the school has been substantially enlarged, notably with a new Technology and Science block. In 2000 the school gained Media Arts College status and now teaches 1,400 children with 130 staff. The old school buildings in Spring Hill became St Martin's Primary School.

The other secondary school in Weston was the County School, which opened in 1922 in huts in Nithsdale Road. The pupils who attended the school referred to it as 'the sardine tin'. It was a mixed school with about 176 pupils and a staff of nine. In 1935 the school moved to new purpose-built premises in Broadoak Road. In the new building, boys and girls were separated and all classes were single sex. No mixing was allowed at any time and even during breaks, boys and girls were expected to keep to their half of the drive!

A prospectus of that period is interesting reading. There was accommodation for 350 girls. The uniform consisted of a navy-blue tunic and blazer with white blouse, black shoes and stockings. For outdoors there was a navy-blue winter coat or mackintosh and a velour hat. In summer the uniform was a cotton dress and light-coloured stockings. A cotton crepe tunic was worn for gymnastics. No jewellery was allowed and long hair had to be tied back with dark ribbons. Hot midday meals were provided at an additional cost or, if students wished to eat their own food, a charge was made for the use of table linen and services. There was a staff of 11 under headmistress, Miss G.E. Farthing, who had a long career with the County School. She began as senior mistress in Nithsdale Road, becoming headmistress at the move

to Broadoak Road. She retired in 1956 and was remembered with great affection for her kindness and the interest she took in every girl. She remained unperturbed during the difficulties the Second World War created, coping effortlessly with the schools evacuated to Weston and the consequent disruption to teaching. She also had to deal with the near-total destruction of the Girls' School when it was bombed in 1942. For several years the girls had to be taught in the Boys' School until rebuilding was completed. After the Second World War the school became the Grammar School for Girls, and the Grammar School for Boys – still strictly segregated!

In 1971 comprehensive education came into being. The Grammar School became Broadoak Comprehensive School and mixed-sex classes came back into use. *The Phoenix*, the magazine for the Girls' Grammar School was filled with articles on the change-over to comprehensive education and how it was going to affect them. Mostly they welcomed it, not least because of the mixed-sex classes. 'It will be better mixed because it will encourage more social life', or 'Friends are going to be split up but work will be easier.' Out went all the old rules about girls not straying onto the boys' playing-fields and so on. Some girls were worried about the larger class sizes and the new teachers. Others were hopeful that exams would become less important! Teachers were more concerned about introducing the changes in what was, by then, a dilapidated and outdated school building. They would have to manage for many years after that. Not until 1999 were brand-new school buildings opened for what had become Broadoak Community School. At the time of writing Wyvern and Priory Schools also cater for the vastly increased population and educational needs of the town.

The School Trip

Excursions were often a valuable part of education. 'The girls of 3 and 3A left the school on an expedition to examine the plant life in a pond at the bottom of Moor Lane.' So reads an extract from the logbooks of Worle County Secondary School in 1941! Other trips out were more exciting, often to Knightstone Theatre or the Tivoli Cinema. However, it was not long before the Education Committee put its foot down and insisted that trips had to have 'educational value', such as an excursion to Cannington Farm Institute or the *Weston Mercury* offices. In 1938 the girls of the County School's Scientific Society had a 'Visit to the Making of Clinical Thermometers at Uphill', whilst in 1949 they visited Weston's gasworks, as well as a production of Moliere's *L'Avare* in French. In 1951 the Festival of Britain offered educational opportunities and a trip to the South Bank Exhibition in London was organised. Unfortunately one boy managed to get lost after dashing off to buy some fruit and rejoining the tail end of a different school party. He had to be collected from a police station and didn't get back to Weston until gone three o'clock in the morning!

After the Second World War schools began offering foreign-exchange visits for pupils. The Bristol/Bordeaux Association was set up in the late 1940s, in order to foster greater links and knowledge between France and Britain. Over 300 pupils in this area travelled in 1966, flying in chartered aircraft from Bristol Airport to Bordeaux. The Grammar School for Boys was just one of the local schools participating in the scheme. In 1963 a party from Worle County Secondary School travelled to Sweden. Brian Saunders recalled:

Nowadays, pupils travel far and wide with total nonchalance but in 1963 it was as though we were travelling to outer space with very little hope of ever returning. I think the family farewells and reassurances took longer than the actual journey.

Today school outings and trips abroad are often an established part of the curriculum. The sight of the grave of a 15-year-old soldier who died on a battlefield in the First World War for example, can give children a better understanding of the realities of war, than hours spent in a classroom. Pupils are encouraged to foster links with other schools, such as Worle County Secondary School's correspondence with Edumfa Grace School in Ghana. In addition, school orchestras or sports teams may go on reciprocal tours abroad. We have come a long way from a pond in Moor Lane!

Weston College

Higher education first started in Weston in 1873 when evening classes in science were run in the National School at the bottom of Lower Church Road. Although it appears there were few pupils, it did not stop the Government School of Art being opened in 1882 in the upstairs rooms of the Church Institute in the Boulevard. This was much more successful with approximately 76 students and

consequently planning began to mark the diamond jubilee of Queen Victoria with a brand-new, purpose-built School of Science and Art in Lower Church Road. The site and building was funded by local donations, by a grant from the Department of Science and Art in South Kensington, another grant from Somerset County Council and a donation from funds left over from the Great Exhibition at Crystal Palace, London, in 1851. The new school was designed by local architect Hans Price and opened in 1893 with 110 students.

Weston College grew from these foundations. Gradually a greater variety of courses were offered, but finding suitable premises grew harder. Different departments were situated in buildings all over the town. Agriculture, art, business studies and women's subjects were in Westcliffe in Kewstoke Road, whilst building, catering and engineering were in the School of Science and Art in Lower Church Road. Finally, general studies were in Burton House in Walliscote Road. And so, in 1970, a new modern building was constructed on the site of St John's School, originally the National School, where the first evening classes had been held. This new college allowed all departments to be combined under one roof, with the exception of the art department, which was returned to the old School of Science and Art next door, and ceramics and sculpture which were taught in the old British School in Hopkins Street until the 1990s, when the building was sold and converted into private housing. Because of the comparatively small size of the site available, the building had to be much higher than any other building in Weston. This, together with its uncompromisingly modern design has attracted controversy over the years. However, a new extension and makeover in 1998 has softened its exterior appearance somewhat.

Weston College has expanded its range of subjects over the years. Nowadays it offers more than 800 full- and part-time courses up to degree level, to over 15,000 students annually. With the Government encouraging new funding initiatives, it has also formed partnerships with schools and businesses and is scheduled to open a new campus in 2005/6 in association with Regency Insurance.

Marriage certificate between George Every, a labourer, and Ellen Price, both of Uphill. They were married in the Wesleyan Regent Street chapel in Weston-super-Mare in 1892. This is now closed and is the Regent Street branch of Barclay's Bank.

Emmanuel Boys' Choir, 2 July 1922. Jack and Wilfred Osmond are standing second and third from the right in the back row.

Dedication of the new Catholic Church of Corpus Christi, June 1934. The Bishops of Clifton, Nottingham and Menevia in Carmarthen, Wales, took part in the ceremony.

God's Word

Religious communities in the area were, and are, very active. In the early days each village just had its parish church. All those in Weston, Worle and Uphill were first begun in Norman times with additions and changes over the years. The Parish Church of St John the Baptist in Weston dates from 1823, when the original church was rebuilt due to its state of disrepair and small size.

As Weston developed, so new Anglican churches opened to cater for the new communities. Up to Victorian times, most people attended a church of some denomination. Emmanuel Church was built in Oxford Street in October 1847, followed by Christ Church in 1855 and Holy Trinity in 1861. All Saints' and St Paul's both started as prefabricated iron structures, until the congregations proved large enough, not only to warrant permanent buildings, but also to raise the funds to provide them. Today, with the decline in church attendance, many of the churches and chapels, have become redundant. Fortunately, few have been demolished, but have found new uses, such as the Bible Christian Chapel in Burlington Street, now a store for North Somerset Museum Service, or the Ebenezer Chapel in Lawrence Road, Worle, which is a community centre.

The Congregational Church, Weston-super-Mare

Nonconformists first met in a room in a house in Stiverd Place on Beach Road, close to Richmond Street. The congregation was small to begin with, but as numbers grew, helped by the seasonal increase in visitors, they were soon able to fund a stone chapel. It was built in 1825 on the corner of Richmond Street and York Street, then called Harvey's Lane. Revd W. Page was the first minister. He was a popular preacher and the congregation grew further until, by 1829, it was decided a new and larger chapel was required. A site was chosen in High Street and the church opened the following year. It was a fine stone structure with a stuccoed frontage and it stood about 20 feet back from the footpath. Paths on either side led to the vestry, schoolroom and, at the rear, a small burial-ground. The old York Street chapel was deconsecrated and sold.

When the Revd Page retired in 1831, a new minister was ordained in the High Street chapel. The Revd Richard Skinner only stayed in Weston for two years but made quite an impression on the Westonians. At the time, the townspeople felt the rector of the Parish Church was not a good preacher and didn't inspire his congregation, and so many of the tradesmen and artisans drifted towards the High Street chapel. This situation was reversed when Archdeacon Law was sent to the Parish Church, and so the Revd Skinner moved on to Devon. A number of ministers then followed in quick succession, none staying more than a couple of years or so. In February 1840, the then minister, Revd John Davie, invited the poor of Weston to a meat tea to celebrate the wedding of Queen Victoria and Prince Albert. To everyone's surprise the lady of the manor, Mrs Smyth-Pigott, came to watch the people enjoying the feast. This was seen as an act of great condescension since Nonconformists were viewed with great suspicion by the gentry at that time.

The Revd Davie stayed for three years and did much to spread the word of God in the area. When a young man was murdered in a house in Worle, he preached a sermon at the scene of the crime. The following Sunday he preached at the house of the murdered boy's parents in Bleadon.

The next minister was Revd Joseph Hopkins of Bradford on Avon. He started a boys' day-school at the High Street chapel, but the Church Meeting (the Nonconformist equivalent of a Parish Council) were not happy with how much of his time the school was taking up, so Hopkins resigned. He continued with his teaching, moving to Weston Lodge in Worthy Lane. This had a large garden which covered part of what is now Waterloo Street and the Boulevard. At the end of the garden was a large field which Hopkins bought as a playing-field for the pupils. When he moved again to Wellington Place he sold the field for building land. The resultant road was named after him – Hopkins Street.

The 1840s were a time of great expansion in Weston. Until now the Baptists had been content to worship in the Independent Chapel, High Street, sharing it with the Wesleyans, but by the 1840s wanted a church of their own. They chose a site in

Wadham Street and, despite objections from the Smyth-Pigotts at Grove House, the Baptist Chapel was opened in 1850. This separation depleted the congregation at the High Street chapel and by 1853 it was on the verge of extinction. It was the arrival of the Revd Richard Pritchett that appears to have saved the day. He was a man of genial disposition and was well educated. Whilst holding to his Nonconformist faith, he was willing to co-operate with the established Church more closely. His father and brothers were architects and, with their help, together with a large donation from Richard Ash of Clifton who was a frequent visitor to Weston, he achieved the rebuilding of the High Street chapel. The new church opened on Sunday 29 May 1858. It had a nave with north and south aisles, an apse at the eastern end and an 85 foot tower topped with a spire. It stood on the corner of Cambridge Place and it is part of this church that can still be seen today, although at the time of writing it is occupied by Woolworths.

In 1874 the Revd Hastings took over the ministry. By this time the resident population of Weston stood at just over 11,000, but with the summer visitors, the church was once again proving too small. Rather than extend the existing church, or rebuild on the same site, the decision was taken to build on a new site on the Boulevard. The new church, the fourth one for the congregation, was designed by a London architect, T. Lewis Banks and built by local builder, John Hando. The High Street chapel was sold and the graves removed to Ashcombe Cemetery. The spire was taken down stone by stone and re-erected at Banwell Abbey. In June 1942, the Boulevard Congregational Church was destroyed by enemy action. A new modern open-plan church was rebuilt on the original foundations and was opened as the Boulevard United Reformed Church in 1959. It is still in use today.

The Children's Church

I am sure there are many people in Weston today who remember Ena Monday's remarkable achievement in the establishment of the first self-supporting interdenominational Children's Church, although I have to confess I had never heard of it until researching this book. Mrs Pratlett first told me of it and produced a wonderful booklet, written by Ena Monday, which recounted its history.

Ena Monday had been a Sunday-school teacher from her teens and, although unmarried and childless, loved children. After a break forced by ill health, she decided to resume her teaching work, but wanted to do something more than just run a class. She called together some members of her previous Sunday schools and together they came up with the idea of a children's church, run by and for the children themselves. Thus it was that in September 1942, the first ever interdenominational children's church opened.

A meeting was held every Sunday morning in Christ Church Parish Hall in Alfred Street, which was hired for a nominal rent. Ena, or Monday as she was known, had decided from the beginning that the church should not rely for funding on other churches and also did not want to 'steal' children from other Sunday schools. So, although she invited every child she met to join, she also encouraged them to remain members of their own churches. This was one reason why services were never held on Sunday afternoons, when other Sunday schools were open. By 1943 the membership stood at 50 but, just as it was taking off, they lost their meeting place when it was announced Christ Church Parish Hall was required for war use. It was this that spurred them to dare to launch a building fund so that they could have their own church. In the meantime the children gathered in Monday's dining-room in Moorland Road every week, where they made handicraft items in wood or needlework, to sell for the building fund. Not all the money was kept, however, and contributions were regularly made to such causes as the Suffering Jews, Blitzed Churches and Prisoner of War funds.

By January 1945, news of the church had begun to reach the wider public and the *Weston Gazette* published an article expressing horror that children might hold religious services. The controversy raged for three months until Mr Chapman, a Methodist preacher from Bridgwater, attended one of the services in question. He followed this up with a long letter to the newspaper headed 'Bridgwater Preacher delighted with Weston's Children's Church' and commented that he '... was astounded by the keenness, capability and sound common sense' of the children. The next week donations flooded in! In March that year Jesse Williams, one of the first members of the church, reached the age of 21 and became co-leader with Monday. In June 1946, by sheer determination, hard work, and unrelenting fund-raising efforts, they were able to purchase two derelict houses in Swiss Road, which came complete with an old builder's yard at the rear. A local builder, Arthur Taylor, gave up his spare time and, together with the children, he set to renovate the houses. By December the *Weston Gazette* wrote:

The Children are building their own church. An inspiring sight in Swiss Road. The Christmas Season this year has a special significance for everyone who has watched the progress of the Children's Church in Weston... Not content with raising £850 for this fund... these children, whose ages vary from two to fifteen, spend their spare time in mixing mortar, carrying and laying bricks, and erecting scaffolding on the site at 39–41 Swiss Road.

Just over a year later their 'dream church' opened. As well as a space for prayer, there were recreation rooms and a crèche for babies. The interior was fitted up properly. Pews were rescued from Wick St

The Independent Chapel in the High Street, Weston-super-Mare, 1870. This church was built in 1858 on the corner of Cambridge Place. It is still possible to see the remains of the side windows, now part of Woolworth's.

Below: The Congregational Church, the Boulevard, 1876. This print shows the church shortly after it was built. It was destroyed by enemy action in 1942 and rebuilt as the United Reformed Church in 1959.

Below left: Ena Monday, founder of the first self-supporting interdenominational Children's Church, established in Weston in 1942.

Members of the Children's Church, Swiss Road, Weston-super-Mare.

Lawrence Methodist Chapel, which was closing, and were stripped and oak-grained for their new setting. The choir pews came from another redundant Methodist chapel at Chiltern Polden, as did the pulpit, in which it was believed John Wesley himself once preached, although this had to be cut down to fit. The grand opening on 29 September 1947 received nationwide publicity and the membership swelled to 100 children, of all ages up to 17.

As well as a Sunday-morning service, there were meetings on Sunday evenings for which speakers were booked or Monday gave a short talk. There were three choirs, including a 'Babies' Den Choir' for children aged under three. All the services were conducted by the children. Monday was delighted when she saw the children of some of the early members come in their turn to the church. Weekday nights there were classes in woodwork or sewing and they had their own cricket, football and rugger teams.

The whole enterprise was built on faith – that God would provide what was needed when it was needed, and it seems that is indeed what happened. Many times the group was told their aim was impossible, that it was the wrong time to raise money, that nothing would come of it and Monday would be a laughing stock, but they battled on and won. Indeed their blazer badge bore one word – tenacity – each letter of which held its own special meaning: truthfulness, endeavour, nerve, accomplishment, character, inspiration, triumph and youth.

The Children's Church has now closed and the building is a Bible Study Centre. Times change and membership had been falling, but Monday was not upset, as she said at the time, 'It doesn't matter how people come to accept Jesus Christ, as long as they do accept him.' Monday died on 29 December 1989 at the age of 94.

The Sunday-School Outing

During his childhood, Leonard Portch took part in many Sunday-school outings to Weston from Bristol. The following is his account of one enjoyed in 1920:

Philip Street Baptist Church always organised an annual outing to Weston. We ran errands trying to earn a few pennies, which we saved for the great day. We kids went free and mothers had to pay a shilling. On the night before the outing we all had baths and went to bed early. The next morning we were up early, mother cutting sandwiches and all of us going mad with excitement. Most of the families in Mendip Road went on the outing, and the platform at Bedminster Railway Station would be packed with women and kids with buckets and spades. Every time a train came in sight, everybody jostled about, women picked up the smaller kids and there was panic and shouts of 'Here it comes!'. There were always lots of false alarms and I found it thrilling and exciting.

Eventually an empty train would arrive and we kept together in the scramble to get a compartment. They would pack in like sardines, with about 25–30 people in each compartment – there were never any corridor coaches on these trains. There were usually six mothers on each row of seats facing each other and the kids stood up, some on the floor and some standing on the seats behind the mothers.

We would arrive at Locking Road Station at Weston and make our way to the beach. I usually managed to scrape together about sixpence to spend and mother always saw to it that we had a donkey ride and an ice-cream cornet. We all had a 'tea ticket', which was free, and at teatime everyone made for the Salvation Army Hall where we had tea, bread and butter and cakes.

At dinner the mothers liked to go to The Britannia, a pub near Grove Park, and have a glass of beer or stout with their sandwiches. Us kids would have a lemonade. There were tables and forms in the pub yard for people to have grub with their drinks.

We would find our way to Locking Road Station about 8p.m. for the journey home, and for days afterwards it was the main talking point, and we often compared sunburns!

Members of the Sunnyside Road Methodist Church Choir on their annual outing, late 1920s.

Weston at War, 1939–45

When the Second World War broke out in 1939, people's lives were changed for ever. It was a dramatic and involuntary change and it is hardly surprising that this period is remembered with so much clarity. What I find astonishing is that it is also remembered with such a degree of affection. So much of what we take for granted today – personal freedom to travel, to choose employment, even what to eat – was restricted or dictated. As Ken Long, evacuated to Uphill, put it:

War heightens, exaggerates and distorts the emotions in a way no other experience can do, and it both elevates and degrades people; it brings out the very best and the very worst.

Looking back I am also amazed by the amount of organisation that went into the preparations for war. Planning had to cover everything from potential large-scale devastation and loss of life to how to feed the homeless, from clothing exchanges to coping with evacuees, from housing those made homeless to tracking down the residents in their temporary accommodation to deliver mail. Considering that, initially at least, much of it was done by volunteers in their spare time, one can't help but wonder how or even if it could be done today. Civil defence units are the prime example of this. They began in Weston in 1936 with efforts to establish the Air Raid Precaution Scheme. It was described later as 'a pioneer's' story of indifference, hard work, disappointment and achievement.'

Air Raid Precautions

In 1935 the Government began to plan for the

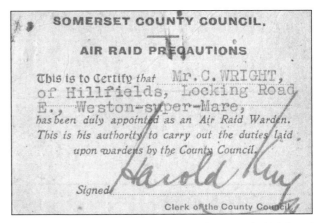

Cyril Wright's national identity card. Every person in the country was issued with a card on the outbreak of war.

ARP identity card for air-raid warden, Cyril Wright of Worle.

Air-raid wardens, Worle, March 1940. This picture was taken outside their warden's post at the Church of England School (now Hillside School), Worle. The picture includes Mr G. D. Waite (one of the masters at the school and head warden) with his wife beside him, A. Tripp, Mr Dunning, R. Durston, ?, Fry, ?, Muxworthy, Mr and Mrs May and Ted Edwards and his wife. Shortly after this picture was taken Mr Waite moved to Wrington and Mr C. Martin (standing with arms folded fourth from left) took over as head warden.

protection of civilians in case of war. A year later the first ARP (Air Raid Precaution) Committee was convened at Weston Town Hall. They decided to form subcommittees to cover the variety of tasks that would need to be done in the event of attack – warnings, medical aid, fire prevention, road repairs and so on. At this stage it was thought sufficient to train 75 air-raid wardens and 12 head wardens for Weston-super-Mare, plus two wardens for each village.

Public lectures were arranged. For example, Boots the Chemists organised a special demonstration of a gas-proof room at the Town Hall. One has to bear in mind that at this stage war had not yet broken out, and indeed might not have, and all preparations had to be financed at local level. Since war was not seen by everyone as an imminent threat, only just over 800 people volunteered for the civil defence throughout Somerset! As late as January 1939 only about one quarter of the required number of wardens had been trained, although equipment began to arrive, including 50 steel helmets, 100,000 sandbags and 50,000 civilian gasmasks, all of which had to be packed and distributed to the public.

When war was declared on 3 September 1939 an Area Organiser, based in a room in the Town Hall, was appointed to co-ordinate preparations. There was still public apathy to overcome but new lectures and

demonstrations inspired a new batch of volunteers.

By this time the civil defence was developing into a highly complex scheme. For training, a tactical table was designed and built, on which a miniature air raid on a housing estate was enacted, especially to train British and American Army units. The exercises were carried out with great realism, with diving aeroplanes, exploding bombs, rescue from debris by Fire Guards, shepherding of the homeless to rest and feeding centres, transport of the wounded, control of traffic, feeding of personnel, messenger work, temporary police stations, enquiry points and a post for 'incident control' with a microphone for the training commentary. By today's standards this all sounds very amateurish, with shades of Michael Bentine's famous exploding scenarios, but it did work and Weston's civil defence personnel received many commendations for their work, especially during the major attacks on the town.

In March 1940, Worle ARP wardens received the comment 'the best display yet seen in the district' at a combined civil-defence exercise. A period of active recruitment and intensive training by the head warden, Mr G. Waite (one of the masters at the Church of England School in Worle, the Hillside First School in 2004), led to this accolade being given. A warden's post was built at the school. Stan Terrell, whose father-in-law, Cyril Wright, was an air-raid warden at Worle, showed me a copy of 'The Warden's Song', sung at a concert to raise funds to furnish the post. It runs to five verses, the first being:

With their hats slung on their haversacks,
They tramp the draughty streets,
With their hats slung on their haversacks,
On their wardens' beats,
They walk for hours and hours and hours on
dark and dirty nights
They rave and curse at Adolf when they're
looking out for lights,
But when they get back to their post they've got
no home delights,
Just their hats slung on their haversacks.

The final verse ends:

So might I ask you people somewhat like we did before,
To give as much as last time or perhaps a little more,
'Cos every bit you give will foil those
Nazis by the score
With their tails tucked between their legs.

The commitment required of the volunteers was tremendous. For the duration of the war – almost six years – men and women finished their daytime work and started a nine-hour night duty with a further 15 hours 'on call' every third or fourth day. Some of these people were well over 70 years old. They also carried a heavy responsibility as it became clear that they would not only be charged with minimising the effects of enemy air attack on civilians but would also be required to co-ordinate military and civil services in the case of invasion. Even children helped. In his farewell message to the invasion committee, the Regional Commissioner gave particular thanks to the parents of the boy and girl messengers who had allowed their children to serve.

The air-raid wardens' service was tested to its limit in the major attacks on the town, particularly on 28 and 29 June 1942, when one head warden was killed, and others injured. In spite of the damage done to their own homes, the wardens continued to work during the raids and the aftermath. The wardens' posts gave a sense of security to the streets and became a centre to which people came for advice and help. So well trained were they that in 1944 local

Weston-super-Mare fire brigade, 1941. The Second World War saw the busiest years for the local fire service with two major blitzes and large numbers of incendiary bombs dropped on the town. Some of these men were part-time in the AFS and held down other jobs as well. Fifth from the left is Joe Sammells, a foreman sign-writer for the Borough Council.

wardens, by then veterans in raid experience, volunteered for duty in London during the flying-bomb attacks, which earned them all the admiration of their London colleagues.

Fire Services

The Second World War provided the busiest time for all fire brigades. On the outbreak of war, Weston's fire service was controlled by the Local Authority and consisted of a professional chief officer with part-time retained officers and firemen. For wartime these were supplemented by a full-time and part-time auxiliary fire service.

When the heavy raids began in 1941, it was considered sensible to amalgamate all the fire services bringing them under one command and so the National Fire Service was formed. This did not bring any great change to Weston-super-Mare beyond the standardisation of training and equipment.

The Fire Guard came into being on a voluntary basis in 1939, by members forming themselves into street parties to protect their own homes. The movement developed and grew until early 1941 when it became a national organisation and the first real test of their capabilities came. Showers of incendiary bombs and several high explosives were dropped on the town, causing deaths, injuries, and damage and destruction to buildings. The fire parties saved many properties from becoming total ruins. At the end of June 1942, the town was again attacked on two consecutive nights. The proven efficiency of the Fire Guard and the results of their operations during this event were such that they received not only the highest commendation from the Government but were also given national publicity.

First Aid

Dr Hugh Powell, St John's Ambulance Brigade Commissioner for Somerset, took charge of the Casualty First Aid Service. In 1940 a first-aid post was set up at the swimming pool. During an alert, a doctor, a nurse, and a staff officer were always on duty, and when the post went into action a second doctor was also present. On three occasions the post itself was damaged by enemy action. In the June raid of 1942 three of the nurses were injured. In all some 200 cases were treated at the post during raids and many who were rendered homeless in the vicinity were passed through.

A house at 105 Moorland Road was taken for use as a base for personnel, a first-aid post, stores, garage and maintenance. Miss L. Rossiter looked after the personnel, drove the ambulances, and opened up and took charge of the emergency first-aid post during raids when the mobile unit was called away. The latter consisted of a caravan, fitted with all the equipment of a casualty theatre in a hospital,

together with a large car for the transport of the doctor, nurse, and a team of Red Cross and St John's Ambulance personnel. This unit could be set up anywhere in a few minutes and it was much used during the raids.

Dr Dennis Clark won the MBE for his work during raids, particularly at the Prospect Place incident where, despite considerable risk to himself, he tended trapped casualties. The casualty service as a whole was awarded one MBE, two commendations for gallantry, seven Red Cross Distinguished War Service Certificates, and seven St John Ambulance Meritorious Service Certificates.

First-aid parties were formed mostly from volunteers from the St John's Ambulance Brigade and the Red Cross. There were eight parties of four manning the two Weston depots, plus drivers and messengers, with three more parties at Worle. Their pre-war training was soon supplemented by on-the-job experience and it was not long before the parties became skilled in the fastest and best way to treat people and get them to hospital as soon as possible.

In the early days of the war those on duty reported to their respective headquarters in Oxford Street and Orchard Street and on alert proceeded to the beach bus station. Subsequently first-aid party depots were opened at the Albert Memorial Hall in Union Street, Glentworth Hall on the sea front, and at Sunnyside, Worle. These were manned every night until the end of 1943, when a little relaxation was allowed.

The ambulance depot in Wadham Street was opened in January 1940. Mrs Wilmot of the Red Cross was in charge and had to overcome a great deal of prejudice as to the suitability of women drivers for this kind of work. At first the facilities in the depot were very poor. The ambulances were ancient canvas-topped vehicles, continually having to be towed home. The cars used to transport sitting-cases were owned by different drivers. To begin with the work consisted mostly of maintenance, delivering equipment, training new recruits, and taking part in exercises. After Dunkirk (1940), however, a large number of wounded and sick soldiers were brought to Weston-super-Mare and the depot provided transport for them, meeting trains and moving them to specialist hospitals. In the raid of January 1941, a bomb dropped next door to the depot. Numerous casualties were brought there for treatment. On the second night of the June raids in 1942, the depot was evacuated during the height of the bombing, and a temporary headquarters set up in a car on the sea front and later at Glentworth Hall, where they managed to give a full service for several days until it was possible to return to Wadham Street.

The second ambulance depot was in Oxford Street. This was mainly a personnel pool for all first-aid parties and reinforcements. Hospitals drew on the pool for extra help in an emergency and it provided relief parties every three hours in the early raids. This depot also suffered in the raids and in June 1942 had to be evacuated owing to serious fires raging all around it. All the furniture and equipment was placed in Emmanuel churchyard for safety until the next day.

Anti-Gas Preparations

After the experience of gas being used in the trenches of the First World War, the authorities had every reason to believe it would be used in any future conflict. Therefore preparations were made to deal with any potential civilian casualties. In August 1940, the first-aid post at the swimming pool established a gas-cleansing section to cope with walking victims. The Sanatorium, taken over as an emergency hospital, also had a cleansing section for stretcher cases, with a large lead bath with overhead showers. A similar set-up was later built at the Kewstoke Convalescent Home, also taken over as an emergency hospital. Various showers for cleansing were also sited at schools and public toilets throughout the town. At Knightstone Baths facilities were set up to deal with contaminated clothing. It was also thought that there should be some provision made for members of the public who might be gassed some distance from the cleansing stations – as such, a 'housewife cleansing service' was established. This involved 430 housewives who volunteered for special training. Mrs Battiscombe was in charge and used role-play to demonstrate the treatment required for various types of gas. Scenes were enacted which showed the possibilities of home treatment while amateur actors, clad in bathing costumes, submitted to being 'cleansed' at each performance!

It was not widely known but there was also a special train equipped for gas-cleansing which remained at Weston station throughout the war.

Rescue Parties

The main job of the rescue service was to free those trapped alive under collapsed buildings and debris and to recover the dead, as well as to take any

Rescue party at work in Weston after an air raid, 1941.

immediate action necessary for the temporary support or demolition of buildings.

At the beginning of the war there were just two rescue parties and two gas decontamination squads in the borough. As the war progressed, it was decided to teach the decontamination squads rescue work. So by 1940 there were 15 rescue parties, with depots at Rector's Way, Eastfield Gardens, and Church Road, Worle. Their job was physically exhausting and mentally harrowing; those who worked in this way for the five-and-a-half long years of the war must have been very special people.

The Police

It was realised even before the outbreak of war that the job of running an efficient service to deal with enemy attacks would be far too difficult for any one service to undertake alone and that the police would need additional support to handle all the duties which might occur. An urgent recruitment drive was started to enrol men as Police War Reserves, who could be called upon to perform the duties of constables. In addition, all retired policemen became members of the First Police Reserve. Reinforcing all of them was the Special Constabulary.

The Home Guard

These men have become well known today as 'Dad's Army'. The first battalion in the Weston area was formed in May 1940. The headquarters were in Salisbury Terrace and the men used the Drill Hall in Langford Road for training. Many men, such as Joe Thomas, volunteered locally. He has written an account of his experiences in Uphill Home Guard:

Being local born and still at school when war broke out in 1939, I wanted to enlist in the Local Defence Volunteers but at 14, I was too young. I waited a year and then went along to the enlisting officer. I told him I was 16, although in fact I was still only 15, but no more questions were asked, they fitted me out with a uniform, gave me a Lee-Enfield rifle and trained me for the local Home Guard as it was renamed.

Every Wednesday night, with five others, we performed guard duty in the Old Tower on Uphill Hill and what a spooky experience it was. More often than not we would be a man short so instead of doing two hours on and four hours off, we would do one-and-a-half hours' single duty, and at three o'clock in the morning on Uphill Hill, on your own, and at only 15 years of age, it was not funny. On a moonlit night with bats flying around, field mice crawling around your feet, the sea mists coming up over the hill and the old church with no roof and the churchyard full of tombstones just 100 yards away, it was no place for faint hearts.

Then suddenly the air-raid sirens would sound and the roar of German aircraft could be heard overhead.

Uphill Home Guard, pictured in Uphill Quarry.

Uphill Home Guard. Left to right, back row: *Rex Coward, Mr Wright, Mr Hort, Mr Brown, Mr Varder, Len Trowbridge, John Thoday, Mr Crawford, Stan Pickett;* middle row: *Mr Pearce, Fred Gamalin, Mr Gamalin, Mr Davidson, Mr Jay, Mr Paulk, Mr Rubins, Mr Milton, Mr Matthews;* front row: *Mr Stonelake, Mr McDonald, Mr Walters, Mr Parsons, David Minifie, ?. Rex Coward was the postmaster at Uphill. Mr Davidson was killed when a bomb was dropped in Malvern Road. Mr Jay ran the mineral-water factory in Jubilee Road. Mr Paulk was a butcher and David Minifie a plumber.*

The searchlight on Uphill Hill would be switched on and this would illuminate the whole area. Then the battery of anti-aircraft guns on Uphill Golf Course would crack into action. As the enemy aircraft flew up the Bristol Channel, all along the Welsh coast the searchlights and guns would open up; what a wonderful sight never to be forgotten. It was the biggest firework display I have ever seen. This would go on for hours until dawn, then it would be time to pack up, descend the hill, have a quick breakfast and then off to work.

I remember Jim Upham, Len Trowbridge, Rex Coward who ran the Post Office, and David Minifie who was the local plumber, but the character of them all was Sergeant Paulk, the local butcher. It was in his house in Uphill Way that we met for briefings before we climbed the hill. The stories he told us about ghosts and happenings in the church were scary. The Home Guard training stood me in good stead when I was called up for the Army at 19 years of age.

Bert Mullen recalled the Uphill Home Guard when he was posted to Weston in 1940 and again in 1941. He was a member of a searchlight unit. The Army huts were at the foot of a cliff near the harbour, and his unit was operating a searchlight on top of the hill on the far side of the Old Church of St Nicholas. German air raids had started and the searchlight beam picked up enemy bombers flying in from the south to hit targets in Bristol, Wales and the Midlands. There was plenty of action and through it all was the possibility of being machine-gunned by enemy aircraft, who had a nicely illuminated target at which to aim – the searchlight beam and its operators. During one bombing raid in the area, dummy fires were started in open countryside to the south in the hope that it would attract the enemy bombs. The searchlight-post men often fraternised with the local Home Guard and visited their headquarters, which was the old windmill near the church. On a cold winter's night they would have a chat and a whisky, and sometimes after the all-clear they went for a quick pint in The Ship Inn at the foot of the hill.

Many local companies, such as the Post Office and the Weston Gas Company, formed their own Home Guard units.

The Women's Voluntary Service

The Women's Voluntary Service was formed as a result of the threat of war. In Weston the organisation was established in April 1939. An office at 29 Oxford Street was taken as headquarters, but it was later moved to 24 Beach Road. It was the first such centre in Somerset.

Women were enrolled for many different types of civil defence and other voluntary war work. For example, 16 women joined the Home Guard, to cook for the men in the event of emergency and rotas of WVS members manned the Parish Church belfry

daily from 9a.m. until dusk in case the bells needed to be rung in the event of an invasion. A mobile canteen was given to the local WVS by the American Red Cross in April 1941, and did splendid service after the raids, working day and night feeding workers and bombed-out people. The Queen's Messenger Food Convoy based in Weston was the only one in the country to be driven as well as staffed by WVS members. This saw active service in Plymouth, Bristol, Bath and Weston-super-Mare, as well as in London during the flying-bomb attacks. The WVS Housewives' Section was started in Weston in June 1940, to help the wardens' service in the event of emergency. They kept up-to-date lists of residents, with their next of kin, etc., which were supplied to the rescue parties after any raids; these were a means of saving lives as well as finding the bodies of people who otherwise may not have been known to be in the area. Housewives took in homeless people, gave immediate aid, looked after children, old people and invalids, cleared up debris, cleaned homes, shopped and cooked for bombed neighbours, traced missing people – the list was endless.

The War and Weston

After all these preparations, all anyone could do was await developments and cope as best they could. This waiting period is often referred to as the 'Phoney War' and lasted until November 1939. After that, the war began in earnest.

Despite everything, most people believed that Weston would be relatively safe, so much so in fact that in September 1939 over 10,000 children and expectant mothers were evacuated here from the East End of London. Ken Long was one of those children:

On Friday 1 September 1939, myself and many hundreds of children were assembled at Napier Road School in East Ham and marched along the High Street which was lined with hundreds of sobbing and worried mothers. We were going to the station to be evacuated somewhere away from London, but no one – not even the parents – knew where! I had my gas mask, a label pinned to my jacket with school name and address and a carrier bag (not a suitcase) holding my pyjamas, a change of underclothes and some sandwiches. A few children brought nothing with them. I was ten-and-a-half years old and without a brother or sister for comfort and support. The eldest child was about 14 and the youngest only five – some young ones were unaccompanied too! Babies and pregnant mothers were mixed in with us on the non-corridor train.

The evacuation was the greatest single movement of population in Britain, a decision taken only the day before, in which ultimately 3,500,000 children would be taken away from their homes to avoid the inevitable bombing and gas raids we had been told would come on the very first day. It was an astonishing feat of

A Tramps' Party for the 'New Neighbours' evacuees at their hall in West Street, which in 2004 is the Oxfam charity shop. The bottle on the table holding the candle, was from Holt Bros, a Burnham-on-Sea brewery.

organisation but certainly not perfect.

Our train from Paddington went to Bristol, then to Weston-super-Mare and we ended up in a little village called Uphill. There we were taken to a large school playing-field, lined up and prodded, checked for head lice and scrutinised by the potential foster parents before selection and allocation to our new billets. The best and cleanest children were chosen first! It was like being auctioned off. Some children didn't understand – they thought they'd been sent away because they'd been naughty!

We, myself and another boy, were first placed with Mr and Mrs Wreford of 'Windyridge', Bleadon Hill. It was a lovely house in a remote village. There were lots of fruit trees, lawns and chickens. It was very much a middle-class home and beautifully furnished – it also had a real telephone! Later that afternoon the authorities realised the nearest school was miles away and it was necessary to re-billet us a couple of miles closer in Uphill. We were collected in the back of a very bloody butcher's van to be taken to our new foster parents.

I was very fortunate to be billeted together with another boy, on a family-run poultry farm. We were in the countryside only 200 yards from a sandy beach and we had a black Labrador dog called Carlo. For two boys from smoky grey London it was just heaven! As it was September, the blackberries were ready for picking and cider apples ready for crushing, all totally new experiences for us. The owners were a childless couple – Mr and Mrs Howe – who treated us wonderfully but it was a slightly different world. We found at mealtimes there were things called serviettes in rings on the table, cutlery was arranged in a special order, we said Grace before every meal and had baths every week! We also had to go to church three times on Sundays!

Ken also remembered the sight most mornings, of mattresses hanging out of the bedroom windows

of the cottages in Uphill Way. They were from the beds of evacuees who were emotionally disturbed by being uprooted from their families and consequently were wetting the bed. Many of them were very young.

Just over half the evacuees were billeted in Weston itself with the remainder going out to villages throughout Somerset. Dave Tyler was another one of the first to be evacuated to Weston from East Ham. He and his mother were initially billeted at 42 Alfred Street.

In 1942 my father got fed up with being on his own and came to Weston and bought a house in Milton Road. He got a job with the Bristol Aeroplane Company at Filton, Bristol. The evacuees had a hall in West Street (now the Oxfam charity shop), calling themselves The New Neighbours. The mothers knitted socks, gloves and scarves for the Forces and the children did things like rolling bandages.

Not every billet proved to be as good as those described above. By Easter the first school Ken Long attended had grown so overcrowded that he and some other children were moved to a different school and so he moved homes to be closer. At his new billet he remembered being beaten by his foster parents' own son and he still cannot bear the smell of faggots, a 'delicacy' often cooked by his Welsh foster mother:

Our new school was just awful, we no longer had our old Napier Road teachers from London, but older local men who appeared to resent us being there. They used any excuse of minor indiscipline to exact heavy physical punishment on a pupil. It was cruel and insensitive and they ignored the plight of the very young evacuees who were away from home for the first time, who had not seen their parents for over six or seven months and were sometimes living with people who only wanted the monetary allowance and gave no real care or affection to their charges! I remember in class I once whispered something to my classmate and was immediately called out to receive six severe strokes with a cane across my palms. The pain was terrible and lasted for the rest of the day.

Unfortunately, after all of this upheaval, Weston did not in fact prove to the be safe haven the evacuees were seeking and a large number were killed in the first major blitz on the town in 1941. Indeed, Dave Tyler recalls:

In 1942 an incendiary bomb came through the roof of our house. Luckily we had an ARP warden living opposite, who doused the flames with sand. Apart from some burning and a hole in the roof there was little damage.

Another company who thought Weston would be safe was the BBC. Based as they were in central London, it was thought best if radio broadcasts were dispersed around the country, and so the Winter Gardens and the schoolroom of the Boulevard Congregational Church were turned into two venues for radio broadcasts. They stayed until the bombing in the town began, after which they moved to North Wales, well away from target cities!

In the spring of 1940 Jean Tolson, wife of the head-master of St Peter's School, remembered the 6th Battalion Somerset Light Infantry were posted to Weston and the Colonel asked permission for his men to train on the cricket field.

They came at 6a.m. each morning to do PT and they jogged in so noiselessly that we never heard them come. They also borrowed our field for their Sports Gala and as a thank-you gesture they presented the school with a silver trophy. Suddenly, a few weeks later in May 1940, the regiment disappeared and I am sorry to say that many of their officers and men were killed in the retreat at Dunkirk.

Cherbourg also fell at about this time and people suddenly felt very vulnerable living on the English coasts. All the open spaces and sands were guarded or spiked with anti-landing defences. In May 1940, Jean Tolson recalled:

We woke up to find guns and gun crews in position on the cricket field. It was a very hot day and, feeling sorry for the soldiers guarding their guns, I walked down the field with an offer of cups of tea. To my astonishment, they appeared like dummy soldiers at Madame Tussaud's and would neither look at me nor speak to me. They had obviously been briefed to have nothing to do with strangers. After a day or two, they vacated our field as the imminent threat of invasion passed.

On 14 August 1940 the first bombs fell on Weston, exploding on the sands. Six days later Worle was hit for the first time. From this point on there were regular incidents, some causing casualties and deaths. When a stick of bombs fell in Albert Quadrant, demol-ishing and damaging many houses and causing casualties, the demolition squads, rescue parties, highway, sewer, gas, water and electrical repair parties were put into operation for the first time.

The following month bombs were dropped in the sea off Knightstone Causeway and at Greenwood Road, Worle, where they caused injury and damage. Ruth Coles recalled that her aunt and uncle had a market garden in Upper Milton and lost the tiles off their roof and all their chickens were killed. Unexploded bombs were being discovered almost daily, putting great pressure on the bomb-disposal squads. By now the Battle of Britain was at its peak and people's nerves were on edge.

On 14 October a stick of 12 bombs was dropped across Weston-super-Mare from the eastern to the northern boundary. A house in Leewood Road was damaged, amongst others, as well as the reservoir in Ashcombe Park. The unusual boating lake shaped like the Bristol Channel was lost that night although the bombs missed the main pumping plant of the waterworks by a few yards.

Pupils and staff of Kingsholme School, Arundell Road, 1941. Most children contributed something towards the war effort, from fruit picking and knitting to acting as messengers or rolling bandages.

The following night the first attempt was made to bomb a train – the railway loop line was targeted. It was unsuccessful. Although December saw the first clear day for several months, a British 'plane crashed into sea south of Brean Down and all the crew drowned. Langford Road was the next place to be hit, with casualties and damage and by the end of 1940 the sirens had sounded 387 times.

Meanwhile, residents got on with daily life, although coping with rationing and new restrictions made everything harder. 'Dig for Victory' led to people digging up their gardens and verges and growing as much of their own food as they could. In October 1941 all the schools across the area were closed to enable the older pupils to help in the fields lifting potatoes. In addition there was a general call to make the most of what wild fruit may be about, and many pupils spent afternoons gathering blackberries and rosehips. At the County School, girls were busy knitting for the RAF and Navy Comforts Committees, making over 200 garments during the war. Part of their playing-field was dug up and potatoes and other vegetables planted, the produce being sold to pupils and friends at reduced rates and the profit used to buy more wool. Some of the sixth formers worked at making camouflage nets, while others volunteered for civil-defence duties or work on the land. The school magazine, reduced to one a year to save paper, printed special wartime recipes amongst the poems about gas masks and blackouts. One rather unappetising method to make butter go further suggested beating it with cold custard and a pinch of salt! In about 1942 Mr Broom's local grocery shop had a consignment of peaches and Mr Broom remembers his mother bought one for him, at 3s.6d. Stan Terrell brought up a more unsavoury aspect of wartime life:

Another side to the war years was the black market. I was not very old but I knew that while some clothes were rationed the coupons which you were allotted had a price on them and it was no secret a clothing coupon was worth 2s.6d., maybe even more to the right person. Although this was illegal it did happen.

Wadham Street after the blitz, January 1941. This photograph was taken from the site of the manse that was destroyed that night.

The First Blitz

At 6.30p.m. on 4 January 1941 the first major concentrated attack on Weston began. Wardens had been warned to expect a heavy raid on Bristol, and AFS pumps were sent there as reinforcements. Two bombs fell in the sea near Brean Down and 35 minutes later a heavy attack began at Sand Bay, came over the hill, and ran parallel with the beach. A bomb caused damage to a nursing home which was quickly evacuated. Directly afterwards, a large bomb and incendiaries fell near the entrance of Grove Park and Glebe House, causing a number of casualties and demolishing the manse to Wadham Street Baptist church, a concert hall, shops and houses, and the beautiful east window of the Parish Church. Mrs Gwen Jones lived in the manse at that time:

My husband, Arthur Jones was the caretaker of the Wadham Street Baptist Church and we lived in Church House, next to the church, with our children, Derek aged six and Ruth aged three. My husband brought down a bed and put it in the sitting-room and when the bombing was bad I would sleep in it with the children. Underneath was a cellar, which my husband had strengthened. The night of a bad raid my husband went to turn off the electricity in the church in case of fire. I began to sing with the children to comfort them. As Arthur came out a bomb fell on Grove Park. He was protected by the doorway and only hurt his back. Some soldiers were passing and heard my singing and scrambled in to rescue us. One of them had a car nearby and took us all to my mother in Sandford Road. As we arrived my mother said that she had been trying to get to our house as the noise was so bad she thought it would be safer there! We lived with my mother for a while until we were able to rent a house in Charter Road.

A serious incident occurred at Rector's Way, when a terrace of houses was damaged by a direct hit. Hundreds of pounds in cash and many articles of value were found here by the rescue parties. This led to emergency police enquiry points being set up at future such incidents, in order to take charge of any valuables. Roy Brunker recalls:

I was eight years old and living with my parents in St Omer, a house in Rector's Way. I was sleeping downstairs in a room which was situated nearest to the place where the bomb fell. I was awakened by a rumbling noise and, on being lifted out of my bed by my father, asked what the noise was. He told me it was the sound of bricks falling because of a bomb blast over the road. I was taken and put under the table in the living-room with the rest of the family. As dawn came, I looked across from a bedroom window and could see smoke rising from the rubble and the ARP and AFS personnel in attendance.

A stick of bombs had fallen in the back gardens of the

Weston during the blitz of 1942.

12 terraced houses on the opposite side of the road to St Omer. Of the 12 houses in the terrace, at least seven of them were completely flattened, and the remainder were severely damaged and unoccupied for some time and were eventually demolished. A group of 17 people, who had been to a dance at the Winter Gardens Pavilion and had gone back to one of the houses, were all killed. Also killed was a little girl who I used to play with. There was an RAF Barrage Balloon detachment in the gasworks field, adjacent to the bomb site and personnel from it helped to rescue casualties. The Mason family lived in one house – husband, wife and their only child, a daughter – all three were killed. In this house an RAF man found 'articles of value', amounting to large amounts of cash and rationed food (butter, sugar, etc.), hidden under floorboards and inside of the settee, etc. It was said that the RAF man wanted to keep some of the cash but someone told the police what had been found. The rescue party depot was the Council Yard, next door to St Omer. I often had long chats with Mr Griffin, the night-watchman, when he sat on his 'box' at the gates of the depot on summer evenings. The bomb site and crater became a playground for the local children.

Daphne Stock also remembers the Rector's Way bombs. In 1940, at the age of three, she was evacuated to Weston with her mother. She stayed with Mr and Mrs Andrews in Drove Road:

I was three when my mother used to lift me up from my bed during a night raid and run downstairs to our indoor shelter. I was seven by the time the war ended. Before we had our Andersen shelter, the local communal one was the shelter at the gasworks. I remember being pushed in my green pram down Drove Road. There was a Mrs Cattle whom everyone knew and kept everyone's morale up. I remember lots of singing – 'Roll out the Barrel' and 'Run Rabbit Run'. I went to a kindergarten and we had to take our own milk, which had to be boiled. One weekend when a raid was on, it was one of the worst. We had a board up at the window. A terrible bang went off nearby followed

by another and the board fell from the window. My friend's father was an ARP man. When the all-clear was sounded, Mum told him to look across to Rector's Way where all the houses were down. She asked him to go and see if her friend, Mrs Beagleston, was alright. Coming back he said she had been killed. Our house was the only one left standing.

St Paul's Church together with its Parish Hall in Whitecross Road, and many houses and shops in the vicinity were all destroyed by fire that night. Reinforcements poured in from Taunton, Minehead, Shepton Mallet, Wells and other areas in Somerset. Mrs Woodward also recalled the incident:

I remember that night when St Paul's Church, its Parish Hall and other buildings were destroyed. My father was fire-watching at Knightstone Baths and how relieved we were when he arrived home in the morning. We had been putting out incendiary bombs falling in the road [dowsing them with sand to stop them setting fire to anything]. There was a canteen for the Forces in the Town Hall. I used to help out with the cups of tea some evenings. Harry Lye arranged concert parties to go to the different [military] camp sites around Weston. I was one of the dancers and most weeks we went out to camps at Wolvershill, Banwell Abbey, Brean Down, Langford, Lulsgate Bottom and even once to Steep Holm.

Ample reinforcements were sent to assist the fire brigade and the AFS, including parties from Exeter. Fortunately many residents had, at their own expense, organised street fire parties, equipped with stirrup pumps, ladders and first-aid kits and many businesses were protected by night-watchmen. These unofficial fire guards were responsible for saving the town from further damage.

There were 72 incidents reported during the raid and yet more bombs were dropped on the sands where they did little damage. Five high-explosive bombs and approximately 3,000 incendiaries fell in the borough; 34 people were killed and 85 injured.

It is interesting that the largest incident from a casualty point of view, occurred at Grove Park, almost on the doorstep of the ambulance depot in Wadham Street, so that casualties obtained treatment immediately. The largest incident from the rescue point of view, was in Rector's Way opposite the rescue party depot. This meant that no time was lost in getting people from the debris. The attack ended at 7a.m. the following morning.

Air raids were frightening for most people, but for some children, not old enough to realise the danger perhaps, they provided a great adventure. Stan Terrell recalls:

Night-time raids meant being woken up by my parents and going to our neighbours' garden, where they had a

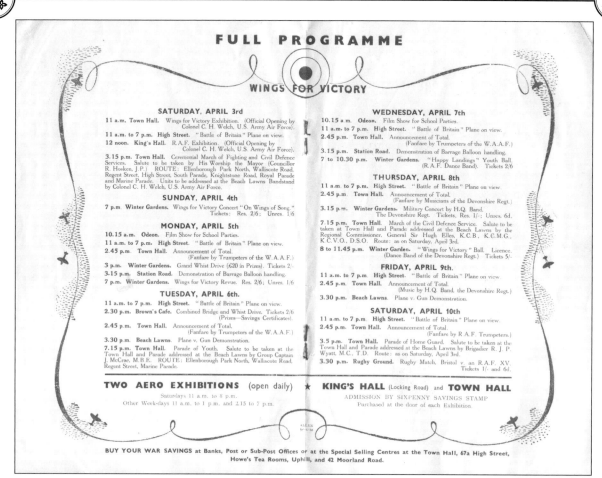

Programme of events at the Wings for Victory Week, 1943.

General view of Weston looking north to the hillside, 1950s. On the right is the sign for the bus station café, in which Eve Mills wrote her married name for the first time, in her new cookery book in 1942.

deep concrete shelter. Looking up into the sky it was easy to see the German aircraft. They were quite low and the sky was lit up with the flares dropped by the aircraft. Before going to the shelter, my parents would have placed a tin chest containing family documents under a wall for safety. On one raid I remember Milton Methodist Church receiving a direct hit by a high-explosive bomb – the noise was frightening.

After an air raid boys, myself included, would try to find shrapnel – pieces of the bomb after it explodes. It was a stupid thing to do and I well remember my mother giving me a good telling off! Going to school after one raid I saw many incendiary bombs (these were live) in the gutter of Grove Road, Milton. Presumably they had been put there by the wardens for collection when convenient and no, I didn't touch them!

Sunday afternoons when the weather was fine, a real treat would have been to see our aircraft practise firing at a white target on the end of Sand Point. We made our way to the top of Monks Steps and got an excellent view. When the firing stopped, some of the older boys would go to the shores of Sand Bay, take off their socks and shoes and walk out into the mud to try to retrieve the shell cases. These were then put in a sack and sold as scrap metal. This was all part of a way of life to put money into the boys' pockets. It was also good for the war effort.

The war effort took many forms, from not wasting food to saving paper and metal for recycling. Stan Terrell remembered one fund-raising drive:

Having lost Marks & Spencer, it gave the town a very large open space to feature a spitfire (at least, that's what I believe it was) as part of a campaign called Wings for Victory Week. Entrance to the site was sixpence and in return for your money you were given a Savings Stamp. The programme of events for this special week included military band concerts at the Winter Gardens and a demonstration of barrage-balloon handling at Station Road! The week ended with a parade of the Home Guard, with a salute taken at the Town Hall. Outside the Town Hall was what looked like a giant thermometer. This recorded how much money had been saved locally for the war effort.

The next few months were relatively quiet although unexploded bombs continued to be found, disrupting traffic. There were also several power cuts, one due to the barrage balloon at Devil's Bridge breaking away and fouling electricity cables. On another occasion a barrage balloon was struck by lightning and caused damage to The Borough Arms Hotel. During this period Eve Mills got married. Her husband was serving in the 1st Battalion of the Suffolk Regiment which was stationed at that time in Cheddar having gone there after the evacuation of Dunkirk. During their brief honeymoon they spent one afternoon in Weston and, after a stroll along the front, they went

into town where her husband bought her a cookery book in WH Smiths. She recalled that it was a thick, hardback book, but rather expensive. They made their way to the bus station and decided to have tea in the upstairs restaurant before catching a bus back to Cheddar. There they sat at a table by the window looking out over the Beach Lawns and, as they waited for the waitress to bring tea, Eve took her cookery book and wrote her name on the fly leaf. It was the first time she had written her married name. Mrs Mills eventually enlisted in the ATS and her husband was sent to North Africa. It was 1949 before they got a home of their own and the cookery book was put to use. She still has it and always calls it her Bristol Tramways cookery book!

Bert Mullen recollected the time when some bombs fell during a raid on Uphill harbour. The traitor, Lord Haw-Haw, broadcast that Weston-super-Mare harbour had been bombed and damaged, but like the majority of his broadcasts, this was not correct and little damage was apparent at Uphill. Later on in 1941 Bert was stationed at Weston Golf Course. The Army took over the main part of the course to site an anti-aircraft unit – four 3.7ins ack-ack guns plus a new weapon which everyone hoped would shorten the war – radar. Bert was by then a radar operator, whose task was to transmit the range, bearing and height of incoming German aircraft to the gunners. Their huts were amongst the trees and bushes near the main road. Close by were the sand dunes – a popular spot for courting couples and a good place to take visiting wives and girlfriends. He remembered that the locals were extremely kind and friendly to servicemen. He said it was fortunate he and his mates didn't have to compete with the Americans for the affections of local girls; he was posted to the Far East before the GIs arrived!

On 28 December 1941 great excitement was caused when a British heavy bomber crashed in a field behind the electricity works, in Locking Road. Although the plane was burnt out there were no casualties and the incident provided good souvenir-hunting opportunities for children!

The Second Blitz

The rest of the winter was quiet and it was not until May that a full alert came. The night coincided with a full moon and people were nervous of reprisals following the 1,000-bomb attack on Cologne in Germany. However, Weston remained quiet and there were no further warnings until the night of 28 June. This blitz was one of the heaviest on the town. One reason was that it was midsummer and Weston was full of munitions workers on holiday. As Louisa James put it at the time in a letter to her son 'Weston has been packed with visitors, the 'No Travel' order not having had much effect.' The raids consisted of mainly incendiary bombs with a liberal scattering of high-explosive bombs, delivered from a low level and highly concentrated in time. The raid began in fine weather with a full moon. Bombers were over the town and the first bombs dropped before the siren sounded at about 1.30a.m. Louisa James, who was wife of the minister of the Victoria Methodist Church, wrote at the time from her home at Annesley House, 21 Southside:

... we were awakened by planes hovering very low, all sounding rather ominous and Teutonic. But as there was no alert we did not worry. Then in a few minutes the siren went and at once flares and bombs were dropped... In less than two minutes, walls, windows and ceilings just crashed in. A bomb had dropped in the garden right opposite... We really thought as it crashed it meant the end, but as already said we were saved, not even a scratch.

Although there were reports of incidents from all parts of the town, the main concentration was in the residential and shopping centre. Ironically, there was a US anti-aircraft battery on Weston Golf Course, but the guns were not allowed to be fired as it was believed the Germans did not know they were there! This was a chance for the reorganised fire services to show their skills, helped by the RAF and stirrup pump parties of fire-watchers. It was following their efforts during this raid that a nationwide Fire Guard plan developed.

One incident involving an incendiary was a fire in the roof of a house in The Shrubbery. Jean Tolson recounted:

Two old ladies lived there alone. They were unaware their house was on fire and did not hear the shouting and banging on their door. Eventually they did hear and opened the door to some soldiers who were billeted quite near, but they refused to leave unless an antique wardrobe was brought into the garden. To humour them the soldiers tried to get it down the stairs but it stuck on the bend and had to be abandoned. Meanwhile we tried to get the fire hose fixed onto a nearby hydrant but the water pressure was so low, owing to the fire engines fighting the many fires in the town, that only a trickle came through. We formed a long line from the hydrant to the house and passed buckets of water along from hand to hand... Eventually we did manage to prevent the fire getting a hold and only the roof and top floor were damaged. Meanwhile the old ladies were being looked after in our cook's cottage. They were, of course, frightened and shocked but, at the same time, wonderfully cheerful.

I find it hard to comprehend the level of dedication of so-called ordinary people during this time. For example, the telephone system never ceased to function, even though operators were working at the top of a high building in the heart of the affected area. In fact, all public services continued despite damage to gas, water, electricity and sewerage systems. Many volunteers in rescue, first aid and casualty-clearing worked the full 48 hours of the raid without rest. Even children worked as messengers and made many journeys through fires and over bomb craters and debris. Part of the letter written by Louisa James recounts the horror of the attack:

Undoubtedly we were saved by the narrow cellar steps. The side wood panelling fell over us... forming a cover. Daddy and Margaret [Louisa's 20-year-old daughter] got more force of it... however we crawled up, thankful we could do so, and went into the kitchen. With the moonlight and blazing fires making a glow we found the kitchen window blown out, also the shutters which were closed... Things on the floor blown off the shelves and awful chaos and confusion. Bombs were falling, whistling ones, others roaring so low and machine-gunning and firing. We just knelt under the table, our arms round each other and could only pray having been spared once, we might be again. For over 40 minutes it was awful, just too dreadful to describe... Presently it became quieter and we hoped they had gone... and they had. We ventured outside round to the front and what a sight met our eyes, fires blazing, lighting up the whole town. The houses opposite too awful for words. One, the Dickens', gone except for one side sticking up like a tower. The road was full of ARP men digging with torches for the Dickens family in the debris.

It was midday on the 29 June before all fires were damped down although a sea mist had drifted across the town by the time the German spotting plane arrived, which led to the German radio report that smoke was still rising from uncontrolled fires. In addition, a large bomb crater and an unexploded bomb at the railway station, combined with the possibility of large numbers of sightseers arriving, led to the station being closed for a time. These two incidents were used by the Germans to report that the town was so badly damaged that no one was allowed to see it.

Many of the town's most well-known and loved buildings were lost, notably Lance & Lance's department store on the corner of Waterloo Street and High Street. Only the solitary lift shaft was left standing. Other losses included Marks & Spencer and the Tivoli Cinema.

Barbara Adams remembered this raid well:

On Sunday afternoons, I and my friends would listen to the band which then still played in the bandstand in Grove Park, or sometimes watch the Boys' Brigade Band march through Waterloo Street. This was before the bombing raids which destroyed Lance & Lance and also the Marks & Spencer store in High Street. They then moved to a new position in Meadow Street. I was one

Blitzed houses in Moorland Road, 1942.

of the new sales girls employed by them to help prepare these premises for the opening, which entailed scrubbing the old floor boards, etc., before the new fittings could be put in. But it was great fun.

During those bombing raids, my mother and I would shelter with other residents in the basement of the building where we had a flat (Queens Road), while my father did fire-watching in the area. He often arrived home with his trouser legs cut from flying debris. We also had our large lounge window blown out in the blast. Luckily the room was protected by the heavy black-out curtain, which was my job to hook up every evening.

I remember my aunt, worried for our safety, coming down from Bristol by bus but not being able to get any further than St Georges, as the buses were being stopped there, and she having to walk the rest of the way into Weston.

The most difficult incident of the first night was at the corner of Moorland Road and Devonshire Road where three separate sticks of large high-explosive bombs landed. Mrs P.A. Willis recalled that night. She was living near the Moorland laundry. When the bombs exploded she was knocked backwards and buried in debris with her baby, Maureen, in her arms. After the all-clear sounded she heard the wardens searching and shouted for help until they found her. She was taken to hospital with a fractured spine and pelvis. Sadly, her baby had been killed. Her husband was fighting in the Far East at the time and never saw his daughter. To add to her distress, whilst in the hospital, more bombs fell the following night hitting the Tivoli Cinema in the Boulevard and shattering the windows of the hospital ward. It is at this point

one should also mention the courage of the young nurses who sat with patients too ill or injured to be moved during the raids.

The bomb-disposal squads were kept busy. Unexploded bombs littered the streets, including one on the sea front and one, which lay in the heart of a narrow shopping centre, that had not only failed to explode, but burst its casing scattering explosive content across the street. It was six months before children playing in Weston Woods found an unexploded 500kg bomb which had been lying at the top of the Town Quarry.

The bombers returned the next night although on this occasion the sirens gave a 30 minute warning before the attack. The largest incident was caused by a group of bombs which fell close together in the Orchard Street area. Houses here contained newly arrived visitors so the correct number of trapped casualties was unknown. The most trying of all problems arising from these weekend raids in the holiday season was the difficulty in finding out the number of people in any house, as the occupiers often had not had time to pass this information to the WVS or the wardens.

It also seemed the enemy was trying very hard to destroy the transport system among other targets. There were groups of bomb craters around five of the six road bridges over the railway. They were deliberately attacked from a very low level, yet not one of them was hit or damaged. Roy Brunker recalls:

I also remember the June raids in 1942, and how the Luftwaffe had tried without success to bomb the railway line, missing it either side in about half a dozen places. One bomb landed between Drove Road bridge and

Weston East signal-box, damaging it. Two other bombs failed to explode and had to be dug out in 1947 with the help of German POWs. My mate and I used to watch them during the school holidays.

Some of the aircraft flew low along some streets, including the Boulevard, machine-gunning anyone unlucky enough to be out in the open.

Another casualty of this night's raid was the Girls' Grammar School, hit by incendiaries. Whilst no one was hurt, the attack nevertheless disrupted the lives of hundreds of children. Rosemary Hodges remembers the incident:

When we arrived on the usual bus on Monday morning the scene was devastating. Although the bus driver and conductor had told us we no longer had a school, nothing had prepared us for the still-smoking ruins and the unforgettable smell of burnt books, chemicals, furniture and gym shoes. We were sent home while the complicated arrangements were put in hand for Barking Abbey and Mitcham Schools, which had been evacuated to us, to leave. Within a few days the staff of both the boys' and girls' schools had organised the sharing of the remaining premises between nearly 800 children. Then began the long years of cramped existence, taking lessons in odd corners, art room, even museum.

Mr Broom was 13 years old and remembers fire-watching in Locking Road that night, complete with tin hat, gas mask, stirrup pump and sandbags.

After the raid fire hoses were seen across the promenade.

It was high tide and all the fire service had to do was run the hoses over the wall into the sea. There was no shortage of water!

Over the two nights of raids, a final tally revealed that approximately 97 high-explosive bombs and 10,000 incendiaries fell, two-thirds of these on the second night. A total of 102 people were killed and 400 people injured. As Louisa James wrote to her son 'I think the German Command is not exaggerating when they say it was one of the heaviest raids. For the size of the town it is.' Her daughter Margaret also wrote to her brother:

Sunday night's raid was even worse and shook our wreck of a house even more. Weston seemed all on fire on Sunday night. The town is a ghastly spectacle – the Germans have said that, for its scale, it has done more damage than any other of their raids, and I can well believe it. All through the town there are relics of burnt out houses... five churches gone, several others damaged. Lances and other big shops along High Street gone, Meadow Street is awful, Orchard Street is an awful sight – an HE bomb did a lot of damage to houses there and it is still roped off; I think there were a lot of casualties there. Out the other end of the town... there is equally bad damage... The railway is damaged... while the goods shed at the station is destroyed.

The Duke of Kent's Visit

As Weston-super-Mare began to pick itself up, news came that the Duke of Kent wanted to pay his

Squad of RAF airmen parading on the sea front at Weston after their six weeks' initial training, 1941.

personal tribute to the people and volunteers for the way in which they had saved their town.

The Duke arrived driving himself in the royal car. He was friendly and eager for information. He expressed concern when he learned of the damage in the residential areas and of all the people now homeless. He was even more impressed when he began his tour. As he saw what Weston had suffered he was moved to remark to the Mayor, Alderman R. Hosken 'Your people are magnificent'. He was so affected that he completely abandoned his official programme and formality vanished as he walked among the people with children clutching at his arms and trouser legs. Among other places, he visited the Bournville estate (Weston's 'Bomb Alley') and Orchard Street, where loss of life during the raid had been heaviest. It was not until the evening, three hours later than planned, that he left Weston, 'holding the wheel with his left hand while he acknowledged their resounding cheers with the other.'

Life then returned to relative quiet with occasional air-raid warnings. In fact there was only one more major incident in Weston during the war.

D-Day

Small numbers of troops had been stationed here for training or defence for some years. Mr Venn remembers the sight of squads of RAF recruits being instructed in the delights of foot-drill on the promenade. There was always an interested gathering of civilians to view the events although they often found the language and attitude of the NCO instructors offensive and even upsetting. Mrs Edwards' late

American GI Lee Mullins with the family with whom he was billeted at 115 Severn Road, 1943.

husband was one of these airmen. She said that he was called up to report to Penarth to be kitted out and then transferred to Weston for the first six weeks of training. Then they got their first leave – one weekend. After that they were split up for specialist training. Leslie Danks was one of three Vickers Aircraft Co. engineers sent to Locking Camp in November 1939 to repair a Wellington bomber that had made a forced landing there. He remembers 3,000 troops had just been billeted in the town, mostly in hotels, but also anywhere else available – 36 soldiers bedded down in the skittle alley of The Borough Arms! Because of this lack of accommodation Leslie had to stay in a caravan at the back of Hill View Farm Hotel in Locking Road for the five weeks it took to repair the aircraft.

In late 1943 even larger numbers arrived in Weston as part of the preparations for D-Day. Many of these were Americans. Barbara Adams remembers them well:

When the American GIs arrived in Weston, things began to change. There was a new aliveness in the town, and the Winter Gardens became much more crowded, as well as noisier. The jive and the jitterbug made the whole place 'jump' as we used to say. It was very exciting, and we all had a wonderful time. We tried to put out of our thoughts what was to come for these young men, who all seemed to be so cheerful.

The first to arrive were the 116th Anti-Aircraft Gun Battalion (Mobile) of the Coast Artillery Corps with the 1st US Army. Later other battalions arrived including gun battalions, anti-aircraft and bomb-disposal squads. The soldiers were billeted in hotels, including Villa Rosa, The Rozel and The Grand Atlantic, or with local residents. In addition a large camp was built on the Beach Lawns.

Dave Tyler recalls this period:

In May 1944 we had three soldiers billeted with us. They took us to the promenade where we watched as they marched down the Grand Pier, climbed down nets hung from the Pavilion end of the pier and waded ashore through the sea. At the time we didn't know why, but a few weeks later D-Day arrived and all became clear. In 1945 we also had an American soldier staying with us. He was a solicitor and had something to do with the Nuremberg war trials. He would go away for weeks and then return with food parcels, which were most welcome as we still had food rationing.

In the main Westonians welcomed the men, taking them into their hearts and homes. There were several GI brides – local girls who married American soldiers. Brian Hector remembered some of the GIs who befriended his family:

Fred Wolf was one of several hundred US soldiers who

were camped in the woods all along the track from Worlebury Post Office to the water tower. He was one of many who made friends with my family when we lived in Green Gables in Worlebury Hill Road. They would call in of an evening just to have a chat and have coffee 'out of a proper cup instead of a tin pot'. They really were a great bunch of young men and to this day I have the greatest respect for the many soldiers that I met, most of whom were only four or five years older than myself. I recall with affection Sergeant Snodgrass from the Bronx, New York, 'where real men are made'! Also Private 1st Class Lee Smart from Maryland who really missed his wife, but who died at St Omer in France. I also recall the padre of the unit who turned down a flight home from Germany to the USA in order to come back to England to thank some of the people who had befriended 'many of my charges'. He ultimately had to return home by sea.

Naturally many black soldiers were among the troops. Black and white troops were segregated at that time and some fights used to break out between the soldiers, especially outside The Queens Hotel in Regent Street. Most locals took little notice but there were some racist incidents. One occurrence even made the national newspapers with the headline in the *Sunday Pictorial* 'Vicar's Wife Insults our Allies'. The article stated that the women of Worle were amazed when the wife of their then vicar attempted to lay down a code to be followed should any black soldier be encountered. There were six points listed: if a black man entered a shop he was to be served as quickly as possible and the assistant should indicate that he was not welcome again; if a lady was in a cinema and a black man should sit next to her she should move immediately; if a lady was walking on a pavement and a black man came towards her she should cross the road; white women should have no social relationships with black troops; on no account should black soldiers be invited into the homes of white women; if a lady was being served in a shop and a black soldier entered she should leave as soon as possible, and if in a queue, immediately. Not surprisingly, the instigator of this 'code' asked the women not to mention it to anyone in case the black troops should hear of it and be offended! However, the ladies were so disgusted by the proposals that one told her husband who was a local councillor. The Ministry of Information got involved and new statements were issued that the women:

... had no intention of agreeing to her decree... Any coloured soldier who reads this may rest assured that there is no colour bar in this country and that he is as welcome as any other Allied soldier.

In the end the vicar's wife received the very treatment that she had recommended for the black GIs.

Whilst the soldiers were here they spent their time training and preparing their equipment, especially for the sea crossing to come. Barbara Adams:

I can remember them training on the Beach Lawns; and in late January 1944, some of them went away on exercises to prepare them for the forthcoming invasion of France, though some of them believed they were already going and would not come back again.

Worlebury Hill Road, sheltered as it was by the trees of Weston Woods, was used to stockpile equipment and vehicles. Stan Terrell:

The American troops were billeted in Weston as part of the D-Day landings in France. There were many with their vehicles in the woods and mainly they were to be seen from the top of Milton Hill to the reservoir and on the Toll Road. I used to run errands for them – I think it was to buy newspapers. It was at this time that America was supplying England with dried egg powder and concentrated orange juice. I remember making up drinks of this orange juice and selling it back to the Americans. It was no secret – they all knew how I had made the drink and happily paid for the privilege! I found them very friendly and generous.

March 1944 saw the last of the large-scale attacks on Weston, although in many respects it was the most difficult raid of the war. The weather was peculiar, with a clear sky and thick, low-lying mist driving in from the sea, which blanketed and muffled sound. It was difficult to locate the planes roaring overhead, and sounds originating from the ground, such as anti-aircraft gunfire and bomb explosions, could not be heard from even a short distance away. The minute that it was known an attack was about to occur, a report was sent to Fighter Command. This brought RAF fighters within minutes, although even before they arrived, the local AA batteries claimed a number of hits. The enemy dropped a number of large fire-bombs over the town, which were spaced as target indicators. In particular, large phosphorus incendiary bombs were concentrated on the Bournville estate and the adjoining bridges. They fell in gardens and railway embankments but failed to explode in the soft earth.

From the form of the attack and type of bombs used it seemed the Germans thought they were attacking a factory of some sort. However, either the sea mist or the layout of the Bournville estate diverted the attack once again to the housing estate, with very little damage.

When the RAF arrived, the enemy scattered south releasing their remaining bombs over any village unfortunate enough to be in its path. The bomb loads contained large numbers of practically every kind of incendiary bomb known to be in use, from the ordinary 1kg through all the variations of steel nose, explosive nose, explosive tail, etc., to the large

VE Day party at Worle, May 1945. Residents of The Rows, Coronation Road and Spring Hill got together in the playground of Worle Infant School, now Mendip Green School.

The Weston Cadet Band parades on the Beach Lawns for VE Day celebrations, 1945.

A VE Day street party in Albert Road, May 1945.

phosphorus-oil bombs. A number of high-explosive bombs of large calibre were also included, one of which caused the only incident involving casualties. This destroyed bungalows on the Oldmixon–Hutton Road, killing four and injuring others.

This raid was the last piece of enemy activity in Weston. On 13 June 1944 the last siren was sounded. In September a great armada of Stirling and Halifax bombers, towing gliders filled with soldiers of the 1st Airborne Division, assembled over the Bristol Channel and flew over Weston on their way to Holland as the Battle for Arnhem and the Rhine began and the war entered its final phase.

VE Day

On 2 May 1945 the order came from London to 'Cease Operations'; the war in Europe was over. Four days later Germany officially surrendered and the celebrations began. Allied soldiers were still fighting in the Far East but for a few days people relaxed and let their hair down.

Locally the civic celebrations had been well prepared. The Mayor made a speech from the steps of the Town Hall paying tribute to the Allied Forces in Europe and concluding by saying:

Finally let us not forget those who rejoice with us but are sad at the loss of their dear ones. Many made the supreme sacrifice, some of them without leaving the safety, as it was thought, of their homes.

This was then followed by a Thanksgiving Service, after which the celebrations could begin. Fireworks were let off and radios and musical instruments were brought out so that there could be singing and dancing. Dances were held at every suitable venue, including the Rozel Bandstand, on the promenade and at the Winter Gardens, where it was estimated 10,000 people came throughout the night. In fact, so many wanted to attend the music was relayed outside, where the road was blocked by dancers.

As night fell the victory lights went on. The blackout was over and for the first time since 1939 the cinemas, Town Hall, Winter Gardens and Knightstone were floodlit. The boys and staff at St Peter's School turned on every light in the building, drew back the curtains, and then went down to the promenade to look back at the building all lit up on the hillside. Then they joined the crowds of joyful people singing and dancing in the streets.

The following day was Children's Day. Street parties were arranged, with neighbours pooling rations so victory teas could be laid on. In Wadham Street a loudspeaker was set up to relay BBC radio for a party of 35 children. The residents of Stradling Avenue had their party near the spot where a 1,000lb unexploded bomb fell. In Alfred Street the tables were arranged on the pavement to avoid the traffic. In Carlton Street they borrowed a horse-drawn coach, decorated it and dragged it round the streets by hand. The residents of Palmer Street made their own 'Siegfried Line', consisting of a rope stretched

The Bridge Road VE Day party, May 1945.

A party of German children in Weston, 1946. They came to England for about six months to escape the appalling conditions at home, staying with local families.

across the road at the Meadow Street end, upon which they pegged out a selection of garments in imitation of the popular song 'We're Going to Hang Out Our Washing on the Siegfried Line'. Stan Terrell recalled that in Milton Brow a party for 100 children was brought to a standstill when it was announced that Hitler had got off the train at Milton Halt and had hidden in a nearby garden. However, he was soon 'caught' and 'executed' on a nearby gallows. The *Weston Gazette* reported that:

One or two seats were used as a bonfire, and on the beach a few deckchairs went up in smoke – generally speaking the ratepayers would not have to foot a very large bill for VE Damage.

Prefabricated houses at Oldmixon, 21 September 1959. Prefabs provided an easy way to solve the postwar housing crisis.

It was another three months before Japan surrendered and VJ Day too was celebrated, although it is hardly remembered much today. Nancy Davis came over from Wales. She said they all had fish and chips from Farrs and slept on the floors of the restaurants. The streets were lit up and people partied all night. The war was finally over.

The Cost

Approximately 55 million people lost their lives in the Second World War – not just soldiers, sailors and airmen, as in most previous wars, but huge numbers of civilians, on all sides. In total, approximately 194 high-explosive bombs and 31,500 incendiaries were dropped on Weston throughout the war. Now that the fighting was over, the authorities had to tackle the problems of reconstruction and the social change the war had wrought. The most vital problem was that of damaged houses, especially as the speed with which repairs were carried out contributed greatly to morale. The total tally of damage stood at 282 premises totally destroyed, 2,655 properties very severely damaged and 5,510 premises less severely damaged. Of these 7,757 were houses, 85 were churches and public buildings, half a dozen were industrial premises, and 581 were shops and offices. Public buildings owned by the council which were damaged in the raids included Clarence Park Pavilion, Grove Park Concert Pavilion, the abattoirs, the Open Air Pool, Knightstone Baths and the public library.

A new era was about to begin.

Pigeon lofts behind 38 Locking Road, 1950s.

Right: *Advertisement for HMV refrigerators from Betteridge Bros of Oxford Street, Weston, 1930s.*

Left: *Advertisement for electric kettles and irons from Betteridge Bros of Oxford Street, Weston. Note the light-socket plug on the iron, which Sue Ryall describes her mother using. This meant the iron could only be used during daylight!*

Chapter 10

Modern Times

After the war, Weston had to find its way into a new era. The 1950s brought many changes, both in social habits and daily life. This was the era of the teenager, rock and roll and coffee bars. The seaside holiday was still very popular and the town could be jammed with tourists in the summer. I found a lovely description of Weston on a Bank Holiday in the 1950s, in *The Phoenix*, the school magazine for the Grammar School for Girls. It was written in 1956 by Fay Robertson:

In our town of Weston-super-Mare a Bank Holiday often means a day when the residents retire like hermits to the comparative peace and quiet of the back garden.

If any person has the courage he will venture out into the streets, and with every hope of solitude he will make his way to some haunt that is usually deserted. However, he will be sadly disillusioned, for he will find the town taken over by conquering hordes of 'day-trippers' from Bristol and Cardiff. All types of speech may be heard; cockney, Welsh, Lancashire, Yorkshire, and perhaps a little broad Somerset from local country lads who have a day off from the farm.

It is dangerous and almost impossible to ride a bicycle or drive a car. The people mill and push their way from shop to café, and from ice-cream kiosk to pier. By far the most comical sight of all is to see the people on the Beach Lawns and the beach itself. The scene is reminiscent of a battlefield, with mangled and twisted corpses lying about in great profusion. By about midday these bodies sit up and turn over to roast the other side in the scorching sun. Weston seems to be full of well-cooked lobsters.

It is hard to imagine the town quite so crowded today, although the long scorching summer of 2003 gave some idea of how the town used to look in its heyday. The 1950s were also the time when street violence began to become more common, especially among the young. Brian Austin recalls his youth and the legendary fights between local gangs:

5 November in the late 1950s and I'm off to town with my leather jacket, jeans, suede shoes and two knives, to witness the annual mayhem of Guy Fawkes day – the last hurrah of the old 'Weston Revel' I suppose.

The whole area in front of the Grand Pier was a mass of teenagers milling around in a kind of quiet riot. Weston Station was blocked off for traffic, as was the bus station, whilst a wrecking crew moved between the two removing windscreen wipers, and putting 'squibs' into car exhausts or throwing them at windows and balconies. Many young men had pockets stuffed with fireworks and were egged on by excited girls. Along the seafront rockets were set off. 'Jumping Jacks' were deployed to frighten the ladies, and some hardier souls fired hand-held Roman Candles, particularly at apprentices from RAF Locking. I remember a show-down between the top Weston gang boss of the time and the then leader of the newly-arrived Greek Cypriot group. They stood about eight feet apart pulling fireworks from their pockets in turn, lighting them and throwing them at the face of their opponent. There must have been several hundred young spectators and a couple of hundred adults who came out to watch us all.

There were several gangs. They were mostly from specific areas such as Milton or the Bournville estate, and they all dressed quite smartly. Those known as Teddy Boys wore smart coloured Edwardian-style jackets with tight drainpipe trousers, sideburns and a front quiff. They tended to come down from Bristol. I recall the feared name 'Sugar', and a lad who added to his ensemble a cowboy hat and toy gun! The girls wore very full skirts, held out by layers of net petticoats and low tops, often covered by woolly cardigans – which rather spoiled the effect! I was more inclined to be individual in my clothes and remember wearing a leather jacket, procured by my father whilst in Germany, and that actually caused fear and trembling in others when I wore it in the street, and so became my first favourite outfit. I remember the first Greek Cypriot lads as very smart, in dark suits and with habits unusual in Weston at that time – one set being pulled over by the police whilst driving around with a shotgun looking for 'the man who insulted their sister'.

In the late 1950s I was angry and naturally rebellious, liable to anti-social emotional outbursts. I was fired up, as were many others, by the arrival of rock and roll music, available on jukeboxes in all the coffee bars, except the ones you took your number one girlfriend to. A large amount of violence was fuelled by the presence of a couple of thousand apprentices stationed at RAF Locking, who regularly came into town of an evening, and who we saw as persistently stealing our (potential) girlfriends. Once, in a coffee bar behind the old Playhouse, I saw a local lad throw a lightweight chair across a dance space, to knock off, with total precision, the cap of a newly-entered RAF lad.

One particular local gang of oddly polite but very tough lads were so well known that they were employed by the Odeon Cinema as bouncers for pop concerts. The Weston v. RAF war ended after the latter marched into Weston with a band, and beat up their tormentors (and anyone else who looked like one). I was on my way to being a potential troublemaker but I made good friends, started doing rock and roll piano-vocal at places like The Salisbury Hotel, which gave me the confidence to go into theatre and become someone else.

Sue Ryall has very different memories of her youth in Worle just after the war. Growing up then, children had more freedom in many ways and often spent the long summer holidays playing out in the fields and woods.

I, my two elder brothers, and Mum and Dad, lived in a 1930s semi-detached house on a large corner plot in Mayfield Avenue just on the edge of Worle village. This was a small cobbled road off Locking Road at the end of the village. There were eight semi-detached houses with a small grassed roundabout at the end. Behind all of the houses were long thin gardens and behind the gardens there were green fields stretching to the railway line and beyond. There was one odd bungalow at the beginning of the avenue, privately built and lived in by one of my childhood friends, Mark Jones. The road leading into the avenue went across a narrow ditch with quite steep banks. There were water-filled ditches all over the place in those days, all gone now, of course. The children spent hours playing on and in them. I remember my brother Tony even tried to sail an old tin bath in one with a friend but it sank!

The garden area was very large and most of it was given over to potato growing. This was just after the war and everyone was still 'Digging for Victory'. Dad grew enough potatoes to keep the family for a whole

Wellsea Rhyne before being conduited, 17 October 1960. Most of the old streams and drainage ditches have now been covered or diverted. The houses on the right are in Cardigan Crescent.

year. After digging up they were kept in large sacks in a green corrugated-iron shed just behind the house. We also grew runner beans, cabbages and sprouts. The soil was a very hard clay so we didn't have much luck with carrots or any sort of root vegetables. Dad's bean sticks were supplied by the gypsies who visited local houses every year selling bean and pea sticks, clothes props and pegs. They were all cut from the hedgerows.

In a large run at the bottom of the garden, again made of corrugated iron and painted green, we kept about a dozen brown hens. We didn't keep a cockerel because they were noisy. If we wanted chicks to replace the hens we ate, I would be sent to Tripp's Farm in the village to buy some fertilised eggs which would be put under the broody hen. I had to walk home very carefully so that I didn't jog or disturb them in any way. When they hatched, Mum would feed them on mashed up boiled egg! On Sundays when Dad worked in the garden he would let the hens out and they would peck around where he was digging, it was my job when I was small to herd the hens back into their run at the end of the day.

Mr Rains from over the road would come around and kill a chicken by wringing its neck when we needed one for a meal. I can see Mum now, in an old apron, sitting in the doorway of the shed surrounded by sacks of potatoes, logs and coal, plucking the dead chicken which lay across her lap. When that was done it would be 'drawn' [the insides removed] and any unformed eggs found inside the bird were used for cakes or the Yorkshire pudding with our roast dinner on Sunday.

We always had a roast on Sundays, usually chicken or pork, served up on the dot at noon. We had roast potatoes and fresh vegetables and sometimes a long sausage-shaped suet pudding which Mum made and tied up in an old unwanted clean vest of Dad's. It was tied at the ends with string and boiled in a saucepan for about four hours. The suet pudding was dished up with the meal and if there was any left over we had it for pudding with sugar and jam. Sometimes Mum put currants in it and then it was called Spotted Dick. While we ate we listened to 'Two Way Family Favourites' on the radio followed by 'Educating Archie' or 'Round The Horn'.

Our meat was bought as fresh as possible because in the early days we didn't have a fridge. Like most people, we had what was called a 'meat safe'. This was a wooden box with the front and back covered with fine mesh. It had a mesh door and a shelf and was kept outside fixed to the wall of the house in the shade. The meat kept fresh for about two days but if it smelt a bit off Mum would wash it in vinegar which took away the smell. Later when Dad built a conservatory on the side of the house we bought our first fridge as we now had somewhere to put it. The old meat safe became a cage for my pet mice!

Mum also used to preserve eggs when we had a glut. She would put the fresh eggs into an old enamel bread bin in an isinglass solution, where they kept for months on the floor of the pantry. Although not completely fresh they were much nicer than the tins of powdered eggs which was all most people had during rationing if they weren't lucky enough to have hens.

Before we had a washing machine, Monday was always wash day. It wasn't an easy job in those days. First Mum would drag out the 'copper'. This was an aluminium boiler on legs with a round lid. The water was heated by gas so the boiler had a rubber hose which was connected to a gas tap which stuck out of the floor in the corner of the kitchen. The washing was sorted into whites and coloureds, the whites were put into the copper and boiled, then heaved into the sink which was full of cold water. After a few good rinses, a 'blue bag' was added to the last sink-full of water, which made the whites look whiter by colouring them a very pale blue. Then the whole lot was carried outside to the mangle at the bottom of the garden. The one I remember was a small rubber mangle on an iron frame, it stood over an old tin bath which caught the water. Mum stood on a slatted board to keep her feet dry.

Ironing was done on a blanket-covered board which Mum balanced on the end of the dining table in the back room. The iron had a round plug on the end of its flex which had to be plugged into the light socket – this meant that ironing could only be done in the daytime. As the iron had no thermostat the light had to be switched on and off depending on how hot Mum needed the iron to be. To test how hot it was she would spit on it or hold the iron very close to her face! If the washing was too dry it would have to be sprinkled with tap water to dampen it down. Our clothes were aired around the fire in the winter on the wooden clothes horse.

Compared with modern kitchens, which are light and airy, our kitchen was small and dark. It had an oblong white china sink with a wooden draining-board across one end of the room. On the long wall opposite the back door we had one of those tall food cupboards with a drop-down enamelled top which gave access to the food. At the other end of the room under the stairs was a walk-in pantry which housed, as well as food, the gas meter. Being under the stairs the pantry ended in a point so all sorts of odd things ended up there along with the spiders. The walls were painted with cream gloss paint and the floor covered with lino.

The front room was the best room. On the wall over the fireplace was a 'Sunburst' clock in gold metal. The room was not used very much until we bought a new floor-standing radio. In my early years the radio was our only form of entertainment, apart from playing cards. My brother and I used to lay on the floor and listen to our favourite programs, 'Dick Barton Special Agent', 'The Goon Show', 'Much Binding In The Marsh', and 'Round The Horn', and every morning the family doctor on the radio would tell the nation how to keep healthy and fit. During the day everyone listened to 'Workers Playtime', 'The Dales' and 'Sing Something Simple'. We had three stations on the radio, the Light Program, the Home Service or the Third Program.

For some reason wallpaper paste was hard to come by

Locking Road shops, c.1959.

so we made our own with flour and water, and each of the decorative corner pieces was cut out by hand and pasted in each corner of the wall, which was considered very fashionable. When you bought wallpaper in those days, you had to cut about half an inch from each long edge before it could go on the wall, then it had to be overlapped by about a quarter of an inch when pasting it up. It's no wonder most people painted their walls with gloss paint as it was a lot less bother and easy to wipe clean.

We used to have our logs and coal delivered. In the early days it came on a flat horse-drawn cart that held a large pair of scales for weighing the sacks of coal. The coal was graded into 'Best' or 'Nutty Slack'. If I was around Mum would make me stand at the back door and count in the sacks of coal carried in on the back of the coalman so that we wouldn't get cheated. The coalman had a leather hood that hung down his back so that his neck and back were protected from the heavy sacks.

Milk was delivered daily when I was young, it came in big churns by horse and cart from Tripp's Farm in Worle. Mum would go outside with her jug, along with everyone else, to get the milk. The ladle would be dipped into the churn and a measure would be poured into the jug. She would leave the milk to stand for the cream to rise to the top. This would be skimmed off and scalded, the resulting thickish cream we had with bread and jam. All the kids in the avenue loved the old milk horse and we didn't like it when Mr Tripp bought a modern electric milk float, so while he was collecting his money one day we filled his float with rubbish from the tip, old tyres, bits of tin and garden stuff. It made no difference of course, we didn't get the horse back and we all got into trouble.

There were quite a few people who travelled the roads selling things. There was the rag and bone man who had a horse and cart and shouted 'Ragabone' as he walked his old horse around the roads. He collected anything. Rags could be sold on, as could jam jars, old china and furniture. There was the man who sharpened scissors, knives and axes. He had a small portable grinding stone on a wheel which he worked with his foot whilst sitting on a little stool. The kids in the avenue used to stand around watching the sparks fly.

The gypsy woman was a seasonal visitor. She sold flowers made from shaven wood which looked like shaggy chrysanthemums. She also sold home-made pegs, the big old fashioned kind. They were made from two pieces of wood with pointed ends, held together at the top with a metal band, and if you needed a clothes prop she could get you one.

We had yearly visits from an Indian gentleman too. He wore a white turban and a double-breasted grey pinstripe. He sold cleaning brushes from a suitcase. All types of brushes for every job you could imagine, soft and stiff ones, twisty long thin ones, tiny little ones for cleaning the teapot spout and scrubbing brushes and broom heads. He even had bright-yellow dusters and dish cloths. He would stand on the front step, open up his suitcase and show you all his stuff, picking things out to show you and trying to get a sale.

Then there was the 'never-never' man; from him you could buy sheets, blankets, eiderdowns and towels, in fact any household linen you needed. It was paid for weekly and when you had nearly finished paying he would persuade you to buy something else and so the payments went on and on and it never, never seemed to end. He came around in a little van that was stacked high with linen. Mum liked Whitney satin-edged blankets and candlewick bedspreads.

Our house was the first one in the avenue to have a phone fitted. It was a large black bakelite one. It was kept in the hall by the stairs on a little shelf that Dad made. At the time it was a mistake as our phone number was soon known by everyone in the road and I was forever being sent to get this neighbour or that to come to the phone and speak to their friends and relations, or the phone would ring and someone would want a message passed on. We had less calls on our phone than anyone in the road! Dad soon got fed up with everyone else using our phone and decided we could manage without it so it was removed.

When I started buying records in the 1950s Dad bought a record player. It was kept in the lounge and made of a dark highly polished wood, it had a drop-down front to get to the record deck which held ten records at a time – these were 45s which had just taken over from the old 78s. The first record I ever bought was Elvis Presley singing 'Loving You'. The main record shop at that time was Milliers and was opposite the Odeon Cinema. Downstairs they sold pianos and sheet music, and upstairs they had the record department where you could sort through the records and take the one you wanted to hear into a little soundproof booth which had a record player in it. It was a great way of spending a Saturday afternoon, just playing record after record with no intention of buying one.

Our first television was bought especially to watch the coronation of Queen Elizabeth in 1953. The programs started at five o'clock with 'Children's Hour' and we watched 'Champion The Wonder Horse', 'Robin Hood', 'Robinson Crusoe', 'Daktari' and many others. For the little ones there was 'Muffin The Mule', and

'The Flowerpot Men'. After Children's Hour came the Six O'Clock News and then four hours of adult programs until close down at ten o'clock. A nice man's voice always reminded you to turn off the TV and have a 'good night', then the National Anthem was played. Nothing of very much interest for a teenage girl until the 1960s and a new program called 'The Six Five Special'. Rock and Roll had arrived!

Children and teenagers today often complain that there is nothing for them to do. In the 1950s and early 1960s, they were much more used to making their own entertainment. Sue Ryall again:

Because we lived in a seaside town, Mum and Dad thought there was never any reason to go on holiday, after all, Weston had a long sandy beach, two piers and lots of other amusements, a lot of them free. When I was about eight I was considered old enough to take the bus and go into town on my own. I would cadge some money from anyone in the family who wanted to see the back of me and maybe spend the afternoon on the pier, or on wet days, under it. When it rained visitors left the beach and went on the pier which cost threepence and like most people who were scrabbling in pockets and purses they sometimes dropped the odd penny or two which rolled down between the planks and onto the beach below where the local kids were waiting! Most of the amusements on the pier were the penny-in-the-slot kind. You could have your fortune told for a penny and try your hardest to grab a toy with a grab hand, which to the best of my knowledge never grabbed anything. You could just wander about and watch other people spend their money!

In Regent Street there were three amusement arcades, the Regent Cinema and a couple of pubs, one of which was The Plough Hotel. This was a long thin pub that was pulled down when the back part of Marks & Spencer was built. My favourite place in Regent Street was the waxworks. I spent a lot of time there when I got older as it was very dim and dark in places. You went in one door and out another so the lady taking the money never saw you come out – this meant you could go in with your latest boyfriend and stay for hours! There were the usual Kings, Queens and pop stars, which if I remember rightly were only Elvis Presley and Tommy Steele, and a separate room housed the torture chamber with all the famous murderers of the 1940s and '50s.

One of the amusement arcades had a jukebox, it was a large floor-standing one with coloured lights down the sides and a see-through glass top, it held about 20 records, the old 45s.

The outdoor pool had been built in the 1930s so it was still fairly new when I was young. It only opened in the summer; I wasn't very keen on it because the water wasn't heated and I hate cold water, but if your friends went there then that was where you went too. You paid to go in and then took your ticket to a stern-looking grey-haired lady in a white coat and collected a large metal hanger with a basket attached to the underneath.

The Plough Hotel, Regent Street, demolished in 1972.

Open Air Pool, where Sue Ryall used to sell programs for the Modern Venus beauty competitions in order to earn a free ice-cream.

Then having found a cubicle in the ladies' changing room, all your clothes were arranged on the hanger, shoes and bag in the basket, then it was handed back to the attendant who sat behind a large counter. She gave out a numbered key with a safety pin attached so you could pin it to your costume.

There used to be a patch of grass to lay on by the pool fountain in the early days but that was concreted over so it was a bit uncomfortable to sunbathe. We considered deckchairs a bit sissy so the only time we used the deckchairs was to build dens when the weather turned cold or it rained. There were two water chutes, one into the shallow end and one into the deep end. There was also a springboard into the deep end as well as the lovely high diving-boards. During the summer there were diving displays from the high boards and a Modern Venus beauty competition was held every week. I used to offer to sell programs around the pool in order to get a free ice-cream. The staff would sell ice-creams from a little box hung around their necks and inside the ices were kept cold with blocks of dry ice.

From the Royal Hospital to the pool you were allowed to roller skate on the prom, but that was a winter pastime, along with mucking about in the shelters and chatting. We often played under the walkway at the Marine Lake or tried to get across the causeway when the tide was coming in, pretty scary when there was a gale blowing.

There were three cinemas in Weston then. As well as the Odeon, which was the biggest, there was the Regent in Regent Street and the Central in Oxford Street. This was a real fleapit, very small inside with extremely itchy velour seats. The balcony upstairs in the Central was so close to the screen you could touch it. Next door to the Central was the local fire station. I remember seeing two fire-engines in there one day when the doors were opened. Both those buildings were pulled down when

Oxford Street with the Central Cinema and fire station, c.1953.

the Dolphin Square area was developed. Somerset House now stands on the fire station site.

There were a lot of things going on along the beach and prom in the summer months – there was the Punch and Judy show, the winkle stall and tea stall. Mum would buy sixpence worth of cockles with lots of pepper and vinegar on them if we were passing that way in the summer. On Sundays there was always a church service on the beach which anyone could join. I think the music came from a portable organ but I'm not sure. There was a first-aid post just up from the pier and at the back of it on the beach was a wooden fenced enclosure where any lost children were taken, they were looked after by large ladies in nurses' uniforms until collected by their parents. I can remember peering through the fence at these poor little kids who were usually crying and wondering where their mums were.

The Dairy Festival was held every year on the Beach Lawns in a large marquee, that was great fun because there were cows and calves and sheep with their lambs, all inside on deep beds of straw. You could watch sheep shearing, milking and butter- and cheese-making demonstrations, and outside you could climb all over the huge farm machinery.

There were boat trips to Steep Holm from Knightstone harbour and day-trips by paddle-steamer down the Channel to Lundy Island from Birnbeck Pier. I can remember watching visitors boarding boats from long wooden landing-stages near the Grand Pier when the tide was right. Birnbeck Pier had a ferry service from Wales which brought over day-trippers. The best time to

The Central Picture House, Oxford Street.

watch them was a Sunday afternoon because there were no pubs open in Wales on a Sunday and hoards of them came over to spend the day in Weston drinking. Then there was always a mad rush to catch the last ferry back; we kids thought it was hilarious watching drunken Welshmen running down the pier, sometimes desperately jumping an ever-widening gap as the steamer sailed off!

You had to pay to go into the Marine Lake. There were a couple of buildings fronting onto the wide pavement with large iron gates and a turnstile in between. It was the only place in Weston where you could always find the tide in! There was a paddling pool for kids and paddle-boats on a larger lake for bigger children. If you wanted to look macho for your girlfriend you could hire a rowing boat. They also had swing boats, lots of clean sand, ice-cream and sunbathing. Mum and Dad would always take any visitors they had down there for the day especially the London relations. There are photos of us all enjoying ourselves at the Marine Lake, apart from the day I fell fully dressed into the water and had to be wrapped in a towel while Dad took my clothes away to be dried. I can remember vividly how lovely and warm they were when he bought them back.

When I was a child, the Winter Gardens were open at the front and you could walk through into the gardens the other side and watch the tennis or sit on benches just inside the tall columns and watch the world go by. Coaches would line up on the sea front and the drivers, to get customers, would call out the places they would be going to the following day or even on a mystery tour that evening.

After the war it took a long time for things to get back to any form of normality. Some food was still rationed until 1953. Stan Terrell recalled this period:

As the war came to an end so life became a little easier. Fresh fruit had been very scarce, almost unobtainable. I remember being told by my mother that there was a little shop on the Milton Road, I believe it was Sage's, selling bananas. My instructions were to go and see if I could buy some. After queuing, yes, I was able to bring home some fruit!

The town was scattered with bomb sites while the owners or the council decided whether to reconstruct properties or demolish even more and totally redevelop areas. Sue Ryall continues:

Weston High Street used to be one-way only and when I was young there were still a few bomb sites in the town area. Lance & Lance was a big store on the corner where Argos is now, that was still a bomb site and was used as a car park. When we went on a bus into town we always asked for a ticket to Lances' Corner. Where Littlewoods and Marks & Spencer are now were empty boarded-up sites. The Boulevard church opposite the Weston Mercury offices had been destroyed during the war and I can remember there being a money box set

into the wall of the old church for people to put money in to help with the rebuilding.

The other end of High Street was called Union Street and was a very narrow road with small houses along it. Every so often one of the front rooms would have been made into a shop, perhaps selling a few sweets in a bowl in the window.

The electricity-board showrooms were in Waterloo Street. They had regular cookery demonstrations in a show kitchen upstairs, where they had overhead mirrors so that the audience could see what was happening. I think it was to encourage people to use electric ovens and to use all the new food that was available after the war. I watched a demonstration once with Rose, my sister-in-law.

The terminus for the buses that ran from Worle used to go as far as the police station and then turn around in that wide piece of road to go back to Worle. The roads were quite dark as there weren't many lights and the ones that we had were not very bright, so travelling on a bus at night was very difficult because you couldn't see where you were. The bus conductor would call out the stops as we came to them.

At Weston's main railway station during the summer holidays you could always find groups of young boys with home-made hand carts waiting for a holiday train to come in. They would offer to carry people's luggage to whatever boarding-house they were staying in – they charged depending how far they had to pull the luggage and the family trotted behind with the address on a piece of paper – people were not prepared to spend money on a taxi; it just wasn't done in those days.

Next door to the library was the hospital [now flats]. There were open balconies at the side and the patients would be wheeled out on nice days to take the air. If you were on the top deck of a bus you could wave to them as you went by. Quite a few of the buildings at that end of the Boulevard were still in use as houses then, and the large house that is now Birnbeck Finance was a private school. There were lovely big trees all the way down the road and the street lights were hung right across the middle of it. When they needed attention a man would have to crank a handle on the pole on one side of the road to bring the light down.

In the event, some parts of Weston were redeveloped, notably the Carlton Street area, which became Dolphin Square. Other radical ideas, which included demolishing Waterloo Street and some of the Boulevard to create a wide, straight dual carriageway to the sea front, did not go ahead. Some bomb sites remained until the 1980s (such as the Tivoli in the Boulevard) and indeed there is still one visible on the corner of Beach Road and Richmond Street. However, the majority of the town returned to being a popular family seaside resort, welcoming thousands of holiday-makers every year – until the onslaught of the foreign package tour! But that is another story.

Above: *Coronation party outside the British Legion Club in New Street, Weston-super-Mare, 1953.*

British Legion Coronation party, New Street, Weston-super-Mare, 1953.

Coronation decorations, Meadow Street, 1953.

Chapter 11

Pot Pourri

This part of the book is filled with all those many fascinating snippets of memories, information and short articles that don't fit into any of the preceding chapters, but I feel are too interesting to leave out of a book of this nature. I have also included a selection of extracts from old newspapers, notably the *Bristol Mirror*, that relate to Weston, Uphill and Worle.

Press Cuttings

The *Bristol Mirror*, 21 June 1806

LOST, Supposed to be Stolen, from Uphill in Somersetshire, on the 29 May last, TWO HAND-SOME GREYHOUNDS; one being a Dog of large size, and answers to the name of Leader, and the other a Bitch of small size, and answers to the name of Dent; the Dog is brindled, and the Bitch fallow, marked with small white spots.

Whoever will restore them to Mr PAYNE of Uphill House, the owner, will be very handsomely rewarded, and if sufficient proof is given of their being stolen or destroyed, so as the Offender or Offenders can be brought to a conviction of the offence, a reward of 20 Guineas will be given, over and above the penalties allowed by Act of Parliament.

The *Bristol Mirror*, 20 June 1807

WORLE ASSOCIATION
We whose Names are here unto subscribed, Proprietors and Occupiers of Land in the said Parish, Do hereby give Notice, that we have entered into an Obligation to prosecute at our joint expense, all Persons who shall commit any Depredation on our respective Property.

John Price, Vicar of Worle   Denis Sheppard Leman
Robert Bishop   John Hammons
James May   John Stabbins
James Hunt   George Henvill
John Woodruffe   Edmund Fry
George Davis   James Bishop
John Walters   George Thayer
William Marston

The *Bristol Mirror*, 10 February 1810

FOR SALE (IN FEE) BY AUCTION... All that neat, convenient and well-accustomed INN and TAVERN, called THE VALIANT SOLDIER, situate in the parish of Worle, in the county of Somerset, now in the occupation of Mr Wm. Marston, the proprietor.

The Valiant Soldier Inn was the three-storey property in Church Road, Worle, at the end of the terrace of cottages at the top of the Scaurs.

The *Bristol Mirror*, 23 December 1813

FOR SALE (IN FEE) BY AUCTION, On Monday the 17 January 1814, between the hours of Four and Six o'clock in the afternoon.

Lot 1. All that well-accustomed INN, called the NEW INN, with the Ball Court, Bowling Alley, Garden, Orchard, Offices, Stables and Coach-House adjoining, the whole containing, by estimation, one Acre and an half more or less.

Lot 2. A Close or very rich MEADOW GROUND, called Cole-Bridge, adjoining Lot 1, and containing, by estimation, 1 acre, 2 rods more or less.

Lot 3. A Close of ORCHARD & GARDEN GROUND nearly opposite Lot 1, containing, by estimation, three quarters of an acre more or less.

Lot 4. A WILLOW BED, containing, by estimation, a quarter of an acre more or less.

The Premises are in the parish of Worle, in the county of Somerset, and are now occupied by Mr Joseph Leman.

The House, Offices, Stables, and Coach-House, were all lately new built, and are well calculated for an Inn, having been erected for that purpose, and are plentifully supplied with water. The situation of the Premises is peculiarly eligible, adjoining the road from Congresbury to that much frequented sea bathing place Weston-super-Mare, distant therefrom only two miles.

The New Inn stands at the end of Worle High Street, and is now called The Woodspring.

The *Bristol Mirror*, 25 December 1813

TO BE LET BY TENDER, The FORMING and

STONING of a PUBLIC ROAD, from Uphill Moor Gate to the corner of the Boundary Wall of Weston-super-Mare new Inclosure, agreeable to a Plan and Specification thereof...

NB A Plan and Specification of the said Road is also left at The Dolphin Inn, in Uphill.

The *Bristol Mirror*, 6 August 1814

The following case of juvenile intrepidity took place at Uphill on Sunday last. A boy, a son of Joseph Norman, farmer, was bathing in a pill [creek] adjoining the river, and disappeared for more than 3 minutes; he would inevitably have met a watery grave, had not a lad, 17 years of age, son of Mr John Worwell, of The Dolphin Inn, (who ran to the spot as soon as the alarm was given) plunged boldly in, and after two fruitless efforts, at last succeeded in saving him. It is supposed he was 20 feet below the surface of the water.

The *Bristol Mirror*, 19 February 1814

TO BE SOLD OR LET, and entered on at Lady-Day next, A Capital DWELLING-HOUSE, with a large Garden, walled round, with choice fruit trees therein, and other conveniences attached thereto; together with a large Shop and Warehouse adjoining, wherein the trade of Linen Draper, Haberdasher and Grocer has been carried on for upwards of twenty-four years by the present proprietor.

The Stock and Fixtures to be taken at a fair valuation (or Sold by Auction) on Monday the 7th day of March next, and following days, unless disposed of by private contract, of which due notice will be given.

Apply to Mr George Henville, Worle, Somerset.

This sale relates to what was commonly known as Gunnings Stores at the top of the Scaurs in Worle. It has now all been converted into private housing.

The *Bristol Mirror*, 17 October 1818

TO BE SOLD (IN FEE) BY AUCTION, in suitable lots, By J.M. Tucker, On Monday the 16th day of November next at two o'clock in the afternoon, at the NEW INN, at WORLE, THE MANOR or LORD-SHIP of WORLE, in the county of Somerset, with the ROYALTIES and APPURTANCES thereto belonging; together with about FOUR HUNDRED ACRES OF LAND, IN THE PARISHES OF Worle and Kewstoke; in the several occupations of Robert Bishop, Isaac Prenter, Mary Davis, James Hunt, and Geo. Hewlett, as tenants thereof.

NB The Estate consists principally of Rich Grazing Land with suitable Farm Houses and Orchards – is situated about 18 miles from Bristol, and 2 from Weston-super-Mare, and it partly adjoins the direct road from Bristol to Weston. The Roads to the Estate are very good; The Land Tax is redeemed, and the Poor

Rates are moderate...

For further particulars and conditions of sale, application may be made to Mr Jarman, Solicitor.

The *Bristol Mirror*, 13 February 1819

To be sold by auction on the Premises, all the extensive and valuable household furniture, dairy utensils and other effects, of Mr John Hammons deceased, at his late residence at Ebdon in the Parish of Worle. Consisting of 7 prime feather beds and bedsteads; 2 mahogany bureaus; 1 ditto chest of drawers; 1 handsome set of mahogany dining tables; 1 mahogany dining, tea, card, dressing and other ditto; six mahogany chairs with hair seatings, and 2 elbow ditto to match; 12 beech chairs with bedroom, fancy, elbow and other ditto; 1 good clock; 1 alarum ditto; folding screen; pier, swing and other looking-glasses; elegant prints and paintings; tea-urn, trays, waiters etc; 1 handsome set of china; a large variety of glass, earthenware etc; hackney saddle, side ditto; 3 large chests; corner cupboard; safe; roasting jack; steelyard; 2 kitchen grates; 2 sets of fire irons; brass and other fenders; tripods, etc.; pestle and mortar; 2 boxes, etc.; heaters; knife-case; 3 dozen of knives and forks; fowling piece; brass and other boilers; with a variety of culinary requisites, brass, pewter, etc.

The Dairy Utensils comprise 2 cheese-presses, complete; 2 milk-leads, 2 cheese-tubs; 1 hand churn, 2 pump ditto; 2 milk-kettles, brass and other milk pans, tubs, trendles, pails, vats, etc., with many other articles. The whole will be sold with reserve.

The above account gives a lovely inventory of a country farmhouse of the period and one can learn much about the man who owned it by the list of contents. The farmer was obviously well-to-do with mahogany furniture, good china and paintings on the wall. The earthenware would probably be used by the staff and labourers. He had a gun – the fowling piece – and rode a horse. He probably had a wife (note the side saddle) who had possibly predeceased him, hence the sale. There was a well-equipped kitchen with good-quality utensils. The farm made milk, butter (trendles are used to salt butter) and cheese.

The *Bristol Mirror*, 13 February 1819, at Uphill

To be LET, for 3 or 7 Years, or a longer Term, a CAPITAL MANSION, elegantly built, and delight-fully situated; consisting of an Entrance-Hall, Breakfast-Parlour, Dining and Drawing-Rooms, 10 Bedrooms, Butler's Pantry, Servants' Hall, Kitchen, and other requisite attached and detached Offices; capital Cellaring, and Stabling for four Horses; Coach-House; together with a good Garden, Orchard, and a Lawn of rich Meadow and Pasture LAND, having therein several Ponds for Fish; containing in the whole about FIFTY ACRES, surrounding the Mansion, which

Above: *A photograph of the Wright family at the Model Village, 1962, taken by their father, Peter. Left to right: Annie Wall, Rosemary ?, Joan Wright, Nicola Wright, Elizabeth Wright, Stewart Wright.*

The Model Village, 1962, with sisters Elizabeth and Nicola Wright.

The summer carnival procession outside the Winter Gardens, 1933. The summer carnival was revived that year and monies raised were given to the St John Ambulance Brigade's funds.

commands a complete view of the Bristol Channel, the romantic Peninsulas attached to it, and the attractive Islands of the Holms, etc.; as well as a most extensive and varied Land View, not excelled in England.

NB With the above may be had a Deputation of the Manor and an extensive Salmon Fishery, wherein are also taken the richest Soles, Silver Eels, and other Fish.

Also, to be LET, for a like Term, a most desirable GRAZING or rich DAIRY FARM, nearly adjoining the above Mansion; consisting of a spacious and convenient Farm-House, called the Manor-House, Barn, Barton, Ox-Stalls and Cow-Houses; Cider-House, and other Offices; Gardens, Orchards, and divers Closes of rich Meadow and Pasture Land, within a ring fence, adjoining the Farm-House; comprising in the whole nearly Ninety Acres, of the greatest variety of rich, sound and healthy land any Farm of its dimensions can produce; having an inexhaustible supply of Pond and Current Water.

The *Bristol Mirror*, 11 September 1819

To be Let, and entered upon immediately, a capital modern-built DWELLING-HOUSE; consisting of 2 large parlours, 5 bedrooms, excellent garrets, 2 kitchens, under-ground cellars, wash-house, and other attached and detached offices, well supplied with both sorts of water; 3-stalled Stable, Coach-house, and 2 Gardens adjoining. The Tenant may be accommodated with from 4 to 12 Acres of excellent Grass LAND, if required. The Premises are pleasantly situated on an eminence, commanding delightful and extensive views of the sea and surrounding country.

The Premises may be inspected on application at FRY'S HOTEL, Weston-super-Mare; and for Rent and Terms of Letting to Mr James Capell of Ebdon, near Worle.

This advert probably refers to Ashcombe House, later a Red Cross Hospital during the First World War and then the Maternity Hospital for Weston. It stood at the top of The Drive and has since been demolished.

The *Bristol Mirror*, 22 January 1820

To be SOLD by Private Contract, several Lots of FREE-HOLD LAND for BUILDING, immediately adjoining The Strand, and fronting the Sea at Uphill, commencing from the South end of the Weston Strand; and forming one of the most desirable situations for Building which has yet presented itself upon the Bristol Channel, embracing the advantages of being about halfway between Weston and the justly-admired village of Uphill; commanding more extensive and varied prospects than any other neighbouring spot, and being perfectly free from any inconvenience arising from the sand.

Persons desirous of treating for any one or more Lot or Lots are requested to apply personally to Mr FISHER, Langford near Bristol.

Personal Memories

In 1919, G. Ritchie, then aged about 5, visited Uphill Church on many an afternoon walk.

For me the church was quite memorable because a few yards from the church porch was a tombstone mounted on top of which was a small model bronze cannon – a field gun. A good model with the barrel being able to be elevated and depressed. Some years ago on a visit to Weston, I walked up to Uphill Church – it was then a ruin and the cannon gone.

A glimpse of the past

Maurice Pitman was seconded to BAC in 1941 to improve the build time for the Beaufighters they were producing. He was billeted in Hampden Road and remembers walking into The Windsor Castle pub and seeing it candlelit and filled with farmers sitting with their beer and cider – a real country inn!

The Coronation, 1953

The coronation of Queen Elizabeth II in June 1953 gave a welcome opportunity for the whole country to celebrate at what was, even then, still a time of austerity. Many people used the opportunity to purchase their first television set, and then suddenly discovered friends they never knew they had, as everyone wanted to watch the event live. At 11a.m. bells rang in all the church towers and prayers were said for the new young queen. Many of the streets in the town were decorated with flags and bunting. Despite the wet and chilly day, street parties were held, with coronation teas of jellies and sandwiches. All the schools had been given a four-day holiday so children could celebrate along with their families. In Grove Park people danced on the lawns to the sound of a band in the bandstand. As dusk fell, beacons were lit on Worle Hill, Bleadon Hill, Brean Down and Brent Knoll. The dancers moved on to the Coronation Ball in the Winter Gardens and danced until dawn – the dawn of a new Elizabethan age.

The Model Village

The famous Model Village on Weston sea front delighted three generations of visitors and locals before constant vandalism resulted in its closure in 1986. It was built in 1962 on land belonging to The Royal Hotel, just next to Spider Lane and officially opened by Armand and Michaela Dennis of television fame. It was a complete country village and included a castle, manor-house and even a hunt with fox and hounds. When it was dismantled some of the buildings were reconstructed at the Castle Café in Kewstoke.

Carnivals

In 1889, Weston Cycling Club held their first illuminated carnival procession in the town. People donned fancy dress and rode their decorated cycles whilst carrying lanterns. They must have provided a spectacular sight! The first illuminated carnival in November was organised a few years later in 1891, the same year that an illuminated ice carnival was held on the frozen clay pits of the Royal Pottery in Locking Road. The first ice carnival was held in Weston in 1861 and it was Conway Warne, the new owner of the Royal Pottery, that decided to revive the event in the 1890s. It must have been a wonderful sight in the wintry darkness as the naptha lanterns flickered around the perimeter and the band played while skaters in fancy dress glided over the ice. The *Weston Mercury* reported that:

On Monday evening a novel and decidedly attractive entertainment was provided by Mr Conway G. Warne, who announced a grand ice carnival on the ponds adjacent to his pits in Locking Road. A portion of the Pottery around the pond had been walled off with high brick walls, forming an entrance, and within this boundary was accommodation for promenaders. Immediately in front of the entrance was a huge coke brazier, and at the extreme end of the ice was built a huge bonfire, which, when lit, shot flames to a height of at least twenty feet. The ponds were illuminated with Chinese lanterns, 'fairy lamps', and naphtha gas lamps – over 1,000 lights being utilised in the general

illumination. On the left of the entrance a handsome and beautifully decorated restaurant had been erected, and here Mrs Sutton, of The Railway Hotel, dispensed such creature comforts as were calculated to induce an amount of warmth. Over 1,000 persons were present. The total area frozen was close on four acres, and on this space the masqueraders and skaters made an effective show, fringed as they were by hundreds of spectators above whose heads were lines of coloured lanterns. Storey's 'Waverley Band' was in attendance, and Messrs Taylor & Son ran brakes at frequent intervals at nominal fares.

The ice carnivals were dependent, of course, upon the weather, but the winter street carnivals ran until 1914 when they were interrupted by the First World War. After the war summer carnivals began to be held, in aid of the St John Ambulance Brigade. These were a lower key affair with a carnival queen elected from local girls. It was 1925 before the winter carnivals began again but the summer ones were kept on also, for holiday-makers to enjoy. The last summer carnival before the outbreak of the Second World War was held in 1938.

The summer carnivals were reinstated in 1958 and ceased again in the 1980s due to the retirement of the main organisers. The November carnivals returned about the same time but are now closely linked to the Somerset carnival circuit that starts at Bridgwater with the Guy Fawkes carnival and ends two weeks later at Weston.

A Bus Journey to Weston in the 1920s

Leonard Portch, a tram driver and bus conductor for the Bristol Tramways & Carriage Co., recalled the sometimes harsh conditions on the buses to Weston:

In those days when I first started on the No. 24 Service, the Bristol–Weston road was a bit different from how it is today. It wound about all over the place. Traces of it are still to be seen. Hedges lined the sides of the narrow road and during the summer the dust came up in clouds from the bus wheels and from the hedges. We were issued with yellow dusters to keep the seats clean and we wore long white dustcoats with blue collars and cuffs.

The entrance to the bus at the rear was rather wide and we had a canvas door blind which had to be pulled across when the road was dry and dusty. There was no other ventilation, so in the summer the front nearside and offside window panes were taken out. A curtain was fixed up beside each, which could be pulled across if it rained, but this, of course, wasn't weatherproof.

There were two seats for passengers on the driver's long seat, and their fares had to be collected from inside through a drop window operated by a strap.

These buses ran on solid tyres and every bump on the road was felt. There were just two side lights and no windscreen wipers. We used to get some real 'pea soup'

Winter carnival float by Walker & Ling, 1933. This tableau 'A Bowl of Iris' won first prize and the Sydney Edwards Cup at the November carnival.

fogs during the winter and often the conductor would have to walk in front with a white cloth hanging over his back and shoulders. The driver carried his own box of tools and carried out any running repairs. Later, when pneumatic tyres were fitted in the late 1920s, the driver and conductor had to do wheel changes on the road if a flat tyre occurred. We were allowed 20 minutes to change wheels and were expected to make up the time afterwards. The spare wheel was bolted on a platform underneath the rear of the bus and whilst the driver was loosening the nuts and jacking up, the conductor's job was to unbolt and get the spare ready and afterwards to replace the old one. The tramway buses were red, white and blue in colour. The body was blue, the wheels were painted red and the roof was white.

To begin with our running time was one and a quarter hours from Bristol to Weston with a quarter of an hour waiting time at each end and they ran every hour at half-past the hour from a stand outside the old Sunlife Assurance Office at the bottom of Clore Street. Then they cut the running time to one and a half hours with a waiting time of a quarter of an hour at Bristol and three quarters of an hour at Weston.

When we arrived at Weston we changed our destination boards and did a journey to Oldmixon via Uphill where we carried passengers as well as parcels which had to be picked up by the recipients at Uphill and Oldmixon. When we got back to Weston we changed boards again and set off back to Bristol.

A Ghost Story

In the early 1970s, Mrs Gwen Page, who lived halfway up the Scaurs, in the cottage which backed onto The Old King's Head pub in Worle, told librarian Jane Saker about the man dressed in the clothes of a farm labourer of the seventeenth century, that she would see walking past her window at regular intervals. At the back of Mrs Page's cottage, in the pub garden, was an area where cockfights were once held and this man headed in that direction. Connecting the pub garden and Mendip Cottage at the top of the Scaurs, is an underground passageway, possibly used in the days of smuggling. The labourer probably knew of that also and may have helped the landlord to store nefarious barrels of French brandy and other spirits. Mrs Page was not worried by these sightings – in fact she grew quite fond of him and missed him if she didn't see him for a while.

Chapter 12

Sports and Pastimes

Langford Rovers AFC, Champions of the Cheddar Valley League, Division One, 1938/39. Left to right, back row: E.J. Palmer (secretary), T. Magor; W. Thorne, K. Burrell (captain), J. Sammells, Herbert Magor, Fred Quick, A. Western (chairman); middle row: W. Rolfe, R. Burrell, E. Webber, E. Day, H.E. Webber; front row: H. Webber, R. Cox.

Uphill Cricket Club outing. Note the two very different coaches. The one on the left has a folding top, much like a charabanc, whilst the one of the right is a more modern vehicle.

Weston-super-Mare UDC Sports Cricket Club 1935. Left to right, back row: *E. Smith (hon. sec.), A. Kent, J. Sammells, F.S. Thornbury, E.G. Cummings, L. Norville, R.G. Jenkins, R.H. Beaven;* middle row: *C.J. Smith, C.C. Collier (captain), T.L. Davies (vice-captain);* front row: *R. Pritchard, D.E. Richards.*

2nd Weston-super-Mare Boys Brigade Co. outside Milton Baptist Church, 1947/48. Left to right, back row: *Gerald Stanton, Gordon Slocombe, Ronald Sims, Pat Tidman, Rodney Dowden;* middle row: *Sgt Brian Hurst, Glyn Williams, L/Cpl Terry Clapp, John Lyons, Geoffrey Blatchford, Cpl Clifford Bradbury;* front row: *John Hicks, Capt. A. Wright, Revd W.J. Hitchcock, Lt. C. Wright, Jack Poole, David Tyler;* seated: *John Ashplant, ?, Michael Davies, Brian Trunks.*

Chapter 13

Chronology

1566	Calamine first discovered in England, on Worle Hill.	1821	Census records 735 residents and 126 houses.
1606	Great floods when the sea defences collapsed. Large numbers of people drowned along this coast.	1822	First guide book to Weston published.
		1823	Trees planted on Weston Hill.
		1824	Weston Parish Church rebuilt.
1644	The Revd Christopher Sadbury imprisoned Puritan rebels in Glebe House, then the rectory.		Stocks and lock-up built in the Worthy Field.
		1825	A market opened at Weston.
1695	Manor of Weston bought by Col John Pigott, who then built Grove House.	1826	An esplanade constructed, from Knightstone to Leeves Cottage.
1702	First school in Weston, a parish school run by Elizabeth Barber.	1828	Whitecross House built.
		1829	Esplanade extended to Regent Street.
1713	Church bells rung in Weston to celebrate the signing of the Treaty of Utrecht after the Duke of Marlborough's campaign.	1830	Knightstone Baths bought by Dr Fox of Brislington.
			Richard Hill opened an Assembly Rooms and library in Regent Street.
1735	An acre of land and a house in High Street sold for £53.	1831	Dr Fox developed Knightstone.
			Census records 1,341 residents.
1769	The poet William Lisle Bowles moved to the Old Rectory, Uphill.	1832	New bathhouse built on Knightstone.
		1833	Causeway to Knightstone raised.
1773	The philanthropist and reformer Hannah More came to Uphill to convalesce.	1837	Chancel of Parish Church rebuilt.
		1838	Tithe Map produced.
1791	The Revd William Leeves of Wrington built himself a summer cottage on the beach. Part survives as the Old Thatched Cottage Restaurant.	1840	Weston-super-Mare & Worle Turnpike opened, from western end of Worle High Street to junction of Locking Road and Baytree Road.
1792	Big fire when an old farmhouse and barn burnt down on the site where The Royal Hotel stands in 2004.	1841	Bristol & Exeter Railway opened together with first railway station in Weston.
			First gasworks built in Oxford Street.
1795	Worle Brewery founded by James May and Mr Castle.		First printing press brought to Weston, by James Dare.
1797	Jane Biss advertised holiday accommodation at Uphill in the Bristol newspapers.	1842	Weston became a town with the Improvement & Market Act.
1808	Work started on the first hotel in Weston, The Royal Hotel at the time of writing.	1843	Albert Buildings built. James Dare publishes The *Westonian*, the first newspaper.
1811	Belvedere, the first house on Beach Road, built for Isaac Jacobs of Bristol.	1844	Villa Rosa built.
		1845	The *Weston-super-Mare Gazette* founded.
	Census records 163 residents.	1846	National School built at the bottom of Lower Church Road.
1813	The New Inn built at Worle (now called The Woodspring).		Wesleyan chapel built in Regent Street.
			First volunteer fire brigade formed.
1815	Weston-super-Mare Enclosure Award.	1847	Royal Crescent built.
1817	Seaview Place built.		Emmanuel Church built.
1819	South Parade built.		Butters' shop opened in High Street.
		1848	Toll Road to Kewstoke constructed.
1820	First public baths on Knightstone opened.	1850	Wadham Street Baptist Church built.

Weston acquires its own fire-engine. Prior to this, one had to be brought from Banwell.

1851 British School built in Hopkins Street.

1853 Glentworth Hall built.

1854 Waterworks opened.

1855 Ellenborough Crescent built.
Christ Church built.
Raglan Circus under construction.

1856 Cemetery opened.
New gasworks built in Drove Road.

1858 Foundation stone for St Joseph's Church laid.

1860 Boulevard and Waterloo Street laid out.

1861 Holy Trinity Church built in Atlantic Road.
Turkish baths opened in Wadham Street.
Town boundaries extended to include White-cross estate.

1862 Goods station built.

1863 The Lodge built in Upper Bristol Road for the Eighth Earl of Cavan.

1864 Foundation-stone for Birnbeck Pier laid.

1865 First hospital built, in Alfred Street.
National School opened at Worle.
Claremont Crescent built.

1866 New larger railway station built, where Tesco is located at the time of writing.

1867 Birnbeck Pier opened.

1868 Royal West of England Sanatorium opened.
Worle Brewery closed.

1870 Worle Church restored.

1871 Shrubbery Road linked to Atlantic Road via toll-gate and lodge.

1874 Christchurch Infant School opened.

1875 Boulevard Methodist Church built.

1879 Worle Brewery buildings converted into a laundry.
Second volunteer fire brigade formed.

1881 Constitutional Club built.
Church Road Baptist Church built.

1883 Work started on Sea Front Improvement Scheme. The two-mile wall and promenade were completed in 1886.
Beach Lawns walled and gated for private use by sea-front properties.
Land for Clarence Park donated by Rebecca Davies.

1884 New and present railway station and loop line opened.

1885 The *Weston Mercury* Office opened in Waterloo Street.
First Atlantic cable laid.
Recreation-ground opened by private company.

1886 St Jude's Church, Milton, consecrated.

1887 Mogg's Band formed.
First experiment to light Weston by electricity.

1889 The Grand Atlantic Hotel opened, converted from The College.
Grove Park acquired for town.
First lifeboat house built on Birnbeck Pier.
Clarence Park opened.

1890 First telephone link with Bristol.

1891 Royal Arcades built.
First winter carnival in Weston.

1892 St Saviour's Church opened.
Foundation-stone laid for the School of Science & Art.
Broad-gauge railway lines dismantled.

1893 School of Science & Art was opened although the current façade was not added until 1899.
Free library opened in Grove House.

1894 Final meeting of Weston Town Commissioners.
Weston Urban District Council formed.

1895 Children's Convalescent Home opened.
Severe fire on Birnbeck Pier.

1896 The UDC buys Knightstone Island.

1897 Weston, Clevedon & Portishead Light Railway opened.
Town Hall enlarged.
The Board Schools opened in Walliscote Rd.

1898 The south-west jetty on Birnbeck Pier added.
Clock added to Town Hall.
Foundations of All Saints' Church laid.

1899 New Post Office built in Post Office Road.

1900 Public library and museum opened in the Boulevard.
Victoria Methodist Church built.
Victoria Bowling Club opened.

1901 Electric Supply Co. opened a generating station in Locking Road.
New fire station opened in Oxford Street.

1902 Tram Company started in Weston.
All Saints' and St Saviour's Churches consecrated.
Ashcombe Park opened.
Knightstone Theatre and Baths opened.
New lifeboat house opened on Birnbeck Pier.
Milton becomes part of Weston-super-Mare UDC.

1903 A gale damaged much of Weston's sea front.
New lifeboat launched and christened the *Colonel Stock*.

1904 Grand Pier opened.

1905 Bungalow Hotel built (later became The Grand Central Hotel).
First part of Bournville Road built.

1906 Drill Hall opened in Churchill Road.

1907 Clarence Park bowling-green opened.
Grand Pier extension opened.

1908 High Street paved with wooden blocks.

Worle Churchyard extended.
Clarence Park Baptist Church opened.
Whitecross Hall opened.
New Masonic Temple.

1909 Major fire at Lance & Lance.
Alexandra Gardens laid out on the site of the old station.

1910 Beach Lawns opened to the public.

1911 Cutting the sod ceremony for St Paul's Church.
B. Hucks flew his monoplane at Weston.
Electric Theatre opened, Weston's first cinema.
Hill Road Wesleyan Church built.
Clarence Park East laid out as a recreation-ground.
New bowling-greens laid out at Clarence Park and Ashcombe Park.

1912 Gaslight Company Workshops and Stores built in Burlington Street.
St Paul's Church built.

1913 Sands Day Nursery opened.
Regent Cinema opened.
First x-rays used at Weston Hospital.

1914 The First World War begins.
Excursion station opened for day-trippers.
Smyth-Pigott estate sold.

1915 Ashcombe House became Red Cross Hospital for duration of First World War.

1916 Grand Pier extension demolished.
New abbatoir opened – 'one of the most humane in the country'.

1917 Cemetery extended to Milton Road.

1919 Weston UDC builds first council-houses in the country under the Addison Scheme.

1920 The 'Dutch Oven' bandstand built at the Rozel.

1921 Central Cinema opened.

1922 War memorial in Grove Park unveiled.
Grammar School opened in Nithsdale Road.

1923 South-west jetty on Birnbeck Pier demolished.

1924 Work began on the Winter Gardens.

1925 The Grand Central Hotel opened.
Italian Gardens opened.

1926 Moorland Road Congregational Church opened.
Milton Baptist Church opened.

1927 Winter Gardens and Pavilion opened.

1928 New hospital in the Boulevard opened.
Marine Lake causeway built.
Belvedere demolished to build bus station.

1929 Colonnade added to Marine Lake.
Corpus Christi Church opened.
The Bournville Housing Scheme commenced.
First World War memorial dedicated in

Weston Cemetery.

1930 Fire destroys Grand Pier Pavilion.
Clarence Park Baptist Church opened.
Milton Methodist Church opened.

1931 Milton Church Hall opened.
Worle and Uphill amalgamated within Weston-super-Mare.

1932 Council purchased Worlebury Iron Age hill-fort.

1933 Western Airways formed.
Weston's boundaries extended.
Grand Pier reopened after fire.
Uphill Hill purchased by the council as an open space.

1934 Victoria Methodist Church burnt down.
Ashcombe Park bowling-green opened.

1935 Floral Clock built.
Odeon Cinema opened.
The new bridge at Uphill carrying the Weston–Bridgwater road over the Great Western Railway was opened.
Grammar School opened.

1936 Weston Airport opened.
Victoria Methodist Church rebuilt after fire.
New police station opened.
Weston High Street becomes one-way.

1937 Weston granted borough status. Henry Butt became first Mayor.
Open Air Swimming Pool opened.
Trams ceased operation.
New Rozel Bandstand built.
Weston Woods bought by the council.

1938 Actress Deborah Kerr was born in Weston.

1940 Weston, Clevedon & Portishead Light Railway closed.
Part of Royal Arcade demolished. The blitz finished the job.
First bombs fell on Weston-super-Mare.
First church on Bournville built.

1941 Weston suffered major blitz destroying the Grove Park Pavilion and St Paul's Church among other buildings.
Birnbeck Pier taken over by Admiralty.
Bournville School opened.

1942 Weston's second major blitz, destruction included Lance & Lance and the Congregational church.

1944 General Eisenhower visited American troops stationed in Weston Woods, part of the run-up to D-Day.

1945 Diana Dors won third place in Modern Venus competition at the age of 14.

1946 Birnbeck Pier released from wartime use.
Ashcombe House opened as a Maternity Hospital.

1951	Cuckoo added to Floral Clock to mark the Festival of Britain.
1953	Princess Margaret visited Weston.
	Second World War memorial unveiled in Grove Park.
1954	Regent Cinema renamed the Gaumont.
1957	Worle mobile library started, the first in the South West.
	St Andrew's Church opened.
1958	Observation tower in Grove Park demolished.
	Garden of Fragrance for the Blind opened.
	Clarks build shoe factory in Locking Road.
1959	Boulevard United Reformed Church opened.
1961	Royal Pottery closed.
1962	Model Village opened.
	Black Rock Pumping Station opened.
1963	Experimental hovercraft service operated between Weston-super-Mare and Penarth.
	The Beatles played at the Odeon for one week.
	Hillman's foundry closed after 150 years.
	Inflatable lifeboat joined the main boat at Birnbeck.
1964	Playhouse destroyed by fire.
	Foundation-stone of St Peter's Church laid.
	St John's School demolished.
1965	First shops opened in Dolphin Square.
1967	Pedestrian bridge built over Beach Lawns.
1968	Production of gas at Weston gasworks ended.
1969	New Playhouse opened.
	Villa Rosa demolished.
	Worle library opened.
	Edwardian entrance to Grand Pier demolished and current one built.
1970	New Technical College opened.
	New divisional police headquarters opened in Weston.
1971	La Retraite School closed.
	Worle School opened in Redwing Drive.
1972	The Plough Hotel in Regent Street demolished.
1973	New Tourist Information Centre opened.
	The Gaumont Cinema closed and became a bingo hall.
	The town's first adventure playground built – at Bournville.
	Glentworth Hall demolished.
1974	Borough of Weston ceased with local government reorganisation and the creation of Woodspring District Council.
1977	The Lodge, Bristol Road, demolished.
	The Queen's silver jubilee tour included Weston.

1979	Albert Memorial Hall demolished.
	Capri Villas built.
	Last regular steamer services from Birnbeck.
1980	New Town Hall extension completed.
	First Weston Air Day.
1981	Great storm on 13 December wrecked the colonnade at Marine Lake and much of the sea front.
	Constitutional Club timber roof removed.
	The Victoria Inn (opposite Floral Clock) demolished.
1982	Diving-boards at Open Air Pool demolished.
1983	Rozel Bandstand and Marine Lake colonnade demolished.
	Tropicana opened, converted from Open Air Pool.
1984	Goods and excursion stations demolished to make way for new Tesco.
	Tivoli Flats completed.
1985	Gunnings Store at Worle closed.
1986	Weston General Hospital opened at Uphill.
	Shrubbery Mews demolished.
	Holy Trinity Church renamed Elim Pentecostal Church.
	Model Village dismantled and sold.
	Heritage Centre opened.
	Ashcombe House demolished.
1988	Sea front bus station demolished.
1991	St Peter's Church tower demolished.
1992	Sovereign shopping centre opened.
	Pedestrian bridge built over Beach Lawns demolished.
	New conference centre at Winter Gardens opened by Princess Anne.
	Knightstone Baths closed.
	Hutton Moor swimming pool opened.
1993	Owen Owen store in High Street demolished.
1994	Birnbeck Pier closed as unsafe.
1995	New motorway link road opened.
	Sealife centre opened.
1996	Local Government reorganisation in April abolished Woodspring District Council. A new unitary authority of North Somerset Council was formed.
1998	Weston College extended.
1999	Broadoak School, the old Grammar Schools, demolished.
2001	Salvation Army Hall demolished.
	Jill's Garden created in Grove Park in July.
	New lifeboat *Coventry & Warwickshire*.
2002	Westlands closed its Oldmixon factory.
2003	The Rozel Hotel demolished.

Subscribers

Christopher Air, Weston-super-Mare, Somerset
Mr William Amesbury, Meadow Street,
    Weston-super-Mare
Ken Arlotte, Weston-super-Mare, Somerset
Pamela O. Armstrong, Weston-super-Mare, Somerset
Brian Austin
Dennis John Austin, Weston-super-Mare, Somerset
Mr Douglas Eric Austin (In Memory of),
    Weston-super-Mare
Mrs Ellen J. Baker (née Bishop), Bridgwater, Somerset
Olga E. Baker, Weston-super-Mare, Somerset
William and Lorna Baker, Weston-super-Mare,
    Somerset
Jean Bancroft
Ken Barber, Worle, Weston-super-Mare
Margaret R.J. Beacham, Wick-St-Lawrence,
    Weston-super-Mare
Betty F. Beakes, Worle, Weston-super-Mare
Barbara Beasley, Weston-super-Mare
Phillip Beasley, Weston-super-Mare, Somerset
Ann E. Bell, Weston-super-Mare
K. and S. Belsten, ex-Westonians
Matt Benjamin, Weston-super-Mare
M.W.N. Bennett, Weston-super-Mare
Ben Benstead, Weston-super-Mare, Somerset
Daphne A. Betteridge, Weston-super-Mare, Somerset
Hugh C. Betteridge, Bristol
Mr David W.H. Bevan, Weston-super-Mare
Brian R. Bewley, Weston-super-Mare, Somerset
Mr D.R. Biddulph, Milton, Weston-super-Mare
Mrs M.A. Bidwell, Weston-super-Mare, Somerset
B.W. Bishop, Weston-super-Mare, Somerset
Michael and Patricia Blackmore, Weston-super-Mare
John Blewitt
Grace Blunt, Sandcroft Cottages, Uphill
Mr Mervyn E. Board, Weston-super-Mare, Somerset
Nigel Boddington, Weston-super-Mare, Somerset
John R. Bohannon, Weston-super-Mare, Somerset
Betty Y. Bostock, Weston-super-Mare, Somerset
Phyliss M. Bradford, Weston-super-Mare, Somerset
Ailsa F. Brent, Weston-super-Mare, Somerset
Pat and Cliff Brent, Bleadon, Weston-super-Mare
Mr R.D. Briggs, Worle, North Somerset
Billy T. Brooker, Weston-super-Mare, Somerset
Maurice W. Broom, Weston-super-Mare,
    North Somerset

R. and L. Brown, Weston-super-Mare
Hilary and Paul Brownett, Weston-super-Mare
Jeff Browning, Sydney, Australia
Roy W. Brunker, Weston-super-Mare, Somerset
Cllr Peter Bryant
Brian Burgess, Weston-super-Mare, Somerset
Mr Graham J. Burgess
Bryan L. Burnell, Weston-super-Mare, Somerset
John and Tryphena Campkin, Wellington, Somerset
Anthony P. Carpenter, Weston-super-Mare
Mr John Carpenter, Lympsham, Somerset
Jean and Gordon Carter, ex-Weston-super-Mare,
    Somerset
Joy Carter, Weston-super-Mare, Somerset
John Wilfred Cashmore, Weston-super-Mare,
    Somerset
David J. Cattle, Weston-super-Mare, Somerset
Ian K. Chancellor, Milton, Weston-super-Mare
Reg and June Charles, Weston-super-Mare
Julian P.M. Charlton, Weston-super-Mare, Somerset
Colin C.C. Charsley, Weston-super-Mare
Colin J. Chrisp, Weston-super-Mare
Terry and Jose Clapp, Weston-super-Mare, Somerset
Mr and Mrs R. Clark, Weston-super-Mare, Somerset
Mr and Mrs C.L. Close and family, Bournville Road
Gemma Cogle/Harris, Weston-super-Mare, Somerset
Marina G. Coles, Weston-super-Mare, Somerset
Brian and Lyn Collard, Worle, Weston-super-Mare
Stanley F. Collard, Weston-super-Mare
G. Collia-Suzuki, Weston-super-Mare, Somerset
Mr Jack A. Collie, Weston-super-Mare, Somerset
Dr John Christopher Coombes, Worle, Somerset
Allan and Lynda Corbett, Hutton, Weston-super-Mare
Mr Tom Couch, Weston-super-Mare, Somerset
Bob Cousins, Milton, Weston-super-Mare
Penelope Jane Cox, Watchet, Somerset
Miss Sheila Cox, Old Mixon, Weston-super-Mare
Richard J. Crook, Weston-super-Mare, Somerset
Mr Les Crowe, Weston-super-Mare
Pat Cuff, Weston-super-Mare, Somerset
Bob and Cilla Cutler, Weston-super-Mare, Somerset
Rachel Daniel, Weston-super-Mare, Somerset
Eric C. Darling, Weston-super-Mare, North Somerset
Michael G. Dauncey, Weston-super-Mare, Somerset
Ruth Dauncey, West Sussex, formerly
    Weston-super-Mare

Mrs Marian Davies, Weston-super-Mare, Somerset
Reginald M. and Jennifer A. Davis,
    Weston-super-Mare
Angela Daw, Kewstoke, Weston-super-Mare
Mr Albert Day, Weston-super-Mare
Mr R.E. Day, Weston-super-Mare
Mr Robert Day, Weston-super-Mare
Jack de Bruin, Weston-super-Mare, Somerset
Steven de Bruin, Weston-super-Mare
Christopher Demirtges, Weston-super-Mare, Somerset
David S.R. Derham, Worle, Weston-super-Mare
Christine M. Dodgson OBE
Joan M. Doolan (née Slocombe), Uphill, Somerset
R.C.F. and B.K. Dore (née Wright), ex-Westonians
John D. Dudd, Weston-super-Mare
Mrs Jennifer Dyer, Weston-super-Mare
Mr Leonard Dyer, Weston-super-Mare, Somerset
Margaret Rosemary Edmonds, Weston-super-Mare,
    Somerset
Jackie and Mike Eggar, Weston-super-Mare, Somerset
Mr Anthony C. Evans (In Memory of),
    Weston-super-Mare, Somerset
Mary D. Farrant, Lympsham, Somerset
Maxine Denise Ferrier, Weston-super-Mare, Somerset
Andrew J. Fisher, Weston-super-Mare, Somerset
Michael G. Fisher, Karalee, Brisbane, Australia
Francesca Fitzsimons, Weston-super-Mare, Somerset
Keith William Fletcher, Weston-super-Mare,
    Somerset
Terry J. Flynn, Weston-super-Mare, Somerset
Anita Foord, Hutton, Weston-super-Mare, Somerset
Ken and Mary Ford, Hutton, Weston-super-Mare
Joan Patricia Forman, Weston-super-Mare, Somerset
Bruce Francis, Cheltenham
Mrs M.D. Francis, Weston-super-Mare
Mr Philip Franklin, Weston-super-Mare, Somerset
Jonathan Frankpitt, Wedmore, Somerset
John Fry, Weston-super-Mare, Somerset
John W. Fuller, Weston-super-Mare, Somerset
John L. Fursland, Weston-super-Mare
Mrs Frances Fussell, Hutton, Somerset
John R. Gair, Weston-super-Mare, Somerset
Jill Gallop, Weston-super-Mare, Somerset
Sidney Gallop, Weston-super-Mare, Somerset
Robert Galvani, Weston-super-Mare, Somerset
Chris Gerlach, Weston-super-Mare
William Gibbs, Weston-super-Mare, Somerset
Annette Gibson, North Worle, Weston-super-Mare
Christine and Terry Gilbert
Anthony G. Gill, Worle, Weston-super-Mare, Somerset
C.W. and Marny Gilluly, Washington DC
Mr Keith Glimstead-Milton, Weston-super-Mare
Maureen and Roy Godwin, Weston-super-Mare,
    Somerset
Allen Gould, Weston-super-Mare, Somerset
Bob Greed, Weston-super-Mare, Somerset
Martin B. Greenslade, Worle, Somerset
Richard P.S. Greenslade, East Grinstead, Sussex
Doreen E. Gresham, Weston-super-Mare, Somerset

Mike and Sylvia Gribble
Joyce and Betty (née) Griffiths, Uphill,
    Weston-super-Mare
Mr Chris Hall, Weston-super-Mare, Somerset
Roger and Marian Hancock, Shenington, Oxfordshire
Stephen J. Harding, Weston-super-Mare, Somerset
Douglas R. Hardwidge, Weston-super-Mare
Edward B. Harper
Steven A. Harrison, Weston-super-Mare, Somerset
David J. Harvey, Weston-super-Mare, Somerset
Margaret Harvey, Weston-super-Mare
Wendy and Alison Harvey, Weston-super-Mare,
    Somerset
P. Hatherall, Weston-super-Mare, Somerset
Mrs W. Havercroft, Brent Knoll, Somerset
Denis Hawkings, Hutton, Weston-super-Mare
Maurice Reginald John Hawkins
Miss L. Heale, Weston-super-Mare, Somerset
Philip William Heeks, Weston-super-Mare
John R. Heenan, Weston-super-Mare, Somerset
John Hess, Weston-super-Mare, Somerset
Nigel Hess, Denham, Buckinghamshire
Tony, Pam, Fred and Frank Hillier,
    Weston-Super-Mare
John M. Hinchliffe, Weston-super-Mare, Somerset
Kenneth Gordon Hole
Neil E. Holman, formerly Weston-super-Mare,
    now Paignton, Devon
Stephanie Holman, formerly Weston-super-Mare,
    now Bury St Edmunds, Suffolk
H.C. and F.L. Hope, Weston-super-Mare, North
    Somerset
Cecil F. Hunt, Weston-super-Mare, Somerset
Mrs J. Hurley, Creech St Michael, Somerset
Mr Ronald John Hurman, Weston-super-Mare
Patricia M. Hutsby, Weston-super-Mare, Somerset
Sally Kay Huxham, Weston-super-Mare, Somerset
Paul A. Ireland, Weston-super-Mare, Somerset
Anthony R. Jakeman, Weston-super-Mare, Somerset
John Jennings, Milton Brow, Weston
Dilywn Johnson, Weston-super-Mare,
    North Somerset
Patricia J. Johnson, Weston-super-Mare
Robert C. Johnston, Worle, Weston-super-Mare,
    Somerset
Christine Jones (née Clutterbuck), Weston-super-Mare
Christopher P. Jones, Locking Road,
    Weston-super-Mare
Patricia D. Jones (Kirby), Weston-super-Mare,
    Somerset
Mr and Mrs John Kaye
Mr R.W. and Mrs C.A. Kearle
Eric K. Keen, Weston-super-Mare
Deanna D.J. Kerton, Weston-super-Mare, Somerset
Jill Klajman, Weston-super-Mare, Somerset
Gwendolin Knight
Michael and Marion Knight, Weston-super-Mare,
    Somerset
Roy F.J. Knight, Cullompton, Devon

Mr and Mrs B.D. Lalonde, Weston-super-Mare
Garner Lamb, Estate Agents and Surveyors
Kathleen R. Latty, Uphill, Somerset
Sharon Ledbrook, Weston-super-Mare, Somerset
Paul Lewis, Weston-super-Mare, Somerset
Mr R.J. and Mrs J. Lewis, Worle, Weston-super-Mare,
    Somerset
Sandra Lewis and Family, Weston-super-Mare
Thomas Lewis, Weston-super-Mare, Somerset
Rev. Monsignor Gabriel Leyden
Danielle and Ben Long
Thelma and Charles Loud, Weston-super-Mare,
    Somerset
Mr and Mrs R.B. Lovell, Weston-super-Mare
David L. Marquiss, Weston-super-Mare, Somerset
Joyce D. Marshall, Worle
Ann McHugh (née Moon), Weston-super-Mare
G.H. McIlveen
Alan and Shirley McMahon, Weston-super-Mare,
    Somerset
Mr W.T. Meakin (deceased), Weston-super-Mare,
    Somerset
Christian J. Metti, Weston-super-Mare, Somerset
Mr and Mrs B. Meyer
Grahame Middle, Weston-super-Mare
Grahame L. Middle, Weston-super-Mare, Somerset
K.R. Middleton, Weston-super-Mare
Elizabeth and Douglas Mitchell
Patricia J. Mitchell
Callum John Moon, Weston-super-Mare, Somerset
Alan Morgan
David J.H. Morgan, Bleadon Hill, Somerset
Frederick F. Mudge, Weston-super-Mare, Somerset
A.H. Mugridge, Weston-super-Mare, Somerset
Mrs Betty Mursell, Southampton
Sybil M. Neads, Weston-super-Mare, Somerset
June Neal, Weston-super-Mare, Somerset
Raymond C. Newbury, Weston-super-Mare,
    Somerset
Andrew Nisbet, Clifton, Bristol
Angus W. Nisbet, Ealing, London
Peter W.W. Nisbet, Weston-super-Mare
Irene M. Norman, Weston-super-Mare, Somerset
Diane Oliver, Nailsea, Somerset
J.C. and J. Oliver, ex-Westonians
Daniel Organ, Weston-super-Mare
John A. Palmer, Weston-super-Mare, Somerset
Ray and Joan Palmer, Worle
Brian and Margaret Parfitt, Weston-super-Mare
Les and Mary Parsons, Weston-super-Mare
Richard and Sue Parsons, Weston-super-Mare
Derek John Patch, Weston-super-Mare, Somerset
Jill and Mike Patrick, Weston-super-Mare, Somerset
Kevin A. and Sharron L. Penney, Weston-super-Mare
Audrey V.M. Perkins (née Francis), Uphill, Somerset
Donald J. Phillips, Weston-super-Mare, Somerset
Elaine Phillips, Weston-super-Mare
Len Phillips, Weston-super-Mare, Somerset
Roma Phillips (née Hillier), Weston-super-Mare,

Somerset
Steven Phillips, Weston-super-Mare, Somerset
Mrs Beryl Piper (née Wilton), Weston-super-Mare
Doris E. Pitman, Weston-super-Mare, Somerset
M.J. Pitman, Weston-super-Mare
Renee Pitt, Alfred Street, Weston-super-Mare
David Plaister, Weston-super-Mare, Somerset
Winifred S. Pollard, Weston-super-Mare
D.J. and C. Poole, Weston-super-Mare, Somerset
Mr and Mrs J. Pope, Weston-super-Mare
Geraldine and John Prescott, Worle,
    Weston-super-Mare
Maureen and Peter Price, Weston-super-Mare
Mr Aubrey Pugsley, Weston-super-Mare, Somerset
Norman Punter, Worle
Mrs Ann Pursey, Cothill, Station Road, Sandford
Mr E.S. Ratcliffe
Edna W. Ray, Weston-super-Mare, Somerset
C.L.G. Reeves, Weston-super-Mare
Graham Reeves, 1935–1998
Shirley Reynolds (née Bradshaw, née Owen), Uphill,
    Weston-super-Mare
Michael John Richards, Weston-super-Mare, Somerset
Alan G. Richardson
Mrs Audrey J. Richardson
Barry Ridge
Mrs Brenda E. Robertson, Weston-super-Mare,
    Somerset
Christine Robinson, Weston-super-Mare, Somerset
Mr D. Ross
Alice F. Rossiter, Weston-super-Mare
Jennie Rossiter, Nelson, New Zealand
Councillor Dave Roxburgh, Weston-super-Mare
Sue Ryall, Kewstoke
Jane Elizabeth Saker, Weston-super-Mare, Somerset
Mr and Mrs D.C. Salisbury, Weston-super-Mare
Theresa P. Scott, Weston-super-Mare, Somerset
Mr Pete Seaton and Mr Mark Western,
    Weston-super-Mare, Somerset
Geof Sheppard, Weston-super-Mare
David and Julie Sheppard, Weston-super-Mare
Barbara E. Sims, Weston-super-Mare, Somerset
Gavin M. Sims, Weston-super-Mare, Somerset
Peter Sinclair, Weston-super-Mare, Somerset
Reginald C. Skelton, Weston-super-Mare, Somerset
G. Skinner, Weston-super-Mare
Joan Sluman, Weston-super-Mare, Somerset
Ernest E. Smart, Weston-super-Mare
Miss Carolyn T. Smith, Weston-super-Mare
Ron (Whiffer) Smith, Weston-super-Mare, Somerset
Margaret A. Snape, Weston-super-Mare
Darren K. Snelgrove, Weston-super-Mare, Somerset
R.M. Sparks, Weston-super-Mare
Phyllis M. Speed, Weston-super-Mare, Somerset
Pam Sperring, Weston-super-Mare
June and Peter Stephen, Weston-super-Mare
Daphne Stephens, Hutton, Weston-super-Mare,
    Somerset
Winifred Ann Stokes

Anne E. Stone (née Kingston), Swansea
Christopher H.B. Stone
Ruth M. Sutton, Shipham, Somerset
Willie S. Tancock, Weston-super-Mare
Mark Taylor
Philip D. Taylor, Weston-super-Mare
Mikel Telega, Weston-super-Mare, Somerset
Joseph Thomas, Weston-super-Mare, Somerset
Derek G. Thorne, Weston-super-Mare, Somerset
Mike, Carole, Jon, Claire and Sam Thorne, Locking Village, Nr Weston-super-Mare
Monty, Dorothy, Mike, Cath and Jan Thorne, Westbury Crescent, Weston-super-Mare
Audrey Todman, Weston-super-Mare
David Tolhurst, Weston-super-Mare, Somerset
Gillian A. Tomlinson, Wick St Lawrence, Somerset
Michael J. Tozer, Pill, North Somerset
Rosemary Trout, Weston-super-Mare, Somerset
Andrea K. Tucker, Weston-super-Mare
Mrs I.M. Tucker (née Hedges), Weston-super-Mare, Somerset
Maureen H. Tucker, Weston-super-Mare, Somerset
Michael James Tucker, Weston-super-Mare
Roger Tully, Weston-super-Mare, Somerset
David and Joan Tyler, Weston-super-Mare, Somerset
Mr E.L. Tyler, Weston-super-Mare, Somerset
Shirley M. Vincent (née Smith), Weston-super-Mare, Somerset
Helen Vukotic, grandaughter of John and Lydia Minifie
Sally Walker, Weston-super-Mare, Somerset
Dave and Pam Wallace, Locking, Weston-Super-Mare
The Wallace Family of Jubilee Road

John F.W. Walling, Newton Abbot, Devon
Patricia M. Walsh, Weston-super-Mare, Somerset
Sheriden, Connor and Jason Walton, Weston-super-Mare, Somerset
Pamela J. Warlow, Weston-super-Mare, Somerset
Dorothy and Gordon Warren, Weston-super-Mare, Somerset
Geoffrey W. Watkinson
Roy Watts, Worle, North Somerset
Lance Webber, Weston-super-Mare
Linda Westgarth, Hutton, Somerset
Kenneth G. Weston
Weston-super-Mare Town Council
Mrs Kim Westwood, Weston-super-Mare
Chris and John White
Phillip A. White, Weston-super-Mare, Somerset
Carol Whittle (née Pegler), formerly of Worle
Ethel E. Wilcox (née Beimingham), Weston-super-Mare, Somerset
Bryan C. Williams
Mrs Patricia Williams, Weston-super-Mare, Somerset
Matthew J. Williamson, Weston-super-Mare
Mr R.W.S. Wilson, Weston-super-Mare, Somerset
Harold Wiltshire
Windwhistle Primary School, Weston-super-Mare
David Wink, Weston-super-Mare, Somerset
Mr P.A. and Mrs M.R. Wintle, Weston-super-Mare
Barbara Wood, Weston-super-Mare, Somerset
Malcolm F. Wood, Weston-super-Mare
Pam Woodburn, ex-Weston-super-Mare
Gordon F. Wride
Robert G. Wright, Weston-super-Mare, Somerset

Community Histories

The Book of Addiscombe • Canning and Clyde Road Residents Association and Friends

The Book of Addiscombe, Vol. II • Canning and Clyde Road Residents Association and Friends

The Book of Ashburton • Stuart Hands and Pete Webb

The Book of Axminster with Kilmington • Les Berry and Gerald Gosling

The Book of Bampton • Caroline Seward

The Book of Barnstaple • Avril Stone

The Book of Barnstaple, Vol. II • Avril Stone

The Book of The Bedwyns • Bedwyn History Society

The Book of Bickington • Stuart Hands

Blandford Forum: A Millennium Portrait • Blandford Forum Town Council

The Book of Boscastle • Rod and Anne Knight

The Book of Bramford • Bramford Local History Group

The Book of Breage & Germoe • Stephen Polglase

The Book of Bridestowe • D. Richard Cann

The Book of Bridport • Rodney Legg

The Book of Brixham • Frank Pearce

The Book of Buckfastleigh • Sandra Coleman

The Book of Buckland Monachorum & Yelverton • Pauline Hamilton-Leggett

The Book of Carharrack • Carharrack Old Cornwall Society

The Book of Carshalton • Stella Wilks and Gordon Rookledge

The Parish Book of Cerne Abbas • Vivian and Patricia Vale

The Book of Chagford • Iain Rice

The Book of Chapel-en-le-Frith • Mike Smith

The Book of Chittlehamholt with Warkleigh & Satterleigh • Richard Lethbridge

The Book of Chittlehampton • Various

The Book of Colney Heath • Bryan Lilley

The Book of Constantine • Moore and Trethowan

The Book of Cornwood and Lutton • Compiled by the People of the Parish

The Book of Crediton • John Heal

The Book of Creech St Michael • June Small

The Book of Cullompton • Compiled by the People of the Parish

The Book of Dawlish • Frank Pearce

The Book of Dulverton, Brushford, Bury & Exebridge • Dulverton and District Civic Society

The Book of Dunster • Hilary Binding

The Book of Easton • Easton Village History Project

The Book of Edale • Gordon Miller

The Ellacombe Book • Sydney R. Langmead

The Book of Exmouth • W.H. Pascoe

The Book of Grampound with Creed • Bane and Oliver

The Book of Gosport • Lesley Burton and Brian Musselwhite

The Book of Hayling Island & Langstone • Peter Rogers

The Book of Helston • Jenkin with Carter

The Book of Hemyock • Clist and Dracott

The Book of Herne Hill • Patricia Jenkyns

The Book of Hethersett • Hethersett Society Research Group

The Book of High Bickington • Avril Stone

The Book of Ilsington • Dick Wills

The Book of Kingskerswell • Carsewella Local History Group

The Book of Lamerton • Ann Cole and Friends

Lanner, A Cornish Mining Parish • Sharron Schwartz and Roger Parker

The Book of Leigh & Bransford • Malcolm Scott

The Book of Litcham with Lexham & Mileham • Litcham Historical and Amenity Society

The Book of Loddiswell • Loddiswell Parish History Group

The New Book of Lostwithiel • Barbara Fraser

The Book of Lulworth • Rodney Legg

The Book of Lustleigh • Joe Crowdy

The Book of Lydford • Compiled by Barbara Weeks

The Book of Lyme Regis • Rodney Legg

The Book of Manaton • Compiled by the People of the Parish

The Book of Markyate • Markyate Local History Society

The Book of Mawnan • Mawnan Local History Group

The Book of Meavy • Pauline Hemery

The Book of Mere • Dr David Longbourne

The Book of Minehead with Alcombe • Hilary Binding and Douglas Stevens

The Book of Monks Orchard and Eden Park • Ian Muir and Pat Manning

The Book of Morchard Bishop • Jeff Kingaby

The Book of Mylor • Mylor Local History Group

The Book of Narborough • Narborough Local History Society

The Book of Newdigate • John Callcut

The Book of Newtown • Keir Foss

The Book of Nidderdale • Nidderdale Museum Society

For details of any of the above titles or if you are
interested in writing your own history, please
contact: Commissioning Editor, Community
Histories, Halsgrove House, Lower Moor Way,
Tiverton, Devon EX16 6SS, England;
email: katyc@halsgrove.com